CREATION AND LITURGY

Ralph N. McMichael, Jr.
Editor

In Honor of
H. Boone Porter

The Pastoral Press
Washington, DC

ISBN: 1-56929-001-6

The Pastoral Press
225 Sheridan Street, N.W.
Washington, D.C. 20011
(202) 723-1254

The Pastoral Press is the publications division of the National Association
of Pastoral Musicians, a membership organization of musicians and clergy
devoted to fostering the art of musical liturgy.

Printed in the United States of America

Contents

The Legacy of H. Boone Porter

Introduction

THE GENESIS OF THIS BOOK REVOLVES AROUND TWO LUNCHES I HAD WITH BOONE Porter. The first occurred in the refectory at Nashotah House during one of Boone's frequent visits to the seminary while he was editor of *The Living Church.* I had been discussing with him his contribution to the *Festschrift* for Thomas Talley (who along with Marion Hatchett and Leonel Mitchell did their doctoral work under Boone). At one point in our conversation, I abruptly asked Boone if anyone was doing a volume in his honor. He replied, "no." The seed was planted, and I began pondering the idea. Later, at a meeting of the North American Academy of Liturgy, I discussed the possibility of a book in Boone's honor with some of my fellow liturgy professors at Episcopal seminaries. I received encouragement to proceed, and this led to the second lunch.

I made an appointment with Boone to see him at his office in Milwaukee, and he suggested that we have lunch. I wanted to let him know about my idea so that if anyone else started this project I would know, and I wanted to get his ideas about a theme for the book and who might contribute to it. We went down the street to the luncheon buffet at the Astor Hotel, and after getting our food I presented him with my desire to edit a volume in his honor. Boone is a humble man, and he was genuinely surprised and delighted by this prospect. I told him that since he was one of the primary architects of the 1979 Book of Common Prayer, I thought it fitting that the theme of the book could be on the future of Anglican liturgy. However, Boone was not so taken aback by my proposal that he could not offer another theme: creation and the liturgy. Throughout Boone's life and career as a scholar he has been concerned with creation, and was an advocate for its greater inclusion in the Book of Common Prayer. Hence, this book is about creation in the liturgy and life of the church.

A look at the bibliography of Boone's publications at the end of this volume attest to the wide range of his scholarship and service to the church. That is, Boone has concerned himself not only with the history of liturgy, but also with rural ministry, stewardship, contemporary practice of ministry and liturgy, and so on. Boone is a witness to the wholeness of the Christian life and its dynamic continuum of *lex orandi; lex credendi; lex vivendi*. Through his writings and work Boone has always been concerned with the interplay of the church's prayer, belief, and life.

I am delighted by the contributions submitted for this volume, and their adequacy to the task of exploring the relationship between creation and liturgy, as well as honoring the broad expanse of Boone's mind. These studies are expositions of *lex orandi; lex credendi; lex vivendi*: creation in the history of the liturgy; in theology; and in the life of the church. In addition to these sections of this volume, the last section provides the reader an appreciation of the scope of Boone's contribution to the church. It must be noted here that the biographical sketch was dictated by Boone to his beloved wife Violet under the pretense that it was for their children, and not for this book. I would like to thank Violet for this, and I would like to thank all the contributors for their good work.

Let me conclude this introduction with an account of another meeting with Boone, this time not for lunch, but for some cheese and crackers and a drink (after all we are both devout Anglicans and do not shy away from the pleasures of creation). I had sent Boone what was to be my second published article in *The Living Church* which was a follow-up on an article on the diaconate. The second article had to do with the relationship between baptism and holy orders, and Boone had encouraged me in my thinking on this matter. However, Boone found the style of the second article to be too strident, and he invited me out to his farm to discuss how I might rework it for publication. The conversation we had that night taught me many things. Boone spoke of expressing one's views in such a way as to convince, and not to condemn. Boone has been a witness to me, and to the church, of what it means to be an authentic scholar of the liturgy, a doxological person; one who ultimately strives for the right worship of God. May this book be a step in that direction.

Ralph N. McMichael, Jr.
Nashotah House
Michaelmas, 1992

Lex Orandi:
**Creation in the
Liturgical Tradition**

1

Christ and Creation: Observations on Anaphoral Structure

Aidan Kavanagh, O.S.B.

ONE OF BOONE PORTER'S MOST ACCOMPLISHED STUDENTS, THOMAS J. TALLEY, has done much to clear up the lines of Christian anaphoral development.[1] With his customarily cautious precision, Talley makes clear what can and cannot be said about the eucharistic prayer or anaphora, its development and contents. Among other things he sheds important light on an apparent anomaly, namely, the absence of a creation-theme in many anaphoras (I use the term loosely) of the first three centuries for which we have texts. This absence, he suggests, was not due to Christian insensitivity about or rejection of creation but to certain matters in the development of anaphoral structure.

Although it would be incautious in the extreme to imply that all early eucharistic prayers developed in the same way at the same time, especially in the second and third centuries, at least one major genetic structure can be identified in the surviving evidence. This is the Jewish table prayer, said at the end of meals over a cup of wine mixed with water, known as *birkat-ha-mazon* (=BHM). This tripartite prayer blessed God for created nourishment, thanked God for revelation, and petitioned God for present and future redemption on the basis of what God had done in the past, thus investing the blessing and thanksgiving sections with the character of anamnesis or commemo-

3

ration. Joseph Heinemann pointed out this association of specific prayer forms with specific motives in 1977.[2] His insight shed precious light on what the Christian table prayer, and indeed the entire event, came early on to be called *eucharistia*, thanksgiving, rather than *eulogia*, blessing, and assumed a strongly anamnetic content focusing on the deeds of God leading particularly to the ultimate revelation of himself as Father in Christ Jesus as Son. Hence also the strongly petitionary nature of the developing eucharistic prayers, which would eventually focus in most traditions on an invocation-petition (*epiclesis*) of the Holy Spirit as agent of redemption both now and in the future. If Heinemann's insight is correct, it provides a clue to how doctrine—in this case that of the Trinity—in its primal stage emerges out of the prayer of the church at worship.

But the question here is why certain early Christian table prayers drop, relocate, or diminish the theme of creation along with its specific prayer-form, that of blessing. One notes the Jewish text:

> Blessed are you, Lord our God, King of the universe, for you nourish us and the whole world with goodness, grace, kindness, and mercy. Blessed are you, Lord, for you nourish the universe.[3]

The content makes clear that this is not a blessing of God for creation pure and simple, but for God's nourishment of "us and the whole world." That such nourishment is through created food and drink may be implied, but the text nowhere makes this explicit.

The point may seem small, but it does not remain small when one turns to the Christianization of BHM in chapter 10 of the *Didache*, that first-century collection of teaching and liturgical materials of Syrian provenance. One notices what happens when the blessing section of BHM, just quoted, is reworked and placed second rather than first in the tripartite sequence of the *Didache*:

> [We give thanks to] You, almighty Master, [who] created all things for the sake of your Name, and gave food and drink to mankind for their enjoyment, that they might give you thanks; but to us you have granted spiritual [*pneumatiken*] food and drink and eternal life through your child Jesus . . .[4]

As Talley notes: "What is missing in *Didache* is the initial, more universally extended benediction of God as Creator of all and pro- vider of food to all, Israelite and non-Israelite alike. That blessing of God as food-giver is transformed in *Didache* 10:3 into a second thanksgiving for the gifts of spiritual food and drink and eternal life, for food and drink that have been assimilated to the covenant relationship, no longer merely the alimentation provided for all by the Creator."[5]

This second section of the *Didache* reworking of BHM is more overt about God as creator than BHM itself; from this it goes on to nourishment, not mainly with natural food and drink but with "spiritual food and drink and eternal life"; and it forsakes the blessing form for the thanksgiving form. God is thanked rather than blessed for creation and nourishment, now through "your child Jesus," the revealer of God.

It cannot be ruled out that "spiritual food and drink" in such a meal context refers to the eucharistic bread and wine themselves, the more-than-natural elements that nourish participants in this meal for a similarly more-than-natural "eternal life." The prayer would, after all, have been said by the senior at table during the conclusion of the meal while holding the mixed cup. It would therefore seem hard to avoid this prayer-text as the earliest attestation outside the New Testament to the quite special character (*pneumatiken*) of the eucharistic elements.

Be this as it may, this second section of the prayer stresses carnal nourishment and creation less than it does "your child Jesus" as revealer of God. This is the burden of the very first of *Didache*'s three prayers:

> We give thanks to you, holy Father, for your holy Name which you have enshrined in our hearts, and for the knowledge and faith and immortality which you have made known to us through your child Jesus; glory to you for evermore.[6]

It is the revealer of the Father, Jesus, who is the motive for this *eucharistia*, to the extent that the Jewish blessing of God first for created nourishment is put now in second place and given *eucharistia* form, as we have noted. Creation and nourishment are not ignored; they are seen rather as functions of the One who reveals, who is ultimate revelation itself—"through your child Jesus," a phrase used in both the first and second prayers.

This shift to *eucharistia* for revelation in Jesus appears to be underway as well in the tradition of reporting the Last Supper found in Luke 22 and 1 Corinthians 11, where Jesus' table prayers are all designated as *eucharistia* with no mention of his having blessed. This is in clear contrast to the other tradition of reporting the supper in Matthew 26 and Mark 14, where Jesus is said to have blessed God over the bread and thanked God over the cup, which would have been Jewish practice. But unlike Luke-Paul, Matthew-Mark report no meal separating the bread-blessing and the cup-thanksgiving: the two happen back-to-back "As they were eating"—in other words, within the meal itself. To me this discrepancy suggests that Matthew-Mark may be reporting the supper in terms of developed liturgical usage in early churches where the meal had dropped out from between the bread blessing and the cup thanksgiving, perhaps due to reasons of disedification reported elsewhere by Paul in 1 Corinthians 11. In this light Luke-Paul seem to report the Supper in more of its historical integrity, with the meal separating the bread event, now become a *eucharistia* as in *Didache* 9, from the cup thanksgiving. In this regard it is helpful to take *Didache*, at least chapters 1-10, not so much as post-biblical as contemporary with the writing and compilation of Luke-Paul, circa 40-60 C.E. Dating *Didache* 9 and 10 earlier rather than later at least ameliorates some problems that otherwise are difficult to deal with, such as the truly eucharistic rather than agape nature of the event described in chapters 9 and 10. In this direction recent scholarship seems to be tending.[7]

In sum, the eucharistic prayers in *Didache* 10, while they do not eliminate reference to creation as a motive for giving thanks, reposition the reference and subordinate it to the non-carnal nourishment of this unique meal that comes to the participants through the revelation of God by "your child Jesus." The emphasis is no longer on creation and the nourishment it affords, but on revelation through Jesus. We shall see this same thing next in the eucharistic prayer found in the *Apostolic Tradition*, attributed to Hippolytus, of the early third century.

The Apostolic Tradition

This is the next undoubted eucharistic prayer text after those found in *Didache* 9 and 10. Its provenance is generally assumed to be Rome, its date around the first two decades of the third century. The earliest version of the *Apostolic Tradition*, containing the eucharistic prayer text, is found in a Latin translation of the original Greek document made around 380, contained in a palimpsest now in the northern Italian town of Verona.[8]

Much has happened to the text since *Didache*'s time. The *Apostolic Tradition* presents a unified text with an institution narrative that mentions the bread and cup back-to-back; a meal as in *Didache*, separating the two, no longer exists. The prayer is now truly a prayer of offering or anaphora, and the whole event is called "the Oblation," distinguished clearly from an agape meal called "the Lord's Supper."[9]

The prayer in the *Apostolic Tradition* opens redolent of *Didache*: "We render thanks to you, O God, through your beloved child Jesus Christ, whom . . ." There follows a series of relative clauses that make creedal statements about how Jesus is the entire motive for this thanksgiving, concluding with his institution of the eucharist at the Last Supper, after which come formal anamnesis and oblation and an epiclesis of the Holy Spirit. There is no mention of creation; the whole is exclusively christic in content. Unlike *Didache*, the petition for the church is now overtly pneumatic but no less ecclesial:

> And we ask that you would send your Holy Spirit upon the offering of your holy church; that, gathering her into one, you would grant to all who receive the holy things (to receive) for the fullness of the Holy Spirit for the strengthening of faith in truth, that we may praise and glorify you through your child Jesus Christ . . .

But the purpose of the prayer in the *Apostolic Tradition*, church unity, is the same, and the language ("through your child . . .") reminds one of *Didache* 9 and 10. That church orders such as *Didache* and *Apostolic Tradition* often build, the later upon the earlier, enhances the possibility that this prayer is working off the earlier document's petitions for the church, unifying them into one within a unified prayer for the Holy Spirit to accomplish its unifying purpose. The tradition of eucharistic thanksgiving and petition remains strong in *Apostolic Tradition* and is unfolding here in what might represent the "birth" of the Holy Spirit as an anaphoral feature along with institution account, anamnesis, and oblation.

The Roman Canon

It is not easy to be clear about the original creation content—or lack of it—in other early eucharistic prayers since in their received form they represent a degree of development that is often considerable. The entry of the *Sanctus* into the euchology of the Table must have had effects on the anaphoral structure; the dates of this, no less than its results in the various eucharistic traditions, are strongly debated among scholars.[10] But once this entry happened, the need to have some introductory wording leading up to the *Sanctus* would have given what may have appeared to some as an opportunity to load such wording with creation motifs, as one sees in the *Yotser-Kaddosh* of the synagogue liturgy. Where *Sanctus* is absent in early eucharistic prayers, as in *Didache* and *Apostolic Tradition*, such an opportunity did not arise. But even with a *Sanctus*, as is apparently the case with the anaphora known as the Strasbourg Papyrus, dating from the second half of the third century and standing at the fountainhead of the Egyptian tradition of St. Mark, creation is a strong motive for thanksgiving.[11] From this it seems that the entry of the *Sanctus* into eucharistic euchology from around 350-400 was not the only factor that led to creation motifs being included.

Nor does the entry of the *Sanctus* necessarily result in creation motifs being included. The old Roman *prex eucharistica* or *canon missae* is a case in point. This prayer still displays the seams that mark the various prayers of western type that have over the centuries made it up. First recognizable references to it appear in his lectures to the newly baptized by Ambrose of Milan around 380 and entitled *De Sacramentis*.[12] Ambrose walks his neophytes through the eucharistic prayer(s) they had heard for the first time on the night of their baptism, concentrating particularly on the "words of Christ" by which the elements were changed into the body and blood of the Lord, He seems to go through the prayer-sections in order, sometimes quoting the very words that survive in the Roman Canon, at other points merely referring, with maddeningly vague allusions, to other parts. Of "the earlier parts" he says: ". . . praise is offered to God; prayer is made for the people, for kings, for others . . ." And while the "prayer" reference may well be to what is contained in the canon's *Te igitur* section, what "praise is offered to God" might mean in specific is unsure. Does this include the *Sanctus* with its lead-in text (later to be called the preface)?[13] That non-Roman western churches subsequent to Ambrose devote much attention to the integrity of the variable preface (the Verona Sacramentary of the fifth century contains 267 of them),[14] and that the *Sanctus* hymn was heavily commented on in both east and west, suggest that had *Sanctus*, at least, been in the Milanese anaphora Ambrose would have said something about it. But the argument is a weak one from silence; other north Italian fragments of the canon have prefaces but no *Sanctus*.[15]

That the canon makes no attempt to connect the hymn to the *Te igitur*, which follows, reveals a seam where an addition has occurred.

Igitur ("therefore") would then, as Spinks argues,[16] refer back to an originally *Sanctus*-less preface thus:

> It is truly fitting and right, our duty and our salvation, that we should always and everywhere give you thanks, O Lord, holy Father, almighty eternal God, through Christ our Lord.
>
> (*Te igitur*) We therefore pray and beseech you, most merciful Father, through your Son Jesus Christ, to accept and bless these gifts . . .

Two things may be noted here. First, whether with or without the *Sanctus*, which arrived in Rome around 450, there is no creation motif. Second, the lines just quoted, down to *Te igitur*, constitute the entire *eucharistia*-thanksgiving section of the Roman anaphora; all the rest of the prayer is constituted by a series of distinct petitionary prayers. It is these that Ambrose quotes or that still remain in the Roman anaphora—*Te igitur, Memento Domine, Communicantes, Hanc igitur, Quam oblationem, Qui pridie* (the institution narrative), *Unde et memores* (the anamnesis and oblation), *Supra quae, Supplices te, Memento etiam, Nobis quoque.* From this point of view the Roman anaphora is the least "eucharistic" of all those in the euchological repertoire of the historic Christian churches, and the most petitionary. And these peculiar characteristics Ambrose already witnesses before the end of the fourth century; they are not evidences of "medieval corruption." Early Hispanic and Italian fragments reveal the same peculiarities.[17]

Conclusions

The two most archaic eucharistic prayers, *Didache* and *Apostolic Tradition*, exhibit certain features which, amid the welter of later developed eucharistic prayers, are shared by the old *prex eucharistica* or *canon missae* of Rome, the full text of which does not appear until the (sixth century?) Gelasian Sacramentary (ms. eighth century). None of the three originally had the *Sanctus*, and none appear to have had creation as a motive for eucharistic praise, focusing instead exclusively on revelation in Christ. In this all three appear to adhere to the canon of Jewish prayer which allocates blessing for created nourishment, thanksgiving for revelation, and petition for present and future redemption. There are no blessing formulas in any of the prayers; if Heinemann is correct about the canon of Jewish prayer, the Christian Table euchology moved away from it almost from the beginning. As for eucharistic and petitionary material, the *Didache* contains the former and latter in a ratio of about 3 to 2, *Apostolic Tradition* of about 2 to 1 (excluding institution narrative and anamnesis and oblation); the Roman prayer is over ninety-five percent petitionary, the weakest Christian Table prayer in eucharistic cursus. But it is the strongest of all, including Egyptian St. Mark,[18] in its petitionary content, which focuses on the eschatological need for present and future redemption "through Christ our Lord." In this the Roman prayer may represent a sort of palimpsest of prayers native to the Italo-Hispanic areas and originating in the earliest Latin-speaking church, that of North Africa.

In all this, however, we are doing no more than lurching, as Talley says, across small stepping stones in a river of ignorance. Yet it remains remarkable how much our knowledge of these matters, so crucial to the faith and well-being of the churches of God, has increased during this century, thanks to the work of such dedicated and superb teachers as Boone Porter and his students. They have blessed us all.

Notes

1. See Talley's two essays, "From Berakah to Eucharistia: A Reopening Question," *Worship* 50 (1976) 115-137, and "Sources and Structures of the Eucharistic Prayer," in *Worship: Reforming Tradition* (Washington, D.C.: The Pastoral Press, 1990) 11-34.

2. Joseph Heinemann, *Prayer in the Talmud: Forms and Patterns*, Studia Judaica, vol. 9 (Berlin and New York: Walter de Gruyter, 1977) 33.

3. R.C.D. Jasper and G.J. Cuming, *Prayers of the Eucharist: Early and Reformed*, 2d ed. (New York: Pueblo Publishing Co., 1980) 10.

4. Jasper and Cuming, *Prayers* 23-24.

5. Talley, "Sources and Structures" 17-18.

6. Jasper and Cuming, *Prayers* 23.

7. Ibid. 20-22; Talley, "Sources and Structures" 17.

8. Jasper and Cuming, *Prayers* 34-36.

9. Although oblatory terminology is new in *Apostolic Tradition*, as is the euchological structure of anamnesis-oblation that contains and focuses it, the association of sacrifice with eucharist is not. *Didache* 14, a chapter that may be somewhat later than the original core of chapters 1-10, speaks of the Sunday eucharist in overtly sacrificial terms centered on Malachi 1:11: "In every place and time offer me a pure sacrifice, for I am a great king . . . and my name is great among the heathen." By the time of *Apostolic Tradition* these sentiments have become expressed in the prayer itself.

10. See Bryan D. Spinks, *The Sanctus in the Eucharistic Prayer* (New York: Cambridge University Press, 1991).

11. Jasper and Cuming, *Prayers* 53-54.

12. Ibid. 144-146.

13. Ibid. 163-166.

14. See J.A. Jungmann, *The Mass of the Roman Rite*, vol. 2 (New York: Benziger Brothers, 1955) 115-128.

15. See Spinks, *The Sanctus* 95. It appears that western churches were just beginning to adopt the *Sanctus* c. 400 and that all the eastern churches had already done so.

16. Ibid. 94.

17. See Jasper and Cuming, *Prayers* 156-158.

18. Ibid.

2

The Creation Theme
in Eucharistic Prayer

Thomas J. Talley

A MAJOR SHIFT IN LITURGICAL UNDERSTANDING IN THIS CENTURY HAS COME
with the recognition that the eucharistic prayer is much more than the
"prayer of consecration" that it was once considered. Beyond that
rather functional characterization, reflective of a limited comprehension of the liturgy itself, appreciation of this central prayer of the
eucharist as *The Great Thanksgiving* asserts its role as the great
profession of faith, the confession of the whole mystery of our
salvation.[1]

Yet in much of our tradition (and not just the Anglican) we find in
this prayer little reference to the doctrine so well addressed again and
again in "The First Article" by the editor of *The Living Church*, the
distinguished scholar and priest whom this volume honors (and
whom I am honored to acknowledge as my *Doktorvater*), namely, the
doctrine of creation. It is with creation that Scripture begins and so do
both the Apostles' and Nicene creeds, but the role of creation among
the themes of eucharistic prayers, although often important, is far
from constant.

The earliest prayers that can be taken to be for the eucharist are
found in chapters 9 and 10 of the *Didache*, a Syrian church order now
dated by most scholars to the first or early second century. However,
these very simple prayers, devoid of any reference to Christ's Last

13

Supper with his disciples or to his death and resurrection, are so unlike what we have come to assume of eucharistic prayer that many have doubted whether they could really be that. Further, the similarity of chapter 10 to a recognized Jewish grace after meals led some scholars to suppose that chapters 9 and 10 of the *Didache* had to do not with the eucharist at all, but only with ordinary meal fellowship.[2] Comparison with that Jewish grace after meals has become a more complex question in recent decades.

In the prayer books (*siddurim*) of the ninth and following centuries, the grace after meals, *birkat ha-mazon*, opens with a benediction of God as creator and provider of food to all humankind, then gives thanks for God's peculiar gifts to his people (the land, the law, the covenant), and then prays for the building of Jerusalem and the restoration of the kingdom of David. Although these prayer books provide the earliest full text of *birkat ha-mazon*, some writers have supposed that it lies behind *Didache* 10, and have argued, therefore, that this was only an agape, not a eucharist.

In fact, we cannot reconstruct the text of that meal grace as it was in the first century for the simple reason that all Jewish prayer in the first century was an oral rather than a written tradition. Even in the *siddurim* there are textual variants, and we cannot know what particular prayers sounded like centuries earlier, if they were in use at all. There is good reason to believe that even where there was a fairly sturdy traditional pattern, verbal variation could be expected even from one occasion to another in the same locale.

However, whatever variety there may have been, we know that a grace after meals structurally similar to the one we find later in the *siddurim* was in use, since a grace of that form is found in *The Book of Jubilees* in the second century B.C.[3] Apart from a fourth benediction said to have been added in the second century of the Common Era,[4] the medieval texts and that in *Jubilees* present the same structure: a benediction of God as creator and provider of food, a thanksgiving for God's saving intervention in history, and a supplication for the future of the elect people. In the later texts, as noted, the thanksgiving is focused on God's gift of the promised land, the covenant, and the law, while the supplication is for the people Israel, the restoration of Jerusalem, and of the kingdom of the house of David.[5] On the other hand, the text encountered in *Jubilees* is put on the lips of Abraham, and that required a content free from those historical references. Nonetheless, Abraham begins by blessing "God Most High who created heaven and earth and who made all the fat of the earth and gave it to the sons of man so that they might eat and drink and bless their Creator." He then gives thanks for a long life lived in peace, in which "The sword of the enemy did not triumph over me in anything which you gave to me or my sons," and then turns to supplication that God's mercy and peace may be upon him and the seed of his sons, "so that they may become an elect people for you and an inheritance from all the nations of the earth."

Didache 10 is also three short paragraphs, and, given the fluidity of Jewish prayer, it is easy to see why *Didache* 10 could be taken to be a Christian version of such a grace after meals. However, the differences between *Didache* 10 and the Jewish grace, when examined carefully, are as interesting as the similarities, and can suggest a quite deliberate Christian revision. There are two points at which this difference appears: (1) there is no initial benediction of God as creator and giver of food to all, leaving a thanksgiving for the Name as the opening section; and (2) that thanksgiving, ended in a doxology, is followed by a second thanksgiving that distinguishes between the natural food and drink given to all in creation and, by contrast, the spiritual food and drink and eternal life given to us in Christ.

> We give thanks to you, holy Father, for your holy Name which you have enshrined in our hearts, and for the knowledge and faith and immortality which you made known to us through your child Jesus; glory to you for evermore.
>
> You, almighty Master, created all things for the sake of your Name, and gave food and drink to mankind for their enjoyment, that they might give you thanks; but to us you have granted spiritual food and drink and eternal life through your child Jesus. Above all we give you thanks because you are mighty; glory to you for evermore. Amen.

Then follows the concluding supplication for the community:

> Remember, Lord, your Church, to deliver it from all evil and to perfect it in your love; bring it together from the four winds, now sanctified, into your kingdom which you have prepared for it; for yours are the power and the glory for evermore.[6]

It is unmistakable here that the creation theme has been subordinated to some degree. No longer the opening benediction, it is mentioned only in the second paragraph and even there is set in contrast to God's special gifts to us, "spiritual food and drink and eternal life through your child Jesus." That could well suggest that the concern of this revision is more the distinctive character of the spiritual gifts than disinterest in creation. Remembering that the thanksgiving in the Jewish grace focused on God's redemptive intervention in history, his gifts to his peculiar people, it is easy to understand this transposition of the reference to the gift of food. What is involved here is not unlike Paul's distinction between ordinary table fellowship, such as was common among the Corinthians, and the *kyriakon deipnon*, the supper of the Lord. Paul asks, indeed, "have you not houses to eat and drink in?" His concern in 1 Corinthians 11 seems to have been to draw a line between ordinary table fellowship and the memorial of the death of the Lord, just as the second section of *Didache* 10 is concerned to distinguish between the food that is the gift of the creator to all humanity and the spiritual food of the eucharist that is an aspect of the peculiar economy of salvation, as were the law and the covenant to our Jewish forebears. That very early distinction between ordinary food and drink and the eucharistic gifts led, I would suggest, to a revision of the common grace after meals that, in effect, suppressed the opening benediction of the creator in favor of asserting the distinctiveness of the eucharist. The resulting double thanksgiving and supplication for the gathering of the church was soon replicated in a similar group of three prayers before the distribution of the eucharist in chapter 9, a thanksgiving over the cup, another over the broken bread, and again a supplication for the gathering of the church.

While it may well be that it was such an assertion of the distinctiveness of the eucharist that subordinated the creation theme in *Didache* 10, that theological deficit was not suffered elsewhere. In Alexandria the anaphora of the Liturgy of Saint Mark opens with a clear benediction of God as creator, through Christ. That strangely constructed liturgy was long known only through medieval manuscripts, but a fragmentary Greek papyrus, evidently written between 300 and 500, was found at Strasbourg and published in 1928.[7] Taken at first to be but a fragment of the already known anaphora of St. Mark, for some time its significance was limited to establishing a much earlier date for that prayer. More recent studies, however, have noted that where the standard text of St. Mark has the introduction to the *Sanctus*, this papyrus fragment has what seems to be a concluding doxology. That could mean that the papyrus fragment represents a complete eucharistic prayer consisting only of a benediction of God as creator, through Christ; an offering of the "reasonable sacrifice" to God, "giving thanks through him to you with him and the Holy Spirit"; and a long series of intercessions leading into the final doxology.[8] An anaphora of that severe simplicity—no *Sanctus*, nor institution narrative, nor memorial of the passion, nor invocation of the Spirit—could well have been framed originally around A.D. 200, G.J. Cuming suggested, and would show an early strong emphasis on creation as a theological theme in the eucharistic prayer. Both Cuming and Herman Wegman, noting that the surviving praise verb in the tattered beginning of the papyrus is *eulogein*, spoke of this prayer as a *berakah* and implied a Jewish background for it. That cannot be categorically denied, but there is no reason to assert it, and structural considerations might argue against it. Indeed, it seems reasonable to consider it a direct Christian composition, though clearly rooted in Old Testament thought. Whether the short text in the Strasbourg papyrus was the complete prayer would impinge, probably, upon its date, but in any case it is clear that this Alexandrian tradition addresses God as preeminently the creator and fully associates the second person with the work of creation.

Even so, however, we find other early anaphoras that do not give clear attention to the doctrine of creation, being focused on thanksgiving for the saving work of Christ and supplication for the outpouring of the Spirit. The best known of these is the eucharistic prayer of a newly ordained bishop in the *Apostolic Tradition*, a church order of the early third century most frequently ascribed to the Roman theologian, Hippolytus.[9] Although the relevance of this document to the life of the Roman Church is disputed, as is its ascription to Hippolytus, the document itself gives valuable insight into liturgical development in the third century apart from questions of provenance and authorship. Of the presently known eucharistic prayers, this is the earliest to include, as the climax of a Christological thanksgiving, the narrative of the institution of the eucharist and the memorial/oblation or anamnesis. The following supplication for the gathering of the church invokes the Holy Spirit, and this is the earliest example of such an epiclesis. Creation is mentioned only in the parenthetical phrase, "through whom you made all things," in the opening Christological thanksgiving whose thrust is primarily soteriological. As with other prayers before this, there is no *Sanctus*.

The same structural characteristics—a Christological thanksgiving with institution narrative and anamnesis, and a supplication including invocation of the Spirit, with neither praise of the creator nor *Sanctus*—are found in an anaphora attributed to Epiphanius, a late fourth-century bishop of Salamis.[10] The theological content of the prayer indicates an even later date (the Christology is clearly Chalcedonian), but its structural similarity to the prayer of the *Apostolic Tradition* suggests that it is an older prayer that has been reworked.

Still another prayer focused immediately upon thanksgiving for the work of Christ, and with no reference to God as creator, is most commonly assigned to the first half of the fifth century in Syria or Asia Minor. This is the anaphora in a church order, *Testamentum Domini*, that is a reworking and expansion of the *Apostolic Tradition*.[11] Here again, although this work was in development at a time when the inclusion of the *Sanctus* was virtually standard in the east, no attempt has been made to incorporate that hymn. Both the *Testamentum Domini* and the anaphora of Epiphanius, in their very different ways, seem to be dependent upon the *Apostolic Tradition*, and may represent conscious archaism.

However, in the course of the fourth century, a praise of God formed the opening section of eucharistic prayers of the type eventually known as Antiochene or West Syrian or Syro-Byzantine. This praise leads into the *Sanctus*, and the continuation of the prayer after that hymn often reflects that fact, repeating the adjective "Holy" in its address to God. Apart from that, the continuation of these prayers after the *Sanctus* is structurally similar to the anaphora of the *Apostolic Tradition*, a thanksgiving for the saving work of Christ culminating in the institution narrative and anamnesis, and a supplication for the community invoking the Holy Spirit, an invocation increasingly focused on the conversion of the gifts and extended in intercessions.

This relationship between Syro-Byzantine prayers and the *Apostolic Tradition* is reasonably overt in the anaphora in Book VIII of *Apostolic Constitutions*, the last of the church orders, from around Antioch and dated ca. 380.[12] The compiler of this document was an avid collector of texts, which he freely expanded. As earlier books are dependent upon other church orders, Book VIII expands upon the *Apostolic Tradition*. Here, however, we find in the opening praise leading to the *Sanctus* perhaps the most elaborate treatment of creation in anaphoral literature, even if in an anaphora that, on the face of it, was never intended for liturgical use. The compiler was also, if not Arian, given to semi-Arian sympathies, and this is evident at several points. Praising first God, "always being in one and the same mode, from whom all things came into being as from a starting point," the prayer proceeds to the generation of the Son, the creation through the Son of the heavenly powers, and then "this visible world and all that is in it." The creation of earth and its creatures is intricately detailed, and the prayer comes then to the "ornament of the world," man, and his fall by disobedience. With that, the author finds himself into the history of salvation under the Old Covenant, and seems unable to find a place to stop that story. The account proceeds through Noah and the patriarchs, Moses and the exodus, reaching finally to Joshua and the conquest of Canaan. At that point the prayer bursts rather abruptly into a renewed declaration of praise that names those who worship the Father: the Paraclete, the Son, and the orders of angelic beings, leading into the *Sanctus*.

By contrast to that celestial hymn in *Apostolic Constitutions* VIII, creation itself joins the praise in the Liturgy of St. James,[13] where God is hymned by the heavens and all their powers, the sun and moon and all the choir of stars, and the earth and sea and all that is in them, as well as by humans and the angelic choirs. The history of salvation is celebrated following the *Sanctus*, and the intercessions following the epiclesis ask for a favorable climate and abundance of harvests, citing Psalm 145:15.

We have no precise date for the anaphora of St. James, but in that connection Robert Taft has recalled an infrequently cited essay of Massey Shepherd that points to a possible citation of the anaphora of James by Eusebius.[14] The text in question is the "Panagyric on the Erection of the Churches, to Paulinus, Bishop of Tyre," included in full in Eusebius' *Ecclesiastical History* X.4. If, as Taft's presentation of the parallels suggests, Eusebius is alluding to the pre-*Sanctus* of the anaphora of James, then the text's references to the worship of creation reveal similar references in the eucharistic prayer familiar to Eusebius. The sermon was delivered ca. 317, and would mark, Taft believes, the earliest datable evidence of the anaphoral *Sanctus*.

Geoffrey Cuming has suggested that the anaphora of James depends on the earliest version of what is commonly referred to as the Alexandrian Anaphora of Basil, the most commonly used eucharistic prayer in the Coptic Church today.[15] He does not assign such a firm date as did Taft to the reference to James, but Cuming has suggested that the earliest form of Alexandrian Basil, perhaps from Cappadocia, perhaps Antioch, could reach back to the late third century. What is clear is that it is Antiochian in structure, and very unlike the Alexandrian prayers that pass from praise of the creator to oblation to extended intercessions before the *Sanctus*. In this early version of Basil, a pre-*Sanctus* prays:

> . . . truly it is fitting and right, I AM, truly Lord God, existing before the ages, reigning until the ages; you dwell on high and regard what is low; you made heaven and earth and the sea and all that is in them. Father of our Lord and God and Savior Jesus Christ, through whom you made all things visible and invisible, you sit on the throne of your glory; you are adored by every holy power. Around you stand angels and archangels, principalities and powers, thrones, dominions, and virtues; around you stand the cherubim with many eyes and the seraphim with six wings, forever singing the hymn of glory and saying: Holy, etc.[16]

Both Taft and Bryan Spinks have given us excellent studies of the *Sanctus* itself and, with that, some attention to its anaphoral context. What appears from this is that, whatever the ultimate origins of the liturgical use of the *Sanctus*, in Antiochian tradition the *Sanctus* forms the conclusion of what will become known as an *oratio theologica*, a praise of God reigning in heaven, and this will most commonly be the *locus* of the praise of God as creator. Such an initial praise of God as creator, of course, was not limited to Antiochian tradition. It has been noted already at Alexandria, and is found also in East Syria. Even in Latin tradition, such a praise of the creator and creation is found in an alternative *contestatio* for the second of the Gallican masses published by Mone, and there is no reason to suppose that this was a unique instance.

If the *Sanctus* first found a place in the fourth-century anaphora not as a hymn inserted between the paragraphs of an existing anaphora but as the conclusion of an opening prayer prefixed to the Christological thanksgiving, the *Sanctus* does seem to be an interpolation into the prayer that emerges as the Roman standard. The roots of that prayer can be seen in *De Sacramentis*, instructions to neophytes by Ambrose of Milan,[17] although it has undergone significant development before we first encounter the Roman text in the Gelasian Sacramentary. Speaking of the eucharistic prayer, Ambrose distinguished between "the other things which are said in the earlier parts . . . by the bishop" and what he characterizes as "the words of Christ." Although Christ's own words are enclosed within what we can only understand to be a fairly stable prayer, it would appear that Ambrose considered the preceding elements ("praise is offered to God; prayer is made for the people, for kings, for others") to be more variable, reflecting the concerns of the *sacerdos*.

Such, in any case, is the situation that confronts us in the earliest collection of Roman mass texts, which we know as The Veronense Sacramentary. There every mass formula consists of a number of short prayers appropriate to the occasion, one of which always begins *Vere dignum*. While occasionally one of these will point definitely toward the *Sanctus*,[18] much more commonly they end simply with the incipit of a concluding formula, *per*; it is entirely possible that some of these, at least, antedate the addition of the *Sanctus* at Rome. The second of two prefaces quoted by an anonymous Arian writer in northern Italy in the early fourth century and edited by Cardinal Mai moves directly from the dialogue through thanksgiving for redemption to prayer for acceptance of the offering, with no suggestion of the *Sanctus*.[19] In fact, as P.-M. Gy has argued, the *Sanctus* probably entered the Roman Canon hardly more than a decade or two before the pontificate of Leo I (440-461).[20]

By the time of the Gregorian Sacramentary, the number of these proper prefaces is severely reduced, and they are provided for only the greater festivals, still with the other variable prayers. Otherwise, there is provided a *praefatio communis* with the *Sanctus* in the *ordo missae*. That common preface merely declares the praise of the heavenly power and the seraphim, and asks that our voices be admitted to theirs with thanksgiving. There is no reference to creation. Otherwise, the proper prefaces are keyed to festivals determined by a liturgical year whose content is fundamentally Christological. Further, the interpolation of the *Sanctus* interrupted the connection of the canon's opening *Te igitur* with the preceding preface, and increasingly the canon alone, with its repeated petitions for the acceptance of the offering, seemed to be the whole of the eucharistic prayer. In that reduced prayer, the praise of the creator for the glories of creation had no part.

There seems little reason to retrace here the history of western eucharistic theology and liturgy from the ninth to the sixteenth centuries. Suffice it to say that in that period the eucharistic prayer was not seen as a great confession of faith, praising and giving thanks to the God who moves in history from creation to eschaton. Indeed, by the thirteenth century at the latest even the thanksgivings for the work of Christ in the proper prefaces were hardly considered a part of the same liturgical unit as the *canon missae*. Increasing preoccupation with the confective power of the words of Christ in the institution narrative left even the canon, apart from those words, of questionable necessity, even in the thought of St. Thomas.[21]

Against this background, the radical abandonment of the traditional canon in Luther's *Formula Missae et Communionis* (1523) is perhaps less surprising. There, in effect, the institution narrative becomes the body of a preface, after which the *Sanctus* is sung as a conclusion. Needless to say, there is expressed here no celebration of creation, nor was there in the *Deutsche Messe* three years later.[22] In both these, Luther shows himself to be deeply tinctured by the liturgical thought of the late Middle Ages, in what he considered essential and in what he thought disposable. His Catholic opponents, of course, continued to respect the authority of the church that imposed the canon, but the issue was obedience, not liturgical integrity.

In the light of the whole western experience, from the fourth century forward, it is rather surprising to encounter in a Protestant document of the sixteenth century a praise of the creator redolent of what we have seen in oriental anaphoras. This is the Cologne church order of 1545, issued by Archbishop Herman von Wied and prepared at his invitation by two outstanding reformers, Martin Bucer and Philip Melancthon. After a standard western dialogue, the preface touches on our creation in the image of God and the appointment of all other creatures to our use:

> It is verily a thing worthy, right, meet, and wholesome, that we give thanks unto thee always and everywhere, that we praise and magnify thee, Lord, holy Father, Almighty everlasting God, through Jesus Christ our Lord, by whom thou madest us of nothing unto thine image, and hast appointed all other creatures to our uses . . .[23]

From that point, the prayer describes the fall, our consequent subjection to death and damnation, and the sending of the Son for our deliverance by the incarnation, the cross, and the gift of the Spirit. This thanksgiving then remembers the gift of the eucharistic sacrament itself, to the end that we may glorify God and sing "with all thy holy angels and beloved children." After the *Sanctus* and *Benedictus* the priest sings the institution narrative. Here a rubric directs the people to "say to these words, Amen, which all the old churches observed, and the Greeks do yet observe the same."

It is generally agreed that Bucer had the major role in the liturgical aspects of the order, but this extended fixed thanksgiving for creation and the history of salvation, and the further reference to the Greek liturgy's singing of "Amen" after the words of Christ over the gifts, might lead one to suspect here the hand of Melancthon, whose favorable disposition to the Greek liturgy was already recorded in the *Apology of the Augsburg Confession*.[24]

Although the Cologne church order, published in English in 1547 as *A simple and Religious Consultation*, is recognized as contributing significantly to the *Order of the Communion* of 1548 and thence to the various prayer books that followed, this fixed prayer leading to the *Sanctus* had no effect on the eucharistic prayers of the Church of England. There a limited number of proper prefaces continued to assign various dimensions of the Christological thanksgiving to particular festivals, a pattern maintained even in the liturgy issued, disruptively, by the Nonjuring Usagers in 1718.

It was different, however, with two other Anglican liturgies that appeared in the eighteenth century, although neither of them could claim any very clear authority. In 1734 Thomas Deacon, representing the conservative wing of what was now a three-way split among the Nonjurors, issued *A Compleat Collection of Devotions, both Publick and Private: Taken from the Apostolical Constitutions, The Ancient Liturgies and the Common Prayer Book of the Church of England*. The eucharistic prayer here opens with a translation, slightly abbreviated, of the beginning of the anaphora of *Apostolic Constitutions* VIII, with the same extended praise of creation and an only slightly attenuated recitation of the salvation history of the Old Covenant.[25] While this may have seen as much actual use as its original, it is doubtful that it saw more. In neither case are we justified in envisioning more than an occasional celebration for the personal gratification of the author, whether in the fourth century or the eighteenth.

Somewhat more frankly ideal was the liturgy adapted by Thomas Rattray from his English edition of the Liturgy of St. James, *An Office for the Sacrifice of the Holy Eucharist, being the Ancient Liturgy of the Church of Jerusalem, to which Proper Rubricks are added for Direction*.[26] Neither this nor his longer study of the Liturgy of St. James saw publication until after his death in 1743. Here, after the dialogue (its first member altered from James to follow 2 Corinthians 13:14), the fixed pre-*Sanctus* praises:

> ... the Maker of all Creatures visible and invisible, the Treasure of all good Things; the Fountain of Life and Immortality; the God and Governor of the Universe: To whom the Heaven and the

Heaven of Heavens sing praise, with all their Hosts: The Sun and Moon, and the whole Choir of Stars: the Earth and Sea, and all Things that are in them: The Angels, Archangels, Thrones, Dominions, Principalities, Authorities, and tremendous Powers: The many-eyed Cherubim, and the Seraphim with six Wings, who with twain cover their Faces, and with twain the Feet, and with twain they fly, crying one to another with never-ceasing Voices, and uninterrupted Shouts of Praise, and saying, Holy, etc.

After the epiclesis, Rattray reproduces as well the petition for climate and harvest as in James.

Although Rattray's works are recognized to have had significant effect on the Scottish Liturgy of 1764, that did not include displacement of the western proper preface tradition, and the prayer after the *Sanctus* continues the soteriological focus of its predecessors of 1637 and earlier. The experiments of Deacon and Rattray, whatever their other value, did not restore interest in creation to the themes of the eucharistic prayer in Anglicanism.

Affection for proper prefaces also prevented their displacement by a fixed pre-*Sanctus* in the anaphora drafted by E.C. Ratcliff, J.C. Winslow, and others for the Bishop of Bombay early in this century.[27] Otherwise, that prayer was deeply colored by the Liturgy of St. James, used by a number of groups in India. After the angelic hymn, the prayer paraphrases James, including the characterization of Christ as he, "by whom thou framedst the worlds." The Great Intercession includes the petition for good climate and abundance noted for James above, including the reference to Psalm 145. Indeed, so faithful is this prayer to James after the *Sanctus* that one feels even more strongly the absence of creation itself giving voice to the great angelic hymn.

In the vast work of liturgical renewal following the Second Vatican Council, the rite of the eucharist was assigned to one of several *ad hoc* commissions, in this case *Coetus X*. That commission produced three new eucharistic prayers (Eucharistic Prayers II, III, and IV) in addition to a modest revision of the Roman Canon.[28] Prayers I and III require proper prefaces, and it is interesting to observe that in many of the new ones the theme of creation is given prominence. Prayer II is based, with obvious changes, on the anaphora in the *Apostolic Tradition*, and contains but the slight reference to the work of the Word in creation in the original. Prayer IV takes much of its wording from the Alexandrian Basil and, apart from an epiclesis before the narrative, follows the Antiochian pattern. Before the *Sanctus* the prayer confesses: "Source of life and goodness, you have created all things, to fill your creatures with every blessing and lead all men to the joyful vision of your light," and the creation theme returns following the *Sanctus*: "You formed man in your own likeness and set him over the whole world to serve you, his creator, and to rule over all creatures."

Those citations are in the ICEL translation, but it was the Latin text, together with the Alexandrian and Byzantine texts of Basil, that formed the basis of *A Common Eucharistic Prayer*, composed by an ecumenical committee of liturgical scholars in 1974, seeking to provide one eucharistic prayer that might find broad ecumenical acceptance, at least in the United States. It appears as Eucharistic Prayer D in the American Book of Common Prayer of 1979. The preceding Prayer C shows, perhaps, the most elaborate development of the creation theme, and is redolent of contemporary cosmology and ecological concerns, especially in its second paragraph:

> At your command all things came to be: the vast expanse of interstellar space, galaxies, suns, the planets in their courses, and this fragile earth, our island home.

The first two prayers of the contemporary language Rite II employ proper prefaces, but there too, the opening of the common preface is careful to give its thanks "to you, Father Almighty, Creator of heaven and earth." That is not true of the common preface in the traditional language Rite I, and its Eucharistic Prayer I, that adopted from the Scottish Liturgy, is exclusively soteriological. However, a revision of that prayer, Eucharistic Prayer II, opens after the *Sanctus*: "All glory be to thee, O Lord our God, for that thou didst create heaven and earth, and didst make us in thine own image."

In sum, we can say that western eucharistic prayers in our time are much more focused on the profession of faith than has been true in the past, and this includes a broader sense of the history of salvation as rooted in the act of creation. This, it seems, is more than just the repair of an unfortunate lacuna in the themeology of the anaphora. It marks a shift in our understanding of the eucharist itself, setting consecration and communion more firmly in the context of the proclamation of the Lord's death and resurrection, and with that the confession of the incarnation and the second coming of the Word, by whom all things were made, so that through our praise and thanksgiving all that is may reflect that creative love in the profession of the faith that justifies.

Notes

1. See *inter alia* Louis Weil, "Proclamation of Faith in the Eucharist," in *Time and Community*, ed. J, Neil Alexander, NPM Studies in Church Music and Liturgy (Washington, D.C.: The Pastoral Press, 1990) 279-290.

2. So, for example, W. Rordorf, "Les prières eucharistiques de la Didaché," in *Eucharisties d'orient et d'occident*, vol. 1 (Paris: Cerf, 1970) 65-82.

3. *Jubilees* 22:5-9. James H. Charlesworth, ed., *The Old Testament Pseudepigrapha*, vol. 2 (Garden City, NY: Doubleday, 1985) 97.

4. By R. Nachman, according to b. Berakoth 48b.

5. See David Hedegard, *Seder R. Amran Gaon* (Lund: Universitets-Bokhandel, 1951) 147-148.

6. Presented here in the version of R.C.D. Jasper and G.J. Cuming, *Prayers of the Eucharist: Early and Reformed*, 3rd ed., revised and enlarged (New York: Pueblo Publishing Co., 1987) 23-24.

7. Ibid. 53-54.

8. E. Kilmartin, "Sacrificium Laudis," *Theological Studies* 35 (1974) 268-287; Herman Wegman, "Une anaphore incomplète? Les fragments sur Papyrus Strasbourg Gr. 254," in *Studies in Gnosticism and Hellenistic Religions*, ed. R. Van den Broek and M.J. Vermaseren (Leiden: Brill, 1981) 432-450; Geoffrey Cuming, "The Anaphora of St. Mark: A Study in Development," *Le Muséon* 95 (1982) 115-129; W.H. Bates, "Thanksgiving and Intercession in the Liturgy of St. Mark," in *The Sacrifice of Praise*, ed. Bryan D. Spinks, Bibliotheca "Ephemerides Liturgicae," Subsidia, vol. 19 (Rome: C.L.V. Edizioni Liturgiche, 1981) 118-119.

9. Jasper and Cuming, *Prayers* 34-35.

10. Ibid. 141-142.

11. Ibid. 138-141.

12. Ibid. 104-112.

13. Ibid. 90-99.

14. M.H. Shepherd, "Eusebius and the Liturgy of St. James," *Yearbook of Liturgical Studies* 4 (1963) 109-123. Taft cites this in a forthcoming continuation of a study of the *Sanctus* of which Part I has already appeared: "The Interpolation of the Sanctus into the Anaphora: When and Where? A Review of the Dossier," *Orientalia Christiana Periodica* 57 (1991) 281-308.

15. This dependency has recently received detailed examination in a fine study by one of Cuming's students, John R.K. Fenwick, *The Anaphoras of St. Basil and St. James: An Investigation into Their Common Origins*, Orientalia Christiana Analecta, vol. 240 (Rome: Pontificium Institutum Orientale, 1992). Fenwick argues that St. James represents an expansion of the early Jerusalem anaphora reflected in the Mystagogical Catecheses of Cyril of Jerusalem by conflation with an early form of Basil.

16. Jasper and Cuming, *Prayers* 70-72.

17. Ibid. 143-146.

18. For example, number 1137 in the edition of Mohlberg concludes: *Et ideo cum angelis*; see L.C. Mohlberg, with Leo Eisenhöfer and Petrus Sifrin, eds., *Sacramentarium Veronense*, Rerum Ecclesiasticarum Documenta, Series Maior, Fontes, vol. 1 (Rome: Herder, 1956) 143.

19. Ibid. 202, formula 1544.

20. P.-M. Gy, "Le Sanctus romain and les anaphores orientales," in *Mélanges liturgiques offerts au R.P. Dom Bernard Botte* (Louvain: Abbaye du Mont César, 1972) 172. Cited here from B. Spinks, *The Sanctus in the Eucharistic Prayer* (Cambridge: Cambridge University Press, 1991) 96.

21. Significant texts are given in P.-M. Gy, "Prière eucharistique et paroles de la consécration selon les théologiens de Pierre Lombard " S. Thomas d'Aquin," *La Liturgie dans l'histoire* (Paris: Cerf, 1990) 214-219.

22. Jasper and Cuming, *Prayers* 191-199.

23. Ibid. 222.

24. *Apology of the Augsburg Confession* XXIV.88. Theodore G. Tappert, ed. and tr., *The Book of Concord: The Confessions of the Evangelical Lutheran Church* (Philadelphia: Fortress Press, 1959) 265.

25. W. Jardine Grisbrooke, *Anglican Liturgies of the Seventeenth and Eighteenth Centuries*, Alcuin Club Collections, vol. 49 (London: SPCK, 1958) 306-312.

26. Ibid. 323-328.

27. Bernard Wigan, ed., *The Liturgy in English* (London: Oxford University Press, 1962) 101-106.

28. The texts of these and other new Roman Catholic prayers may be examined in a valuable study by Enrico Mazza, *The Eucharistic Prayer of the Roman Rite* (New York: Pueblo Publishing Co., 1986).

3

The Offering of the Firstfruits of Creation: An Historical Study

Paul F. Bradshaw

The Old Testament

WITHIN ANCIENT ISRAELITE RELIGION TWO KINDS OF OFFERING OF FIRSTFRUITS CAN be distinguished: the consecration to God of the firstborn of male children or animals, which presumably arose among a nomadic people, and the annual presentation of the firstfruits of the harvest of the fields (grain, wine, and oil), which must have originated in an agrarian civilization. Both of these must also be distinguished from those sacrifices in which a victim was totally "given to God" by ritual destruction. Although the latter may have been a very early way of consecrating one's firstborn child, and although there are recorded instances of some Israelites adopting the Canaanite custom of infant sacrifice (see Jgs 11:30ff.; 1 Kgs 16:34), Pentateuchal legislation required instead that firstborn male children be "redeemed," at first by the substitutionary sacrifice of an animal (Ex 13:1, 11-16; 34:19-20; cf. Gn 22), and later by a monetary payment (Nm 18:16). Even in the case of firstborn male animals, which were slaughtered, the emphasis did not fall on their destruction: the sacrificial victim was to be eaten by the owner's household "before the Lord" (Dt 12:6-7, 11-12, 17-19; 15:19-23).

In both the consecration of the firstborn and the offering of the firstfruits of the harvest, the purpose was the same. A part of all that will be produced is presented to God—*presented* rather than given because it belongs to God already—and serves as representative of the whole. By this ritual action those who make the presentation acknowledge who it is that is the true owner and giver of all, and so are granted the right to take and use the rest. It is important to distinguish this offering from the *tithe*. In the case of the firstfruits, the stress falls on the fact that it is the first and the best which is presented; in the case of the tithe, the emphasis is rather upon the quantity of what is brought. The former is a token gesture; the latter has to be an exact proportion of the whole.

In the course of time two developments took place which to some extent modified the significance of this liturgy. The first was that the oblations became an important part of the financial support of the cultic officials. Deuteronomy 18:4 directs that they are to keep for themselves the firstfruits of grain, wine, oil, and "the first of the fleece of your sheep," but Numbers 18:12-18 adds to these provisions the flesh of animals also, with only the blood being sprinkled on the altar and the fat being burned as an offering to God. We should also note here the statement in 2 Kings 4:42, where a man from Baalshalishah is said to have brought to the prophet Elisha loaves of barley and ears of grain as firstfruits. This would appear to support the claims of some biblical scholars that some prophets exercised a cultic role.

The second development was that these celebrations ceased to be purely the anamnesis of God's lordship over creation and became also remembrances of God's redemptive activity. Thus, the agrarian feast of Unleavened Bread, which had originally marked the beginning of the barley harvest, was combined with the Passover as a commemoration of the Exodus. The feast of Weeks, which Numbers 28:26 calls "the Day of the Firstfruits" and which marked the wheat harvest, retained its agricultural character somewhat longer but was eventually related to salvation-history: Deuteronomy 16:12 attempts to introduce into it the notion of the remembrance of slavery in Egypt, and it ultimately became a commemoration of the covenant at Sinai (Ex 19:1; 2 Chr 15:10; *Jubilees* 6:17-21). Similarly, the general directions about the offering of firstfruits of the harvest in Deuteronomy 26:1-11 make a very clear association with the Exodus ("A wandering Aramean was my father; and he went down into Egypt . . ."): the goods which the worshiper enjoys are the result of God's gift of the land to the people of Israel. The same development can also be seen in the case of Sukkoth, "the feast of Tabernacles/Booths": originally the feast of ingathering (Ex 23:16; 34:22), held when all the produce of the field had been harvested and the olives and grapes had been pressed (Dt 16:13), it eventually became a commemoration of the sojourn in the wilderness (Lv 23:33-43).

The New Testament

The early Christians took over the image of the firstfruits as a theological concept and applied it in at least three different ways:

1. To Christ. It was employed by Paul to describe the relation between the resurrection of Christ and the resurrection of all: "Christ has been raised from the dead, the firstfruits of those who have fallen asleep . . . For as in Adam all die, so also in Christ shall all be made alive. But each in his own order: Christ the firstfruits, then at his coming those who belong to Christ . . . (1 Cor 15:20ff.). Here God is seen as reaping the eschatological harvest, while in Romans 8:29, Colossians 1:15,18, Hebrews 1:6, and Revelation 1:5, Christ is described as being "the firstborn."

2. To the Spirit. In Romans 8:23 Paul speaks of Christians as having "the firstfruits of the Spirit," and closely related to this is the idea of the Spirit as a pledge or down-payment in 2 Cor 1:22 and 5:5.

3. To the Church. Paul refers to certain converts to Christianity as being the firstfruits in their locality (Rom 16:5; 1 Cor 16:15), while the Book of Revelation extends the idea to the 144,000 who have been redeemed from the earth (Rv 14:4), and the Epistle of James seems to apply the image to all believers (1:18).

In all these cases, the stress seems to be upon the idea of the *beginnings*—of the glorious harvest that will be reaped, of the whole family that will be born, of the fullness of the kingdom that will be enjoyed—rather than upon the presentation to God of what rightfully belongs to God, although that idea is no doubt still there in the background (and, indeed, is articulated in Jas 1:17). This shift of emphasis raises the question as to whether the actual liturgical offering of firstfruits still lay within the early Christians' experience, or whether the concept was no more than a literary metaphor, building perhaps upon such Old Testament passages as Exodus 4:22 ("Israel is my first-born son"), Jeremiah 2:3 ("Israel was holy to the Lord, the firstfruits of his harvest"), and Jeremiah 31:9 ("I am a father to Israel, and Ephraim is my firstborn").

Jews in the first century still redeemed their firstborn sons, a practice alluded to in Luke 2:22f. (although here confused by the author with the sacrifice offered for the purification of the mother, in accordance with Lv 12). But this now only involved the handing-over of a monetary payment and no other ritual act. It is also possible that the prescriptions of Deuteronomy 26 were still being observed as late as the first century, but they would only have been practiced by those directly involved in agriculture and so would not necessarily have been familiar to many of the Jewish converts to Christianity. Furthermore, when we take into account the ambivalence felt by many early Christians towards the observance of the Law and participation in the Temple cult, and the crisis which would in any case have been precipitated by the eventual destruction of the Temple, it would not be surprising to learn that the liturgical practice soon disappeared within the Christian tradition. However, as we shall see, this does not seem to have been the case.

The Didache

What is apparently the earliest reference to the Christian adoption of the offering of firstfruits occurs in *Didache* 13:

> 1. Every true prophet wishing to settle among you is worthy of his food.
> 2. Likewise, a true teacher is himself also worthy, like the laborer, of his food.
> 3. Therefore you shall take all the firstfruit of the produce of the winepress and of the threshing-floor and of oxen and sheep, and you shall give the firstfruit to the prophets, for they are your high-priests.
> 4. But if you do not have a prophet, give [it] to the poor.
> 5. If you make bread, take the firstfruit and give [it] according to the commandment.
> 6. Likewise, when you open a jar of wine or oil, take the firstfruit and give [it] to the prophets.
> 7. Of money and clothes and every possession, take the firstfruit, as it seems good to you, and give [it] according to the commandment.

The first question that needs to be addressed here is the integrity of the passage. Jean-Paul Audet regarded verses 3 and 5-7 as the work of an interpolator because they use the second person singular, like several other verses elsewhere in the *Didache*, whereas in the rest of the document the second person plural is employed. Verse 4, however, where the second person plural is used, he explained as a second level of interpolation. In his view, therefore, the directions in verses 1 and 2 were orignally simply a continuation of the instructions about hospitality towards Christians who arrive from other places found in chapter 12.[1]

Stanislas Giet, on the other hand, thought that 13.2 might be an addition to the original text, since teachers are not mentioned again in the rest of the chapter and only reappear in chapter 15. Moreover, the repetition of words from 13.1 and the more literal reference to Matthew 10:10 in this verse ("the laborer [is] worthy of his food") also suggested that it was an interpolation. Yet he did not think that the use of the second person singular in the other verses indicated the work of a later interpolator. They were simply the detailed application of the prescriptions about firstfruits in Exodus 22:29 and Deuteronomy 12:6, and continued the use of the second person singular found in the Exodus text. The repetition of the verbs "take" and "give" in verses 3, 5, 6, and 7, and the alternation of the conclusion "to the prophets" in verses 3 and 6 with "according to the commandment" in verses 5 and 7 created a rhythmical pattern, suggesting that the material had originally been used as part of oral teaching. There was nothing to prove that it had been composed specially for a Christian community. The compiler of the *Didache* had added to this older nucleus the phrase "for they are your high-priests" in verse 3, as well as the whole of verse 4, cast in the plural used in the rest of the document.[2]

Like Giet, Willy Rordorf and André Tuilier in their edition of the *Didache* thought that the reference to teachers in verse 2 interrupted the sequence of the text and belonged to a stage when teachers were replacing prophets as ministers of the word. They also believed that the substitution of the second person plural in verse 4 for the second person singular found in the other verses perhaps pointed to this verse also being an interpolation, albeit an ancient one.[3]

If Giet's explanation of the evolution of the text has any merit, it suggests that the offering of the firstfruits was not an innovation that the *Didache* was introducing into the Christian tradition but was already an established custom which was merely being reinforced. The prescriptions are interesting, for they include firstborn oxen and sheep, as well as firstfruits of the winepress and of the threshing-floor, but there is no reference here or elsewhere to the redemption of firstborn sons. Verses 5 and 6 extend the obligation to offer firstfruits from the primary producers to consumers who make bread or open a jar of wine or oil, and verse 7 takes it even further and applies it to all possessions, thus effectively turning it from a harvest offering into a tax on total income.

The wide-ranging nature of these ordinances and the repeated direction that the firstfruits are to be given to the prophet suggest that the primary concern was not theological but economic. Prophets needed to receive material support if they were to be free to exercise their ministry, and hence the Old Testament commandments were invoked to justify the provision of that support by the Christian community. What is really in view here, therefore, is a tithe for the financing of the prophetic ministry rather than an offering of firstfruits as an expression God's lordship over creation. Only the apparent interpolation in verse 4 gives a hint that the practice might continue when no such support was required, and even here the motive is charity towards the needy rather than the worship of God.

A more direct citation of the Numbers 18 passage about the rights of the priests and Levites to the offerings reappears in the *Didascalia Apostolorum*, a third-century Syrian church order, where it is used as the authority for the community's obligation to provide financial support for its clergy and the relief of the poor. Here firstfruits and tithes are mentioned together, with no distinction being drawn between them: "set apart special offerings and tithes and firstfruits for Christ the true high-priest, and for his ministers, as tithes of salvation . . ."[4] Other patristic writings show the same tendency to regard firstfruits and tithes as synonymous and to lay stress on the quantity that ought to be given to provide for the adequate support of the clergy and the poor. In general, the Fathers criticize Christians for being less generous in their giving than the Old Testament law had required. So, for example, Origen complains: "How can our righteousness exceed that of the scribes and Parisees? For they did not dare to eat anything of the fruits of their fields until they had given the firstfruits to the priests and paid their tithes to the Levites. I, however, do not do any of this at all, but claim and use the fruits of my field for myself so that the priest does not know of them and the Levite does not see any part of them."[5]

Only in Irenaeus do we find a different, and more traditional understanding of the purpose of the presentation of firstfruits, although he relates this to Christ's institution of the eucharist: "the Lord instructed his disciples to offer firstfruits to God from his own creatures, not because God needed them, but so that they themselves might not be unfruitful or ungrateful."[6]

The Apostolic Tradition

We are unable to tell from the *Didache* or *Didascalia* whether or not the handing-over of the firstfruits involved an actual liturgical rite which might have given expression to the sort of understanding of its purpose reflected in Irenaeus' eucharistic theology and so helped to counterbalance the more usual interpretation of its meaning found in patristic writings. In the ancient church order known as the *Apostolic Tradition*, however, we do encounter just such a rite:

> Let all hasten to offer the new fruits to the bishop as firstfruits. And as he offers them, he shall say the blessing and name him who offered, saying:
>
> > We give you thanks, O God and offer to you the firstfruits which you have granted us to receive; you nourished them by your word, and ordered the earth to bear all fruits for the joy and nourishment of humans and for all animals. In all these things we praise you, O God, and in all the things with which you have helped us, adorning for us the whole creation with various fruits; through your child Jesus Christ our Lord, through whom be glory to you for the ages of ages. Amen.
> >
> > Fruits indeeed are blessed, that is, grapes, figs, pomegranates, olives pears, apples, mulberries, peaches, cherries, almonds, plums; but not pumpkins, melons, cucumbers, onions, garlic, or any other vegetable. But sometimes flowers also are offered. So let roses and lilies be offered, but not others. And in all things which are eaten, they shall give thanks to the holy God, eating to his glory.[7]

There is no suggestion here or elsewhere in this document that what was offered was intended for the support of the clergy or of the needy, and indeed the restriction of the offering to new *fruits* as such and not vegetables would rather imply that this was not the case. The prayer concentrates entirely upon the theme of thankgiving for what God has given, and does not contain any element of petition at all, nor even provision for the naming of the offerer mentioned in the opening direction. By contrast, brief prayers elsewhere in the document which are to be used whenever people offer oil, cheese, or olives are almost entirely petitionary in character, although as they are apparently intended for use at the conclusion of the eucharistic prayer itself, the element of thanksgiving would be supplied by that oration.

The *Testamentum Domini*, a later derivative of the *Apostolic Tradition*, reproduces the firstfruits prayer in an expanded form, adding to it a brief petition for the blessing of the offerer, who is mentioned by name (II.14-17). The fourth-century *Canons of Hippolytus* develops this section of *Apostolic Tradition* considerably: what is to be presented are not just fruits alone but "the first of their floors and of their presses, oil, honey, milk, wool, and the first of the produce of the work of their hands . . . and the first of their trees," and the compiler specifically includes vegetables in this. The prayer is considerably changed: only the first sentence now gives thanks for the gifts, and in the rest God is asked to satisfy the needs of the poor and to bless the giver (who is named) and his household.[8] *Apostolic Constitutions* also modifies the prayer quite drastically, but retains its original character as a thanksgiving and does not introduce any petitionary elements into it.[9] Elsewhere in this composition, however, it is made clear that the firstfruits are to be used for the support of the bishop, presbyters, and deacons, with tithes for the support of other clergy, virgins, widows, and the poor.[10]

The East

We cannot be sure, of course, that the various provisions of these early church orders accurately reflect what was really going on in the life of third- and fourth-century churches and are not merely the product of their compilers' imaginations. However, the existence of both canonical legislation and also liturgical texts relating to the offering of firstfruits in the later eastern rites does lend some support to their authenticity. The oldest legislation actually occurs in the collection of canons appended to the *Apostolic Constitutions*. Canon 3 prohibits the offering on the altar itself of anything except ears of new wheat and bunches of grapes, while canon 4 directs that all other firstfruits should be sent to the home of the bishop and presbyters for distribution. Later the Sixth Ecumenical Council (A.D. 680) sought to put an end to a custom that obtained in some places of distributing the grapes together with the sacramental wine (canon 28) and to condemn a practice said to take place sometimes in Armenia whereby people would offer to the priests in the church parts of meat they had roasted, in accordance with the Old Testament prescriptions (canon 99).

Perhaps surprisingly, the later *euchologia* include as the liturgical formulary for the offering of firstfruits the prayer from the *Apostolic*

Tradition, together with its list of the fruits that may be presented (but omitting the statements about vegetables and flowers). However, because even in the oldest manuscript (Barberini 336, of the eighth century) the Greek text is in a defective state,[11] and because its restriction of the offering to fruit alone does not correspond with the canonical legislation cited above, we may have suspicions that this was not a prayer in current use but simply a piece of venerated antiquity copied out from generation to generation.

The fact that the *euchologia* contain other texts for use at the presentation of firstfruits increases this suspicion. There is a "prayer for those offering firstfruits," which, after referring both to God's command that everyone should bring to God "your own of your own" (perhaps an allusion to 1 Chr 29:14) and to God's acceptance of the widow's mite, asks that what has been brought may be accepted by God and lead to an abundant reward in this life and in eternity.[12] Some manuscripts also include a special "prayer at the partaking of grapes," which asks God to "bless this new fruit of the vine" which he has brought to maturity, so that it may bring gladness to those partaking of it and forgivness of sins to those who have offered the gift.[13] Although in the patriarchal liturgy of Constantinople this offering of grapes took place on 15 August, it was observed on 6 August in other places, presumably because the climate brought grapes to maturity a little earlier there.

We may note that these last two prayers lay more stress upon petition for the benefits which may accrue to the offerer than upon the expression of thanksgiving for God's goodness in creation, continuing a trend which can already be observed in the *Canons of Hippolytus* and in the *Testamentum Domini*. The later liturgical books adhere to this, omitting entirely the prayer from the *Apostolic Tradition*, and continuing to use the prayer for the grapes on 6 August in regions where vines are grown. In other regions apples are offered instead on this day, with the "prayer for those offering firstfruits" being used for this purpose.

The West

Similar traditions can also be observed in the west—so similar that they clearly share a common ancient root. While eastern legislation permitted wheat and grapes alone to be offered on the altar itself, at Rome beans and grapes might be offered there, according to the *Liber Pontificalis*.[14] The Gelasian Sacramentary provides a prayer for the blessing both of these new fruits, which turns out to be a shorter version of the "prayer at the partaking of grapes" found in the eastern tradition, omitting the request for the forgiveness of sins for those making the oblation and simply asking that they may partake with thanksgiving—an apparent allusion to 1 Timothy 4:3-4. Antoine Chavasse has compared the two versions and concluded that the Latin is translated from a Greek original, but that this does not mean that the prayer is of oriental provenance.[15] He suggests that it may have originated in the ancient Roman liturgy when the language of that rite was still Greek and not Latin. Be that as it may, it is clear that in some respects the Latin preserves a more primitive version than the existing Greek text.

The prayer appears twice in the sacramentary in slightly varying forms, once among the mass formularies for Ascension Day (where it is intended for beans alone), and once in within the miscellaneous collection of prayers and blessings later in the manuscript under the title *Oratio ad fruges novas benedicendas*, "Prayer for blessing new fruits," where it can be used for grapes or beans. In both cases it is meant to be said within the eucharistic prayer itself.[16] In the light of the eastern version, it was probably first used for grapes alone and only later extended to the blessing of beans. The Gregorian Sacramentary employs it for grapes among the propers for 6 August, as in the eastern custom.[17] The Gelasian Sacramentary also provides an alternative prayer for the blessing of new fruits (which Chavasse has argued, on the basis of its contents, was originally intended to be used before the fruits had achieved ripeness[18]), and another for the blessing of the first apples of the season.[19]

In some later western texts the prayer for grapes was adapted for the blessing of apples;[20] and in others we find quite different prayers for the blessing of firstfruits.[21] In some cases the blessing took place on the occasion of an existing feast. So, for example, in some places the blessing of apples was done on St. James' Day, 25 July.[22] In other cases, there was a complete mass for the blessing of firstfruits with its own propers. The lectionary of Luxeuil, for example, provides as the readings Joel 2:21-27; 1 Corinthians 9:7-15; and for the gospel a pastiche consisting of Matthew 12:1-8, John 4:35-38, and John 6:48-52.[23]

The blessing of the first ears of wheat found in the early eastern tradition was not entirely forgotten in the west. In England 1 August was kept as a feast of thanksgiving for the firstfruits of the harvest and known as "Lammas Day," the name being derived from the Anglo-

Saxon "Hlafmaesse," that is, "Loaf-mass," since on this day bread made from the new wheat was presented at the Mass and solemnly blessed.[24] The custom disappeared at the end of the Middle Ages, and all that was left was the secular, weekday "harvest home"—a festal meal held at the conclusion of the ingathering of the crops. Although the title "Lammas Day" was restored to the calendar of the 1552 Prayer Book of the Church of England, this was not intended to promote any religious observance but was for the purposes of secular reckoning, as it was one of the days in the year on which rents fell due. Special thanksgiving prayers were authorized in the Church of England in a few years when there was a very abundant harvest (1796, 1801, 1813, 1842, 1846, and 1854), and in 1847 a complete form of service with appropriate readings was issued by the Queen's command, but no regular, annual liturgical provision was made. In 1843 the Rev. R.S. Hawker revived the Lammas custom in his parish in Cornwall, and used bread made from the first ripe wheat as the sacramental bread of the eucharist, but on the first Sunday in October instead of on 1 August. The date chosen was close to the usual time of the harvest home, and part of his purpose was to redeem the secular character of that celebration. Thereafter many local churches took it upon themselves to institute annual services of thanksgiving for the harvest and these became very popular, especially in rural areas. Eventually, in 1862 the Church of England made official provision for such a service, and similar forms have been included in many recent revisions of the Prayer Book throughout the Anglican Communion.[25]

Harvest celebrations of various sorts also existed in other parts of Europe in the Middle Ages. In Hungary and in many other places, for example, they took place on 15 August. But the most common occasion for a harvest thanksgiving in medieval times was 11 November, the feast of St. Martin of Tours, and this was a public holiday in several countries. In some places this celebration has continued into the twentieth century. As will be clear from its date, it marked the conclusion of the ingathering rather the offering of firstfruits (although it did include within its festive meal the drinking of the first wine made from the grapes that had been harvested), and apart from attendance at Mass it was largely secular in character. It was from this celebration, continued in the Netherlands even after the Reformation, that the Pilgrim Fathers inherited the Thanksgiving observance which they introduced into North America.[26]

Conclusion

In its long history within the Judeo-Christian tradition the offering of firstfruits has served many purposes. In early times it came to be used for the financial support of religious leaders and for the charitable relief of the poor. In later Christian times the emphasis fell upon the blessing of the oblations themselves together with intercession for the material and spiritual benefit of those offering them. In more recent centuries the celebration has been transferred from the beginning to the end of the harvest and focused upon thanksgiving for its abundance and successful completion. Each of these developments has tended to obscure the primary significance of the ritual act as an acknowledgement of God's lordship over all that exists. Perhaps, therefore, this is another case where retracing our steps could lead to a recovery of a richer and more profound liturgical heritage.

Notes

1. *La Didachè: Instructions des apôtres* (Paris: Gabalda, 1958) 455-458.

2. *L'Enigme de la Didachè* (Paris: Ophrys, 1970) 226-231.

3. *La Doctrine des Douze Apôtres*, Sources chrétiennes, vol. 248 (Paris: Editions du Cerf, 1978) 190-191.

4. *Didascalia* 9, cited from Sebastian Brock & Michael Vasey, *The Liturgical Portions of the Didascalia*, Grove Liturgical Study, no. 29 (Nottingham: Grove Books, 1982) 11.

5. Origen, *Hom. in Num.* 11.2. For other examples, see Lukas Vischer, *Tithing in the Early Church* (Philadelphia: Fortress, 1966) 15-30.

6. *Adv. Haer.* IV.17.5; see also IV.18.1.

7. Chs. 31-32 in Bernard Botte, *La Tradition apostolique de Saint Hippolyte* (Münster: Aschendorff, 1963) 74-79.

8. Canon 36. See Paul F. Bradshaw, *The Canons of Hippolytus*, Alcuin/GROW Liturgical Study, no. 2 (Nottingham: Grove Books, 1987) 33-34.

9. VIII.40.1-4; English translation in W. Jardine Grisbooke, *The Liturgical Portions of the Apostolic Constitutions*, Alcuin/GROW Liturgical Study, nos. 13-14 (Nottingham: Grove Books, 1990) 90.

10. VIII.30; see also II.25ff.; VII.29.

11. Critical edition in Giovanni Mercati, "Una Preghiera antichissima degli Eucologi medievali," in *Alcuni scritti e brevi saggi di studii sulla Volgata* (Rome, 1917); English version in R.H. Connolly, "An Ancient Prayer in the Mediaeval Euchologia," *Journal of Theological Studies* 19 (1918) 132-137, who attempts to reconstruct original Greek of the *Apostolic Tradition*.

12. J. Goar, *Euchologion sive Rituale Graecorum* (Vienna, 1730) 522.

13. Ibid. 553.

14. L. Duchesne, ed., *Le Liber Pontificalis*, 2d ed. (Paris: Boccard, 1955), vol. 1, 159.

15. A. Chavasse, *Le Sacramentaire gélasian* (Tournai: Desclée, 1958) 464-466. His reference in n. 96 to the 1730 edition of Goar should be to p. 553 and not p. 522.

16. Nos. 577 and 1603 in L.C. Mohlberg, ed., *Liber Sacramentorum Romanae Aeclesiae Ordinis Anni Circuli* (Rome: Herder, 1960) 89, 232-233.

17. H.A. Wilson, ed., *The Gregorian Sacramentary*, Henry Bradshaw Society, vol.49 (London, 1915) 92; see also 221.

18. Chavasse, *Le Sacramentaire* 466-468.

19. Nos. 1604 and 1605 in Mohlberg, *Liber* 233; see also Chavasse, *Le Sacramentaire* 468-489.

20. See for example E.A. Lowe, ed., *The Bobbio Missal*, Henry Bradshaw Society, vol. 58 (London, 1920) 170-171.

21. See for example H.M.J. Banting, ed., *Two Anglo-Saxon Pontificals*, Henry Bradshaw Society, vol. 104 (London, 1989) 123.

22. See E. Martène, *De Antiquis Ecclesiae Ritibus*, vol. 4 (Antwerp 1738) 570-571.

23. P. Salmon, ed., *Le Lectionnaire de Luxeuil* (Rome, 1944) 187-188.

24. The Pontifical of Egbert includes prayer texts for this purpose: see Banting, *Two Anglo-Saxon Pontificals* 124.

25. For further details, see "Harvest Festival" in George Harford and Morely Stevenson, *The Prayer Book Dictionary* (London: Waverley Book Co., 1912), and in J.G. Davies, ed., *The New Westminster Dictionary of Liturgy and Worship* (Philadelphia: Fortress, 1986).

26. For further details, see Francis X. Weiser, *Handbook of Christan Feasts and Customs* (New York: Harcourt, Brace & Co., 1952) 267-272.

4

Deus Mundi Conditor

Leonel L. Mitchell

WHEN H. BOONE PORTER JOINED THE FACULTY OF GENERAL THEOLOGICAL Seminary I was a doctoral student in church history and liturgics. It was he who first initiated me into the mysteries of the Latin sacramentaries, and especially the old Gelasian, *Codex Vaticanus Reginensis* 316, with its important initiatory material. I noticed at that time that the Gelasian[1] did not contain the *Exultet* but a prayer for blessing the candle with the incipit *Deus mundi conditor.*[2] It was not germane to the work I was then doing, but I promised myself that I would come back to it. That prayer will be the subject of this essay.

Vaticanus Reginensis 316

The old Gelasian Sacramentary is preserved in a single manuscript, *Vaticanus Reginensis* 316, dating from about 750, and probably written near Paris, possibly at St. Denis.[3] Antoine Chavasse, author of the major study of the manuscript, considers its earliest stratum to represent the seventh-century liturgy of the *tituli Romani*, the parish churches of the city of Rome, the so-called "titular churches" of the cardinal presbyters.[4] In the form in which we possess it, the Gelasian has also assimilated a certain amount of material both from the papal

43

liturgy of the Lateran and from the Gallican and North Italian liturgies.

According to Chavasse's analysis,[5] the blessing of the candle is not a part of the earliest liturgical and literary stratum of the Gelasian, which is readily identifiable by the use of the second person singular in the rubrics, but of a unique ordo for the Paschal Vigil which has been inserted into the text at nn. 425-430 and 443. This ordo has been divided into two parts to permit the insertion from the older stratum of the prayers which follow the vigil readings. The clue that this has been done is the final rubric before the insertion:

> After this the priest gets up from his seat and says the prayers of the vigil of Easter *as contained in the sacramentary.*[6]

Chavasse establishes that the *Ordo qualiter sabbato sancto ad vigiliam ingrediantur*, its title in the Gelasian, describes the Great Vigil of Easter in the *tituli Romani*, the parish churches of the city of Rome.[7] Unlike the papal liturgy, which used two torches and did not have a blessing of the light at this time, this ordo contains clear directions for the blessing of a wax candle (*cereus*):

> The archdeacon comes before the altar, receives the light which had been hidden on Friday, makes the sign of the cross over the candle and lights it and completes the rite with this blessing of the candle.[8]

Notice that there is not yet a "new fire." The light is that which was hidden on Good Friday. The distinctive thing about this candle is precisely that it is not a lamp or taper of tallow, but a candle of beeswax. Such candles were unusual, expensive, and impressive at that time. The blessing is assigned to the deacon, not to the presiding priest. Chavasse traces this blessing of the paschal candle by a deacon back into the fifth century in Italy, and into the first part of the sixth century in the suburban part of the diocese of Rome.[9] Ennodius, bishop of Pavia from 517 to 521 is credited with composing the earliest surviving blessings of the candle,[10] although later literature often claims Augustine of Hippo as the author of the Exultet.[11]

Although a great deal has been written about the Exultet, *Deus mundi conditor* has been almost totally ignored. In addition to the old Gelaisian. it appears in the Eighth Century Gelasian (or mixed Gelasian) Sacramentaries, such as the Sacramentary of Gellone and the Sacramentary of Angoulème,[12] and in Ordo L, the *Ordo Romanus*

Antiquus, a part of the Germano-Roman Pontifical, written about 950.[13] Herman Schmidt, S.J., one of the few writers to discuss it at all, believes that it not an original part of the Roman liturgy, but, like the Exultet, made its way into Rome from North Italy or southern Gaul. He suggests Pavia, Bobbio, or some other Gallican or North Italian center.[14] It was, in any event, replaced by the Gallican Exultet, even in Rome.[15]

Text of the Blessing

As we have seen, the Gelasian does not contain the Exultet, but the deacon blessed the paschal candle with *Deus mundi conditor*, the text of which immediately follows the rubric quoted above.

> O God, creator of the world, author of light, maker of the stars, O God, who have reclothed in bright light a world lying in darkness, O God, by whose ineffable power the brightness of all things took its beginnings, we call upon you in[16] your works, in this most holy night of Vigil, and we humbly offer your majesty from your gifts this waxen candle, not polluted with animal fat, not marred by profane grease, not contaminated by sacrilegious fire, but fashioned of wax, oil and papyrus, kindled in honor of your Name and offered with the deference of religious devotion.
>
> Therefore the great mystery and marvelous sacrament of this night must redound with with worthy praises. In this mystery the age-old darkness perceived daylight thrust upon it by the miracle of the Lord's resurrection, and death, which once had been condemned to eternal night, was astonished to be dragged as a captive in the Lord's triumphal train by the coming of the light of true brightness, and that which had been condemned to slavery when our first parents lied with dark audacity shines with the splendor of freedom through the miracle of this night.
>
> As we therefore approach this awesome festival with all of the spiritual fervor that human devotion permits, we show forth to you, O God, lights pleasing for the brightness of their flame, so that as the wax melts away your creatures proclaim your praises with undiminished faith. The light of the flame is indeed to be acclaimed. Through it the power of the godhead deigned to appear to Moses. It led your people as they went forth from the land of slavery by its saving light. It preserved by its very gentle caresses the lives of the three young men placed in a furnace by the decision of a tyrant.

For, as the terror of darkness is excluded by this light for which we have given thanks, so, O Lord, may the burden of sins be dissolved by the light-giving command of your majesty.

When therefore we marvel at the origin of this substance we must praise the bee as its source.

Bees are indeed frugal in expenditures and, most chaste in procreation. They build cells fashioned from waxen liquid which the master art of a human artisan cannot match. They pass over flowers with their feet, and no injury is done to the flowers.

They do not give birth, but they yield swarms of offspring gathering them in their mouth,[17] as by a wondrous example Christ came forth from the mouth of the Father.

Virginity without childbearing is fruitful among them. The Lord, in fact, out of love for virginity, determined to follow this example when he deigned to have an earthly mother. Therefore, Lord, such gifts are worthily offered at your altars, with which Christian devotion does not hesitate to delight you.[18]

Light and Darkness

The opening phrase praises God as the universal creator, but especially as the creator of light. This sets the stage for a description of the resurrection in terms of a battle between light and darkness. This is, of course, the classic view of the atonement as a battle between death and life to which Gustaf Aulén gave the name of *Christus victor*.[19] Darkness and death find themselves thrust into daylight and paraded as captives behind the chariot of the triumphant light of the risen Christ in the manner of a classic Roman triumph, the parade given to a general after winning a great victory. It is no longer the dead who are bound in darkness, but through the mystery of Christ's resurrection, they are set free and death itself has been bound, as darkness is overwhelmed by a bright light. Of this the brightly shining candle is the symbol, but, the prayer is, even though the wax melts and burns up in the flame, the faith of us who lighted it will continue to shine undiminished. These are certainly appropriate, if not original ideas.

In Praise of the Bee

The passage in praise of bees beginning "Apes vero sunt frugales in sumptibus" is especially interesting. There is a parallel, but different passage in praise of the bee in the Exultet.[20] Bee keeping was an established part of agriculture in the ancient world, and had been from prehistoric times. Both Varro[21] and Virgil[22] included discussions of it in their treatises on farming. The Septuagint version of Proverbs 6:8 contains a section on bees which is not in the Hebrew. It immediately follows the example of the industriousness of the ant:

> Or go to the bee and learn what a worker she is, and how seriously she does her work. Both kings and commoners bear its drudgery in proportion to their health, for it is desired and expected of all. And though her strength be small, since she has prized wisdom she has increased.[23]

The industriousness and wisdom of bees are commonly praised, as is their social organization. Virgil, for example, writes:

> Come now, the qualities which Jove himself has given bees, I will unfold . . . They alone have children in common, hold the dwellings of their cities jointly, and pass their life under the majesty of law. They alone know a fatherland and fixed home, and in summer, mindful of the winter to come, spend toilsome days and garner their gains into a common store . . . Some have taught that the bees have received a share of the divine intelligence.[24]

The utopian quality of life in the hive seems, at least to Virgil, to embody the ideals of Plato's *Republic*. Amazingly these qualities do not appear to interest the author of *Deus mundi conditor*, although they do figure in the *laus apum* of the Exultet, but our author has clearly been influenced by this passage in Virgil:

> Yea, and you will marvel that this custom has found favor with bees, that they indulge not in conjugal embraces nor idly unnerve their bodies in love, or bring forth young with travail, but of themselves gather their children in their mouths from leaves and sweet herbs, of themselves provide a new monarch and tiny burgers, and remodel their palaces and waxen realms.[25]

The procreation of bees was a great mystery in antiquity. It was not until the seventeenth century that Jan Swammerdam, the Dutch biologist, discovered the role of the queen, who was universally called the king in antiquity.[26] The most significant ancient study was by Aristotle.[27] It begins, "The generation of bees is a great mystery," and concludes, "But the facts have not been sufficiently ascertained; and if at any future time they are ascertained, then credence must be given to the direct evidence of the senses more than to theories—and to theories too provided that the results which they show agree with what is observed." He considered three possible methods of reproduction:

> Bees must either (a) fetch the offspring from elsewhere (some hold this view); in which case the offspring with either have generated spontaneously or have been produced by some other animal; or (b) generate the young themselves; or (c) fetch some and generate some (this, too, is a view held by certain people, who maintain that the young of the drones only are fetched).[28]

Virgil clearly held view (a). Varro opted for (c).[29] Aristotle's own view was more complex. He believed that workers, drones, and "the leaders" were all generated "without copulation", the "kings" and the workers, whom Aristotle simply calls "bees", by the "leaders" and the drones by the workers.[30] He admits that some believe the drones to be male and the workers female, and others visa versa, but this he considers to be unreasonable:

> Nor is it reasonable to hold that "bees" are female and drones male; because Nature does not assign defensive weapons to any female creature; yet while drones are without a sting, all "bees" have one. Nor is the converse view reasonable, that "bees" are male and drones female, because no male creatures make a habit of taking trouble over their young, whereas in fact "bees" do . . .

> So far as generating is concerned ["bees"] are female, yet they contain in themselves the male as well as the female <factor>, just as plants do; and this is why they posses the organ for self-defense, for of course it is wrong to apply the term "female" to creatures where no separate male exists.[31]

The *a priori* assignment of gender roles to bees based on patriarchal stereotypes produces astounding scientific nonsense, even in the hands of an Aristotle, and its use as a basis for theological conclusions, needless to say, results in theological nonsense. The results of the application of such stereotypes to human beings similiarly results in sociological and theological nonsense, but that is beyond the scope of this study.

The idea of the bisexuality of bees was widespread in antiquity. We find it, for example, in the (probably fifth-century) apocryphal Apocalypse of John, which says that human beings at the resurrection will be like the bees, not some male and some female, but all the same, tying this to a reference to Matthew 22:30.[32] Bees were associated with the ideal state, whether the Saturnian golden age, Plato's utopian republic, or the resurrection life. Their presence was a sign of divine favor.[33] Clearly for the author of *Deus mundi conditor* it is the supposed ability of the bee to reproduce "without copulation" that is most significant. In this he sees a parallel to the virgin birth of Christ.[34]

It is difficult to understand why our author thought that bees brought forth their young from their mouths. His words "ore legentes" are from Virgil, but Virgil believed that bees fetched their offspring "gathering them in their mouths from leaves and sweet herbs."[35] Perhaps the diligent activity of the bees in feeding the larvae in the cells of the comb was thought to include placing the larvae in the cells.

The reference to Christ coming forth from the mouth of the Father is to Sirach 24:3, in which Wisdom says, "I came forth from the mouth of the Most High,"[36] a passage paraphrased in the well-known Advent antiphon *O Sapientia*:

> O Wisdom, which camest out of the mouth of the Most High, and reachest from one end to another, mightily and sweetly ordering all things: Come and teach us the way of prudence.[37]

The whole point of this excursus into zoology is, of course, to show that beeswax is the ideal substance out of which to fashion a candle to burn in honor of the creator of light and of bees to celebrate the brightness of the resurrection of Jesus Christ. An ascetic, undoubtedly monastic, spirituality which values virginity above marriage and identifies purity with abstinence from sexual relations clearly underlies the entire composition. Wax candles yield a bright, clean light unlike sooty, smelly tapers of animal tallow—so obviously "of the flesh", as the virgin bee is superior to other animals.

* * * * * * * * * *

It is not difficult to understand why this prayer, in spite of some expressive imagery, has languished in obscurity. It lacks the poetry and the scope of the Exultet. To us the passage in praise of the bee bases questionable theology on false biology. This was not evident to those who lived before the seventeenth-century discovery of the bees' method of reproduction, and the passage in praise of the bee in the early versions of the Exultet is similarly flawed. It nevertheless represents an attempt to use the natural phenomena of the created order as analogies to the supernatural operation of their creator in the work of salvation of the human race, and we can still join in giving thanks to the creator of the world not only for light but for the bee, whose production of honey and wax is a miracle of nature, and rejoice with the unknown authors and singers of this prayer that a wax candle can enlighten both our environment and our hearts with the light of Christ's victory over darkness and death. "The light shines in the darkness, and the darkness did not overcome it."[38]

Notes

1. *Liber Sacramentorum Romanae Aeclesiae Ordinis Circuli (Sacramentarium Gelasianum)*, ed. Leo Cunibert Mohlberg, Rerum Ecclesiasticarum Documenta, Series Maior, Fontes, vol. 4 (Rome: Herder, 1960). This will be abbreviated *Gel.*, followed, when appropriate, by paragraph numbers from this edition.

2. *Gel.* nn. 426-448.

3. Klaus Gamber, *Codices Liturgici Latini Antiquiores*, Spicilegii Friburgensis Subsidia, vol. 1, pars prima (Freiburg, Switzerland: Universitätsverlag, 1968) 299-303.

4. Antoine Chavasse, *Le Sacramentaire gélasien (Vaticanus Reginensis 316): Sacramentaire presbytéral en usage dans les titres romains au VIIe siècle* (Tournai: Desclée, 1957).

5. Ibid. 96-97.

6. *Gel.* n. 430. Italics mine.

7. Chavasse, *Le Sacramentaire* 97-107.

8. *Gel.* n. 425.

9. Chavasse, *Le Sacramentaire* 103.

10. Herman A.P. Schmidt, *Hebdomada Sancta, Volumen Alterum, Fontes Historici, Commentarius Historicus* (Rome: Casa Editrice Herder, 1957) 627-650, 809-826. This contains the Latin texts of the documents and the author's commentary on the Rite of the New Fire and the Light.

11. For example, in the Eighth Century Gelasian Sacramentary of Angoulême this title precedes the *Exultet*: "Item dicta beati Augustini Episcopi quam adhuc diaconus cum esset edidit et cecinit feliciter." *Liber Sacramentorum Engolomensis*, ed. Patrick Saint-Roch, Corpus Christianorum, Series Latina, vol. 159 C (Turnholt: Brepols, 1987) n. 732. A similar title appears in the Gallican sacramentaries, *Missale Gothicum* and *Missale Gallicanum Vetus. Missale Gothicum*, ed. Leo Cunibert Mohlberg, Rerum Ecclesiasticarum Documenta, Series Maior, Fontes, vol. 5 (Rome: Herder, 1961) n. 225. *Missale Gallicanum Vetus*, ed. Leo Cunibert Mohlberg, Rerum Ecclesiasticarum Documenta, Series Maior, Fontes, vol. 3 (Rome: Herder, 1958) n. 134.

12. *Liber Sacramentorum Engolomensis*, n. 731; *Liber Sacramentorum Gellonensis*, ed. A. Dumas, Corpus Christianorum, Series Latina, vol. 159

(Turnholt: Brepols, 1981), n. 676. In both manuscripts it is immediately followed by the *Exultet*.

13. Michel Andrieu, *Les Ordines Romani du haut moyen ge*, vol. 5, Spicilegium Sacrum Lovaniense, Etudes et documents, fascicle 29 (Louvain: Spicilegium Sacrum Lovaniense, 1961) 265- 267; Cyrile Vogel and Reinhard Elze, *Le Pontifical romano-germanique du dixième siècle*, vol. 2, Studi e Testi, vol. 227 (Vatican City: Biblioteca Vaticana Apostolica, 1963) 95-96.

14. Schmidt, *Hebdomada Sancta*, vol. 2, 638.

15. Its appearance in *Ordo L* is anachronistic, but typical of the compiler of the ordo, who could not bear to omit a prayer of which he had a copy. In *Ordo L* it is said "humili voce" by the pontiff or presbyter, who makes the sign of the cross over a candle, while the choir sings the seven penitential psalms. The light is then carried into the church in procession, where the *cereus magnus*, the paschal candle, stands in its candlestick in the middle of the church before the altar. This is blessed and lighted by the archdeacon, who sings aloud, "Exultet iam angelica turba." *Ordo L* also contains the rubric originally from Ordo XXVI stating that the blessing of the light does not take place in the Lateran, i.e., it was not yet a part of the papal liturgy. Andrieu, *Les Ordines*, vol. 5, 264-271; see Chavasse, *Le Sacramentaire* 102-104.

16. The exact meaning of *in* here is unclear. It may mean "in the midst of," or "through," or possibly even "because of."

17. This clause is by no means clear. "Partus non edunt, sed ore legentes concepti fetus reddunt examina." Is "concepti fetus" genitive or nominative plural? What does the participle "legentes" modify, and how should it be translated? Other possible translations include "Conceived breedings passing from the mouth yield swarms," or "Speaking from the mouth they yield swarms of the brood which has been conceived." The phrase "ore legentes" is from Virgil's *Georgics* 4.201, where it clearly means that the bees gather their young in their mouths from leaves and sweet herbs. The author of *Deus mundi conditor* does not appear to have so understood it.

18. *Gel.*, nn. 426-428. The translation of the Latin text is my own. If an English translation has been previously published, I have not found it. I am indebted to my colleague at Seabury-Western, the Rev. Richard I. Pervo, Th.D., Professor of New Testament and Patristics, for reading my translation and making helpful corrections and suggestions for emendation, as well as for putting his encyclopedic knowledge of the ancient world at my disposal.

19. Gustaf Aulén, *Christus Victor*, trans. A.G. Hebert (New York: Macmillan, 1969).

20. The passage is omitted from the version of the Exultet in *Ordo L* (ed. Andrieu, 270) and subsequently from the *Missale Romanum* in the editions of both Pius V and Paul VI. It is found in the Supplement to the Gregorian Sacramentary known as *Hucusque* (*Le Sacramentaire Grégorien*, ed. Jean Deshusses, Spicilegium Friburgense, vol. 16 [Freiburg: Editions

Universitaires, 1971] n. 1022b.), in Gallican sacramentaries such as *Missale Gallicanum Vetus* (Rerum Ecclesiasticarum Documenta, vol. 3, n. 134) and *Missale Gothicum* (Rerum Ecclesiasticarum Documenta, vol. 5, n. 225), and in Eighth Century Gelasian Sacramentaries, such as Gellone (Corpus Christianorum 159, n. 678b) and Angoulême (Corpus Christianorum, vol. 159 C, n. 734).

21. Varro, *De Re Rustica* 3.16, (English translation *Cato and Varro On Agriculture*, text and trans. W.B. Hooper and H.B. Ash, Loeb Classical Library (London: William Heinemann; Cambridge: Harvard University Press, 1967) 498-521.

22. Virgil, *Georgics* 4. text and trans. H.R. Fairclough, Loeb Classical Library (London: William Heinemann; Cambridge: Harvard University Press, 1947) 196-237.

23. Proverbs 6:8a-c LXX, ed. Alfred Rahls, *Septuaginta*, vol. 2 (Stuttgart: Deutsche Bibelgesellschaft, 1935) 192.

24. *Georgics* 4, lines 149, 153-157, 219-229, trans. Fairclough.

25. *Georgics* 4, lines 197-204.

26. "Even Aristotle did not know that the queen bee was the common mother of the hive. This discovery, made by Swammerdam in the seventeenth century, is the beginning of the modern knowledge of the subject." *Cato and Varro On Agriculture* 502, n. 2.

27. Aristotle, *Generation of Animals*, text and trans. A.L. Peck, Loeb Classical Library (London: William Heinemann; Cambridge: Harvard University Press, 1953) 3.10, 332-347.

28. Aristotle, *Generation* 333.

29. "Bees are produced partly from bees, and partly from the rotted carcass of a bullock." *Varro* 3.16.4, ed. Hooper and Boyd, 501.

30. Aristotle, *Generation* 341-343.

31. Ibid. 335, 339.

32. *Apocalypsis Iohannis* 11, in Konstantin von Tischendorf, *Apocalypses Apocryphae* (Leipsig: 1866; reprint Hildesheim: Georg Olms, 1966) 76-77.

33. Bees are supposed to have alighted on the cradle of St. Ambrose, presumably making him honey-tongued. The episode is described in Paulinus, Vita Ambrosii 3, and a plate showing a bronze relief depicting the event is in Angleo Paredi, *St. Ambrose: His Life and Times*, trans. M. Joseph Costelloe (Notre Dame: University of Notre Dame Press, 1964) 443.

34. The *Exultet* likewise praises the bee for its virginity:

"O truly blessed and wondrous bee, whose chastity the male sex do not violate, offspring do not shatter, nor children destroy, but like the holy virgin Mary conceived, gave birth as a virgin, and remained a virgin." lines 105-110. Critical edition in Herman Schmidt, *Hebdomada Sancta*, vol. 2, 643.

Obviously not only the virginal conception of Jesus but his birth "as light passes through glass" is here expounded, and it is not only the fruitful virginity of the bee, but what Deus mundi conditor calls "fecunda sine partu virginitas," the added fact that bees do not give birth, which creates the parallel for the author of the *Exultet*. This is an astounding theological edifice to be constructed on such a foundation of mistaken biology and "pious" speculation.

35. *Georgics* 4.200-201; see also note 17 above.

36. N.R.S.V. The Vulgate text (24:5) is, "Ego ex ore Altissimi prodivi."

37. Translation from *The English Hymnal* (London: Oxford University Press, 1933; 10th printing 1953), Hymn 734.

38. John 1:5 (N.R.S.V.).

5

In Defense of 1552

Bonnell Spencer, O.H.C.

THE PREVAILING OPINION AMONG LITURGISTS, ESPECIALLY IN THE EPISCOPAL Churches of Scotland and the United States, is that Cranmer produced an excellent Communion Office in the 1549 Book of Common Prayer and then proceeded to ruin it in 1552. In 1549 Cranmer did translate the eucharistic liturgy of the Latin Sarum Missal with skill and accuracy. He restored its theology to what he rightly considered its original meaning, and expressed it in sonorous English that has been difficult to match. Above all, although he incorporated material from other sources, he kept the basic structure of the Sarum rite.

As a result, those who wanted to keep the current Catholic concepts of the eucharistic action, but who were willing to use a vernacular liturgy, were able to continue to celebrate and interpret the Mass in the old way. This was disturbing to the Reformers, because they were determined to get rid of popular eucharistic doctrines and practices that they considered to be contrary to the word of God. Accordingly, Cranmer decided that the erroneous concepts had to be more explicitly eliminated and produced the 1552 book to that end.

The eucharistic practice most offensive to the Reformers was the claim that the priest could offer the Masses he celebrated as propitiatory sacrifices for the living and the dead. The sacrifice of Masses was based on transubstantiation—the doctrine that at the consecration the substance of the bread and wine was changed into the substance of the body and blood of Christ. The primary objection to the doctrine was the way in which its concept of Christ's eucharistic presence could be used. It taught that Christ was present existentially in the consecrated elements. Although the outward appearances of the bread and wine—their accidents—remained unchanged, so that they looked and tasted the same, their substance—their true being—was changed into the substance of the body and blood of Christ. The priest, by virtue of his ordination, effected that change when he said over the elements the words that Christ used at the Last Supper: "This is my body" and "This is my blood."

The transformation was permanently and objectively made. Once the consecration had been accomplished, the priest held in his hands the body and blood of Christ. He could lift up to the Father once more the atoning death of his beloved Son on Calvary as a propitiatory sacrifice for the living and the dead. This was believed to be especially efficacious in shortening a soul's stay in purgatory, and the more Masses offered the better. Because only a priest could perform this service, he was allowed to receive a stipend for it. Chantries were endowed to provide for them, and relatives of the departed could be persuaded to give money for their celebration. That was an important element in church finance. The Mass was put into the same class as indulgences, against which Luther fired the opening gun of the Reformation with his ninety-five theses.

Another objection to transubstantiation was that it "overthroweth the nature of a sacrament."[1] It holds that the substance of the bread and wine disappears when it is changed into the substance of the body and blood of Christ. The integrity of the sacramental sign is destroyed. The incarnation principle should be extended to the sacraments. Just as Jesus took a real human nature and lived a real human life, so he makes himself available to us sacramentally through real bread and wine. His humanity was not diminished or overridden by his divinity. Neither are the bread and wine when they become his body and blood. Christ makes himself present, and the substance of the bread and wine need not be eliminated in the process.

Luther got rid of the sacrifice of Masses by asserting that the Mass was not a sacrifice of any kind. Not only was the body and blood of Christ not offered as a propitiatory sacrifice, but not even the alms or the unconsecrated elements were presented to God. Nevertheless,

Luther wanted to maintain the objective presence of Christ in the elements for the purpose of communion. Since there was no sacrificial oblation, he felt that he could safely maintain that Christ was substantially present to be received by the faithful. Luther rejected transubstantiation—the substance of the bread and wine remained in the consecrated elements—but he believed that Christ's risen body is ubiquitous. He can make himself present anywhere, and does so in the bread and wine when it is consecrated. Luther insisted that Jesus' words "This is my body" and "This is my blood" had to be taken literally, or else the integrity of both the Gospel and the sacrament would be undermined.

Zwingli and the Calvinists repudiated the sacrifice of Masses in a different way. In rejecting transubstantiation, they denied that the substance of Christ's body and blood was present objectively in the consecrated elements. They did not deny that Christ was really and truly received in the eucharist. But his presence was not directly associated with the bread and wine as such. Rather, he was received by the partaking of them in penitence and faith. The action of the meal was the *locus* of the presence, not the elements themselves. Therefore the celebrant did not have Christ in his hands to be offered to the Father. This concept did not mean that the presence of Christ was effected by the communicant's faith, but that only those who partook in faith could receive Christ who made himself present.

The great tragedy of the Reformation was this division between Luther and the Swiss Reformers. Philip, landgrave of Hesse, at the instigation of Martin Bucer, the pastor at Strassbourg, called a conference between Luther and Zwingli that met at Marburg in 1529. On most points they were able to agree—except the eucharist. Luther insisted that Christ's risen body had to be objectively present in the elements for communion. Zwingli and the other Swiss Reformers could not agree because their defense against the sacrifice of Masses required that Christ's presence not be directly associated with the bread and wine. Bucer kept striving to effect an agreement, but never succeeded.

Cranmer invited Bucer to England in 1549, appointed him professor of divinity at Cambridge, and asked him to write a critique of the 1549 book. The result was what is popularly known as *Censura*, in which Bucer stated his position on communion:

> The bread and wine are symbols of the body and blood of Christ in which he offers to us himself. Apart from this use they are just

like any other bread and wine, for there is no change in their nature and Christ the Lord is not offered in them but in the minds which are firm in faith.[2]

Christ is experienced as present not in the bread and wine themselves, but in their use in communion.

But during the Middle Ages the concept was corrupted:

All these things were so diminished and distorted that some kind of magic change was supposed to affect the bread and wine so that it became the body and blood of the Lord. Certainly the Holy Fathers understood from these words no other change in the elements than one by which the bread and wine, in their own nature and in the permanence of all circumstances of their natural characteristics, were changed from their usual and ordinary use and were, as we might say, "transelemented," so that they became symbols of body and blood and thus of the whole Christ, both God and man.[3]

In these mysteries they are nothing other than signs of the body and blood of the Lord, but not of things altogether absent. They are signs of a kind by which in association with his words the Lord offers himself to us again and again, communicates and unites himself to us.[4]

Through the eucharistic action the elements become efficacious signs, which do not just point to something absent, but when rightly used, effect what they represent—union with Christ.

The controversy between the Lutheran and Swiss theologians focused attention on how Christ was received in communion, whereas the true issue was how to state the real presence in such a way that the sacrifice of Masses and transubstantiation were repudiated. Accordingly, it has often been said that Cranmer, in response to English representatives of the extreme Swiss position, shifted from the objective spiritual presence of Christ's body and blood in the bread and wine, that he held in 1549, to a presence associated only with the action of communion in 1552, and that the inferiority of his second Prayer Book is the result of that shift. Actually, I believe that the principal difference between the two books was the way Cranmer expressed his concept not of the sacramental presence but of the eucharistic sacrifice.

The best place to trace the development of Cranmer's concept of the presence is the epiclesis—the petition that God effect the consecration—in the eucharistic prayer. In the Sarum rite what is left of it is the *Quam Oblationem*:

> Which oblation do thou, O God, we beseech thee, vouchsafe to
> make altogether bles+sed, ap+proved, rati+fied, reasonable,
> and acceptable, that it may be made unto us the Body and Bl+ood
> of thy most dearly beloved Son our Lord Jesus Christ.

Whatever is the antecedent of "which oblation" grammatically, if
any, the crosses indicated that the prayer intends it to refer to the
bread and wine. They are being consecrated so that Christ's body and
blood can be "acceptably" offered to the Father.

Cranmer turned the *Quam Oblationem* into a real epiclesis:

> Heare us (o merciful father) we beseech thee: and with thy holy
> spirite and worde, vouchsafe to bl+esse and sanc+tify these thy
> gyftes, and creatures of bread and wyne, that they maie be unto
> us the bodye and bloud of thy moste derely beloued sonne Jesus
> Christe.

For Cranmer the process of consecration was effected by the Holy
Spirit, as in the eastern liturgies, followed by the "word"—the
narrative of the institution at the Last Supper—which was considered the means of consecration in the western rites.

Cranmer carefully omitted the word "made" from the Sarum
prayer. It suggested too much of a change in the elements themselves.
The words "be unto us" could signify to us Christ present to be
received in communion. A rubric after the narrative of institution
forbids other usages:

> These wordes before rehersed are to be saied, turning still to the
> Altar, without any eleuacion, or shewing the Sacrament to the
> people.

The rubric rejects two practices: first, the lifting up of the consecrated
host that suggested the offering of Christ to the Father as a propitiatory sacrifice; second, the showing of it to the people, so that by seeing
and reverencing it they could fulfill their obligation of worship
without receiving communion.

But those who believed in transubstantiation could still interpret
the 1549 epiclesis accordingly. Bucer suggested a substitute:

> Hear us O merciful Father, bless us and sanctify us by the Word
> and Holy Spirit, that with true faith we may receive in these
> mysteries the body and blood of thy Son to be the food and drink
> of eternal life.[5]

This avoids any action directed toward the elements. Instead, it prays
that we may have the faith to receive Christ's body and blood.

That was too much for Cranmer, but he did feel that transubstantiation must be more clearly ruled out. In 1552 he substituted:

> Heare us O mercyefull father wee beeseche thee; and graunt that wee, receyuing these thy creatures of bread and wyne, accordinge to thy sonne our Sauioure Jesus Christ's holy institucion, in remembraunce of his death and passion, maye be partakers of his most blessed body and bloud.

This emphasizes that we receive the bread and wine in their natural state, but when we do so in accordance with Christ's institution, we partake of his body and blood.

In the 1549 prayer of humble access, Cranmer used the language of John 6:54 to express the reality of our communion:

> Graunt us therefore (gracious lorde) so as to eate the fleshe of thy dere sonne Jesus Christ, and to drynke his bloud in these holy Misteries, that we may continuallye dwell in hym, and he in us, that our synfull bodyes may bee made cleane by his body, and our soules washed through hys most precious blood.

Bucer highly approved of that prayer and wrote eight pages defending—on the basis of his concept of the efficacious sign—our genuine eating of Christ's body and drinking of his blood in a real though spiritual manner. Cranmer retained the prayer in 1552, omitting only the words "in these holy Misteries, that we may continuallye dwell in hym, and he in us."

It is possible that Cranmer held Bucer's concept in 1549 but in the exhortation to communion he reminds us:

> As the benefite is great, if with a truly penitent heart, and liuely faith, we receiue that holy Sacrament; (for then we spiritually eate the fleshe of Christ, and drinke his bloude, then we dwell in Christ and Christ in us, wee bee made one with Christ, and Christ with us;) so is the daunger great, yf wee receyue the same unworthely; for then wee become gyltie of the body and bloud of Christ our sauior, we eate and drinke our owne damnacion, not considering the Lordes bodye.

When we partake without penitence and faith, we still receive the body and blood of Christ. His presence is so objectively real that unworthy reception of the elements is a desecration of Christ and a grave injury to the recipient.

The passage could indicate that in 1549 Cranmer's doctrine of the presence was closer to Luther's. But the passage is repeated in 1552, with only two changes: the word "made" is omitted from "we be one with Christ," and instead of "become," "then we be giltie." Apparently Cranmer did not think his concept of the presence had changed between the two books. The respect he still had for the consecrated species is shown by his specifying in 1552 that they were to be received by the people kneeling.

By then some of his colleagues objected to that practice, claiming that it implied worship of the bread and wine or of a real and essential presence of Christ's natural body. Cranmer staunchly refused to remove the kneeling requirement and added the so-called black rubric that explained and defended the practice:

> whiche thynge beyng well mente, for a sygnificacion of the humble and gratefull acknowledgyng of the benefites of Chryst, geuen unto the woorthye receyuer.

And Cranmer stated his position on Christ's presence:

> For as concernynge the Sacramentall bread and wyne, they remayne styll in theyr verye naturall substaunces, and therefore may not be adored, for that were Idolatrye to be abhorred of all faythfull christians. And as concernynge the naturall body and blood of our sauiour Christ, they are in heauen and not here. For it agaynst the trueth of Christes true natural bodye, to be in moe places than in one, at one tyme.

Thus Cranmer rejected both transubstantiation and Luther's doctrine of the ubiquity of Christ's risen human nature.

But Cranmer believed that Christ's presence remained efficacious in the consecrated elements, so that communion by the reserved sacrament was valid. In the Communion of the Sick he provided:

> Yf the same daye there be a celebracion of the holy communion in the churche, then shall the priest reserue (at the open communion) so muche of the sacrament of the body and bloud, as shall serue the sicke person, and so many as shall communicate with hym (yf there be any.) And so soone as he conueniently may, after the open communion ended in the church, shall goe and minister the same.

If there is no Mass that day in the church, provision is made for its celebration before noon in the sick persons' house.

Bucer in his comments on the Communion of the Sick raised no objection to these provisions. Nevertheless, Cranmer deleted the above rubric in 1552. I do not think, however, the omission reflected a change in his concept of Christ's continuing presence in the elements for communion apart from Mass. Rather, it was the way Cranmer handled the eucharistic sacrifice in 1552 that caused him to remove the rubric. The liturgical expression of the sacrifice is the real difference between 1549 and 1552.

In 1549 Cranmer followed Luther in eliminating a liturgical offering. What Cranmer called the offertory was the collection of alms that the people themselves put in "the poore mennes boxe." In 1552 the church wardens collected the alms and put them in the box. After those who were intending to receive communion had moved into the choir, the 1549 book directed: "Then shall the minister take so muche Bread and Wine, as shall suffice for the persons appoynted to receiue the holy Communion." The elements were set upon the altar without any action of offering. The 1552 text does not even say when they were placed there.

Yet Cranmer did retain the concept of sacrifice in the eucharist, still carefully excluding the sacrifice of Masses. In the Sarum consecration prayer the anamnesis (*Unde et Memores*), after remembering the passion, resurrection, and ascension of Christ, proceeded:

> [We] do offer to thine excellent Majesty of thine own gifts and bounties a pure + oblation, a holy + oblation, a spotless + oblation, the holy + Bread of eternal life and the Cup + of everlasting salvation.

This was held in Cranmer's day to be the offering of Christ to the Father as a propitiatory sacrifice for the living and the dead that was the basis of the sacrifice of Masses. For this Cranmer substituted in 1549:

> Wherefore, O Lorde and heauenly father, accordyng to the Instytucyon of thy derely beloued sonne, our sauiour Jesu Christ, we thy humble seruauntes do celebrate, and make here before thy diuine Maiestie, with these thy holy giftes, the memoryall whyche thy sonne hath wylled us to make, hauyng in remembraunce his blessed passion, mightie resurreccyon, and gloryous ascencion, renderyng unto thee most hartie thankes, for the innumerable benefites procured unto us by the same, entierely desirying thy fatherly goodness, mercifully to accepte this our Sacrifice of praise and thankes geuing.

The holy gifts are the means by which we make a grateful memorial of the mighty acts of Christ.

This is a eucharistic and not a propitiatory sacrifice, and it is made by receiving the bread and wine in communion according to Christ's institution, not by offering Christ to the Father on behalf of the person for whom the stipend is paid. Rather, we pray that

> by the merites and death of thy sonne Jesus Christ, and through faith in his bloud, we and al thy whole church, may obteigne remission of our sinnes, and all other benefites of hys passyon.

The sacrifice is offered for the whole church, and as members of the church we participate in its benefits.

Therefore we render to our sacrifice of praise and thanksgiving by offering ourselves to be united to Christ through partaking of communion:

> And here wee offre and present unto thee (O Lorde) oure selfe, oure soules, and bodies, to be a reasonable, holy, and liuely sacrifice unto thee: humbly besechyng thee, that whosoeuer shalbee partakers of thys holy Communion, maye worthely receiue the most precious body and bloude of thy sonne Jesus Christe: and bee fulfilled with thy grace and heauenly benediccion, and made one bodye with thy sonne Jesu Christe, that he maye dwell in them, and they in hym.

By worthily receiving communion we become one with Christ in his body and blood as "this our Sacrifice."

In light of the above passages we can see that in 1549 Cranmer considered the eucharistic sacrifice to be a memorial sacrifice of thanksgiving offered in the two ways urged in Hebrews 13:15-16:

> Through [Christe], then, let us continually offer a sacrifice of praise to God, that is, the fruit of lips that confess his name. Do not neglect to do good and to share what you have, for such sacrifices are pleasing to God.

The vocal sacrifice was expressed in the anamnesis. The offering and presenting of "oure selfe, oure soules and bodies" indicated our willingness to do good and share what we have. All this culminated in the communion meal, as did the Hebrew peace offerings—a feast on the victim of the sacrifice, part of which was offered to God in the altar fire, and the rest consumed by the worshipers in the sacrificial meal.

The *New Revised Standard Version* calls them "sacrifices of well-being" in the Old Testament. The phrase is appropriate to the eucharist, since it celebrates the reconciliation and union with God accomplished when Jesus Christ on the cross made

> (by his one oblation once offered) a full, perfect, and sufficient sacrifyce, oblacion, and satysfaccyon, for the synnes of the whole worlde, and did institute, and in his holy Gospell commaund us, to celebrate a perpetuall memory of that his precious death, untyll his coming again.

The making of that memorial sacrifice and the renewed participation in its benefits is what a devout eucharistic communion accomplishes.

At first glance it looks as if 1552 drastically changed the rite. Most of the items in the service have been shifted to another place. The consecration prayer is reduced to one-third of its length. It is all very confusing and would seem to indicate a complete change in the understanding of the service. But there is a clue in 1552 that makes sense of the process. It is the way Cranmer handles the anamnesis. In 1549 it was made vocally. In 1552 it was made in action—by receiving communion, the meal by which the sacrifices of well-being were consummated. So the anamnesis prayer was deleted, and the administration of communion put in its place.

That the communion was fulfilling the purpose of the 1549 anamnesis is indicated by the 1552 words of administration:

> Take and eate this, in remembraunce that Christ dyed for thee, and feede on him in thy hearte by faythe, with thankesgeuing.

> Drinke this in remembraunce that Christ's bloude was shed for thee, and be thankefull.

Both words assert that the receiving of communion is a memorial thanksgiving.

That being their purpose, they do not suggest that in changing the words Cranmer was denying or lessening the reality of Christ's presence in the elements. Furthermore, the 1549 words were not an assertion of the presence, but a prayer:

> The body of our Lorde Jesus Christe whiche was geuen for thee, preserue thy body and soule unto euerlasting lyfe.

The prayer asks no more than had already been requested in the consecration prayer and the humble access. But because enough people thought that the presence was diminished in the 1552 book, the 1549 words were combined with those of 1552 in Elizabeth's Prayer Book of 1559, to reassure those who were disturbed. Doctrinally, it was not necessary. It is worth noting that the current liturgies of the Episcopal Church use the 1552 sentence in the bidding to communion, not 1549's.

In 1552 Cranmer brilliantly expressed his concept of the eucharistic sacrifice. The omission of the anaphora of 1549 removed the possibility of interpreting we "make here before thy diuine Maiestie, with these thy holy giftes, the memoryall whyche thy sonne hath wylled us to make" as offering the sacrifice of Masses. Instead, the first prayer printed out after the communion in 1552 asks God "to accept this our Sacrifice of prayse and thanks geuing." That prayer also still contains the offering of "our selfes, our soules and bodies, to be a reasonable, holy, and liuely Sacrifice."

The association of all this with the reception of communion brings out the full significance of that act. Too often, especially in pietistic circles, communion has been considered primarily as a means of receiving pardon and grace. The emphasis has fallen on what we get, rather than on the offering of our worship and ourselves. The importance Cranmer attached to its sacrificial aspect is the reason, I think, why he dropped the communication of the sick from the reserved sacrament. He did not want communion to be administered apart from the grateful remembrance of Jesus Christ's "one oblacion of hymselfe once offered," made in the opening ascription of the consecration prayer. The prayer was short enough to be included in ministering to the sick even on emergency occasions.

Clear as all this becomes as soon as we recognize that Cranmer made the communion the anaphora, it has been misunderstood down the centuries. The 1552 book was used for only a few months, and when the Prayer Book was restored in 1559, the concern of many was that 1552 had diminished the reality of Christ's presence and botched up the liturgy in the process. But Cranmer himself made two mistakes that obscured the concept he was expressing. First, he directed that the Lord's Prayer be said immediately after communion, before continuing with the remainder of the 1549 consecration prayer. Second, although he kept the essential parts of that prayer in a condensed form, he made it an alternative to the 1549 thanksgiving for communion. If used for that purpose, it is no longer seen as an essential part of the great eucharistic thanksgiving.

Cranmer might have better conveyed his concept had he required the recitation of the end of the consecration prayer right after the communion as the explanation of its sacrificial character. Then the Lord's Prayer and the thanksgiving could follow. But whether understood clearly or not, the 1552 form of the service, with the changes in 1662 which were mostly cosmetic, remained the required Anglican eucharistic liturgy until the revisions and alternative services of the twentieth century—except in the Scottish Communion Office and the Prayer Book of the Episcopal Church. The emphasis on the sacrifice of thanksgiving and on the reception of communion as essential to the offering of it prepared the way for the changes that the modern liturgical movement have wrought. We owe a tremendous debt to Cranmer not just for 1549 but even more for 1552.

Since the theme of this book is the relationship between creation and liturgy, it may be wondered what this article is doing in it. Cranmer was a man of his age, when sin and redemption were the principal concerns of the church, especially in the eucharist. Cranmer rejected the propitiatory sacrifice of Masses, but his sacrifice of thanksgiving was primarily for the redemptive aspects of Christ's death as "a full, perfect and sufficient sacrifyce, oblacion, and satysfaccyon, for the synnes of the whole worlde." And we pray that by participating in it by communion "we and al thy whole church may obteiyne remission of our sinnes, and all other benefites of hys passyon."

The other benefits were not specified by Cranmer's liturgies. But once the theological emphasis shifted from sin and redemption to creation and re-creation, it was a simple matter to add creation and incarnation to the thanksgivings in the ascription of the consecration prayer. The sole emphasis on the satisfaction theory of the atonement could be broadened to include other concepts. When Cranmer recognized that the eucharist, as its name implies, is a sacrifice of thanksgiving, he opened the door to more affirmative and creative spirituality than he or his age could have conceived.

Because in 1552 Cranmer put the reception of communion after the institution narrative as the anamnesis, other items in the service had to be shifted. The intercessions that in 1549 were an introduction to the prayer of consecration were put earlier, followed by the penitential preparation for communion. Intruding the humble access between the *Sanctus* and the great thanksgiving, to which the *Sanctus* is an essential introduction, was a blunder. But on the whole the order of 1552 is satisfactory.

When 1662 introduced the offering of the bread and wine at the altar, the recognition of them as representing us and the world—created by God and utilized by us—became possible. Cranmer's rejection of transubstantiation affirmed that the bread and wine retain their natural integrity so that they, and we in them, share in Christ's self-offering throughout. Together with the collection of alms, however, the offertory needs to be closer to the great thanksgiving, so that offering, consecration, and communion are seen as one continuous action. Cranmer's contribution to their union—whether conscious or unconscious—was the identification in his second Prayer Book of the communion with the anamnesis that made its reception the offering of the sacrifice of thanksgiving. The eucharist is the genuine sacrament of our self-oblation to Christ and his to us.

Anglicanism is an excellent example of *lex orandi, lex credendi.* Our liturgy has not only reflected the best insights of its day, but also, because Cranmer was not too precise in expressing his dogmas or perhaps because they were not clearly understood, the door has been open for growth. We have never had an "incomparable liturgy," and for this we may be humbly thankful. But we have had a living liturgy, and 1552 made no small contribution to it.

Notes

1. Articles of Religion XXVIII, *Book of Common Prayer* 1979, p. 873.

2. E.C. Whitaker, *Martin Bucer and the Book of Common Prayer*, Alcuin Club Collections, vol. 55 (London, 1974) 42.

3. Ibid. 56.

4. Ibid. 76.

5. Ibid. 52.

6

Military Prayer Books

Marion J. Hatchett

ONE OF BOONE PORTER'S CONTRIBUTIONS TO THE LITURGICAL LIFE OF THE Episcopal Church was as editor of *A Prayer Book for the Armed Forces 1967*. This book was radically different in many ways from previous books or rites designed for the use of Anglicans in military service. It also anticipated various changes that would come in the subsequent Episcopal rites for trial use, the Book of Common Prayer 1979, and *The Hymnal 1982*.

To appreciate the significance of *A Prayer Book for the Armed Forces 1967* we need to look at the long line of special prayers, forms of prayer, and military prayer books designed for use by Anglicans in time of war which preceded it and to look at the book which has recently succeeded it.

Early Anglicanism

As a matter of fact, the very first official service published in the English language, the Litany, was put forth with the expressed aim of encouraging greater attendance and participation in prayer in a time of war. In 1544 Henry VIII was at war with both Scotland and France. On 11 June he wrote to Archbishop Cranmer:

> We greet you well; and let you wit that, calling to our remem-
> brance the miserable state of all Christendom, being at this
> present, besides all other troubles, so plagued with most cruel
> wars . . . we have set forth certain godly prayers and suffrages,
> in our native English tongue, which we send you herewith.[1]

In "An exhortation unto prayer, thoughte mete by the kinges majestie, and his clergy, to be read to the people in every church afore processyons," the people are bid:

> And here, specially let us pray for our most dear and sovereign lord,
> the King's majesty . . . who at this present time hath taken upon him
> the great and dangerous affairs of war . . . Let us pray for our
> brethren, that bend themselves to battle for God's cause and our
> defence . . . Let us pray for ourselves, that remain at home . . .[2]

The concluding section of the Litany[3] is dependent on material from the Sarum Processional for use in time of war.[4] It was also influenced by Luther's litany, which had been prompted by conditions of war.[5]

The Litany was included in the first English Book of Common Prayer of 1549. In the 1552 revision some "Occasional Prayers" were inserted, among which was a prayer for use "In the tyme of Warre":

> . . . save and deliver us (we humbly beseche thee) from the
> handes of our enemies: abate their pride, assuage their malice,
> and confound their devises . . .

From the days of Queen Elizabeth onward various Occasional Forms of Prayer were put forth by authority for use during times of crisis, principally times of war.[6] One of these Forms of Prayer from 1589 might be called the first Anglican military prayer book, "A Forme of Prayer, thought fitte to be dayly used in the English Armie in France."[7] In structure this is a drastically abbreviated order for Morning Prayer and Litany. The General Confession, Absolution, and short form of the Lord's Prayer from Morning Prayer are fol-lowed by three "psalms" ("or one of them") and four prayers. The "psalms" are printed in a manner which indicates they are to be said responsively. The first consists of selected verses from Psalm 44. The second of the "psalms" is really a cento composed of verses loosely quoted from Psalms 3, 5, 7, 10, 22, 59, and 74.[8] The third is Psalm 115. The second "psalm" had been used as early as 1572 in a form put out at the time of the massacre of the French Hugenots by Charles IX; it had also been used in another form which appeared in 1588, the year of the Spanish Armada.[9] The other psalms and prayers are not found in earlier forms. The first of the prayers, about seven hundred words in length, is more self-righteous and vindictive than the psalms.

> . . . Avance [sic] thyself like a mighty Giant with a swift and terrible judgment against them: frustrate the counsels of all their *Achitephels*: break them down with an iron rod like an earthen vessel: send an host of Angels to scatter their armies both by sea and land: confound them as thou didst the host of the *Assyrians*: Let thine own sword fight for us and devour up them; be thou as fire unto them, and let them be as stubble before thee. Finally let them be as *Oreb* and *Zeb*; yea, like unto *Zebah* and *Salmanah*, and be made as dung on the face of the earth . . .

The second prayer, a little over three hundred words in length, is of much the same tone. The other prayers, "A Prayer for the Queen's Majesty" and "In the time of War," are from the 1559 Prayer Book. The whole of this Form of Prayer, with added material, was reissued in 1590, when another Spanish invasion was expected,[10] and the first two prayers were included that year in "Certaine Praiers to be used at this present time for the good successe of the French King against the enemies of Gods true religion and his State."[11]

At the time of the English Civil War the Puritans published, under the "Imprimatur" of Edmund Calamy, a sixteen-page pamphlet with a descriptive title, *The Souldiers Pocket Bible: Containing the most (if not all) those places contained in holy Scripture, which doe show the qualifications of his inner man, that is a fit Souldier to fight the Lords Battels, both before the fight, in the fight, and after the fight; Which Scriptures are reduced to severall heads, and fitly applyed to the Souldiers severall occasions, and so may supply the want of the whole Bible, which a Souldier cannot conveniently carry about him: And may bee also usefull for any Christian to meditate upon, now in this miserable time of Warre.*[12] The booklet consists of about 139 verses or parts of verses, quoted (some very loosely) from the Geneva Bible, arranged under eighteen headings. Of all the verses quoted only seven are from the New Testament. Under the heading "A Souldier must love his enemies as they are his enemies, and hate them as they are gods enemies" (Mt 5:44; 2 Cr 19:2; Ps 139:21-22) it is the Psalmist rather than Jesus Christ who has the last word.

The Cavaliers also published a military prayer book, *Certain Prayers fitted To severall Occasions and Are to be used in His Majesties Armies. Published by His Highnesse Command.*[13] The first page gives references for psalms "to be Said or Sung" on particular occasions. A three-page cento, "A Psalm preparatory,"[14] follows. The remainder of the book is given over to prayers. Most of them are long, after the manner of the time, and are replete with quotations from the Bible and the Prayer Book. The first is "A Prayer to be said at the setting forth of an Army, or before they March":

> ... It is not Ambition, or Malice, that hath thrust us into this posture, but the necessary defence of thy Church, thy Truth, our Laws, our Liberties, and the Obedience which we owe, under thee, unto thine Anoynted ...

A petition in a prayer "for a place besieged" reads:

> ... As for those who now come about them like Bees, let them be extinct as the fire among the Thorns, deal with them, O Lord, as thou didst with the Host of *Senacherib*, or if not so, yet fasten thy Hook in their Nostrils, and turn them back at least with shame, and dishonour ...

Early Days of the American Church

During the formative days of the Episcopal Church in the United States, the Interstate Meeting of September 1785 adopted for the Proposed Book of Common Prayer a service for July Fourth, modelled after the "State Services" of the English Prayer Book.[15] It met with resistance in some places[16] and was not included in the first American Book of Common Prayer of 1789. During the next century, however, it was authorized from time to time by various bishops.[17]

During the early decades of the nineteenth century, many American bishops and clergy published books of family devotions. William Berrian of Trinity Church, New York, who published such a book,[18] prepared another along these lines "for the Executive Committee of the Army and Navy Convention," *The Sailor's and Soldier's Manual of Devotion*, which was published in 1844. It includes the Forms of Prayer to be used at Sea, the Office of the Visitation of the Sick, and some of the Occasional Prayers from the Book of Common Prayer. In addition, there are many long prayers of penitence (for example, "A Prayer for a grievous Sinner, who has long delayed his repentance," and "Another Prayer after a long course of wickedness and impiety," the first two prayers in the book), prayers for spiritual graces (including one "for obedience to Commanders on Land or at Sea"), and prayers for various occasions (including "A Prayer to be used by an Officer on Court Martial when Sentence of Death may be passed").

The Civil War

The years immediately preceding the Civil War were marked by discontent with the current liturgical provisions and practices of the church. There was a desire for more variety and greater brevity in the public services.[19] The metrical psalms were losing favor, and there was a desire for official recognition of more hymns. A need was felt for special services for mission situations.[20]

During these years a booklet titled *Mission Service* was published in at least three undated editions by the Protestant Episcopal Society for the Propagation of Evangelical Knowledge, which had been incorporated in 1848. This booklet would set the pattern for the military prayer books of the Civil War. It included Morning Prayer, the Litany, Ante-Communion, and Evening Prayer, omitting most of the alternative forms. It also included a few psalms, several Occasional Prayers, and a limited selection of metrical psalms and hymns from the "Prayer Book Collection," the Hymnal of 1826, and the metrical Psalter of 1832, which was bound with the Book of Common Prayer.[21]

In 1861 a twenty-page booklet was published in Cincinnati, *An Order of Public Worship to be used by all Ministers of the Protestant Episcopal Church, when Officiating at any Encampment, or other Depot of Troops, in the State of Ohio; set forth and appointed by the Right Rev. Charles Pettit McIlvaine, D.D., Bishop of the Diocese of Ohio.* It is an abbreviated form for use as either Morning or Evening Prayer. Inserted after the Prayer for the President is "A Prayer for the Country in the present need" and the prayer "in behalf of all present" from the Visitation Office. The remainder of the booklet contains eleven hymns and one metrical psalm from the "Prayer Book Collection."[22]

The Protestant Episcopal Book Society of Philadelphia published that same year *The Soldier's Prayer Book. Arranged from the Book of Common Prayer; with Additional Collects and Hymns.* The Preface, dated 13 June, 1861, was signed by Alonzo Potter, Bishop of the Diocese of Pennsylvania.

> ... I hereby certify my approbation of the book, and recommend
> it for adoption in cases where the full service cannot be cel-
> ebrated with advantage.

The "Public Service" is an abbreviated form of Morning Prayer. This is followed by ten "Occasional Collects" taken from various places in the Prayer Book, and four "Additional Collects," the first of which,

"For Unity," is from the Accession Service of the English Prayer Book. The prayers are followed by eight "Selections from the Psalms."[23] The *Gloria in excelsis* and the Decalogue are printed after the Selections. The next section of the book includes twenty "Hymns from the Prayer Book," followed by twenty "Additional Hymns," many of which were popular among evangelical Protestants at the time. These are followed by "Special Hymns," two each "For the Hospital," "For a Funeral," and "The Christian's Death." The book ends with the "Funeral Service," an abbreviated form of the Prayer Book Burial Office.

In 1862 the Margaret Coffin Prayer Society of Boston published *Selections from the Book of Common Prayer for Missionary and Temporary Services: For morning and evening prayer with the Ante-Communion service.*

In 1862 Bishops Potter and McIlvaine joined with clergy of several denominations in recommending a manual compiled by Charles W. Shields for use "in cases where our own respective rules and customs of worship cannot be exclusively maintained." The book was published in Philadelphia with the title *A Manual of Worship, suitable to be used in legislative and other public bodies, in the Army and Navy, and in Military and Naval Academies, Asylums, Hospitals, etc.*

In this period the Rebels as well as the Yankees published military prayer books. At the November 1862 meeting of the General Council of the Protestant Episcopal Church in the Confederate States of America, a committee was empowered to publish an edition of the Book of Common Prayer with the changes necessitated by the political situation, "and also, in order to supply in part the urgent need of copies of the Prayer Book for our soldiers and sailors, a selection of such portions thereof as are used in public worship."[24] This project was carried out in 1863 by Bishop Stephen Elliott of Georgia, the chairman of the committee on the Prayer Book. He had difficulty with the printer, R.J. Maynard of Atlanta, and wrote to him: "I have received the Copy of the Mission Service and am deeply mortified at the appearance . . . The first two forms, are upon the paper you sent me. The latter forms are upon the commonest newspaper trash." He complained that the cover had been used for advertizing and ordered that plain white covers be put on all that had not been issued. He concluded by saying: "I shall take care how I am caught in any such scrape again." Five thousand copies of this book, which was a reprinting of *Mission Service* with appropriate additions, were printed.[25]

The best known and most widely circulated of the Confederate military prayer books were those published by the Diocesan Missionary Society of Virginia. The first of these was the *Prayer Book for the Camp*. Ten thousand copies of this sixty-four page book were printed in Richmond by Macfarland and Fergusson in 1863.[26]

In 1864 this society issued the *Army and Navy Prayer Book*. Twenty-four thousand copies were printed in 1864,[27] and another edition was issued the following year. In his address to the Diocesan Convention of 1864 Bishop Johns described it as suitable to be a soldier's "valuable *vade mecum* on every march."[28]

Several other abridgments of the Prayer Book were printed in the Confederate States for the use of military personnel. One, an octavo pamphlet of sixteen pages, was published in Charlottesville, Virginia, in 1861.[29] Another was compiled by Joseph W. Murphy, chaplain of the 32nd Regiment, North Carolina Troops, and published by St. Paul's Church, Petersburg, Virginia.[30] Another was published in Mobile, Alabama, in 1862.[31] In 1863 J.W. Randolph of Richmond, Virginia, published a small booklet, *The Psalter, or Psalms of David*, which consists of the Prayer Book Psalter, complete with the ten general "Selections of Psalms," and the centos for the major Holy Days from the 1789 Book of Common Prayer. Evans and Cogswell of Charleston, South Carolina, published for the Female Bible, Prayer-Book and Tract Society a twelve-page booklet, *Prayers and other Devotions for the Use of the Soldiers of the Army of the Confederate States*. Among the prayers is one entitled "The Soldier's Prayer in Camp":

> . . . Let not the defenders of a righteous cause go away ashamed, nor their counsels be brought to nought . . . Place a guard of angels, O Lord, about the Commander-in-chief, and uphold him with the defence of Thy right hand, that no unhallowed arm may do him violence . . .

The Rev. Charles Todd Quintard, one of the most outstanding of the Southern chaplains and later Bishop of Tennessee, compiled *The Confederate Soldier's Pocket Manual of Devotions*. A reviewer in the *Church Intelligencer* commented on this manual:

> . . . It is made up of more or less original, practical matter for the government of Christian life, of prayers well adapted to the wants and circumstances of our soldiers . . . while enough is intermixed to guard the faith against the errors and mistaken liberality of the times by adding the Creed and a judicious selection from the collects and daily services . . .[32]

Quintard sent four copies of this manual to General Polk, who wrote on the fly-leaves of three the names of Generals J.E. Johnston, W.J. Hardee, and J.B. Hood: "With the compliments of Lieutenant-General Leonidas Polk." These were "taken from the breastpocket of his coat, stained with his blood, after his death, and forwarded to the officers for whom he had intended them."[33] Quintard also prepared another devotional manual, *Balm for the Weary and the Wounded*, for those who had exchanged "active service in the field for the harder and more wearing service in the hospital."[34]

The Civil War prayer books from both sides indicate dissatisfaction with the church's provisions for public worship. They indicate a desire for briefer and more flexible services, and they reflect the disuse of the metrical psalms and the desire for more hymns. In this respect they foreshadow the additions to the "Prayer Book Collection" of hymns in 1865 and the complete revision of the hymnal and absorption of the metrical Psalter in 1871 and 1874. The omission of certain canticles and of the optional portion of the Litany in many of these books probably indicates that these were not normally used in actual practice. The fact that the whole of the Communion Service is not included in any of these books indicates the infrequency of its celebration in this period. The failure to include the baptismal rite in any book may indicate either a lack of stress on the sacrament at this period or an assumption that any person who had reached the age for military service had already been baptized.

The metrical psalms, hymns, and prayers which show up with great consistency must certainly be indicative of the popular piety of the period. Only two metrical psalms appear with great frequency:

> 79. "With one consent let all the earth" (Psalm 100)
> 82. "O bless the Lord, my soul" (Psalm 103).

A dozen hymns are included in most of the collections:

> 32. "Welcome, sweet day of rest"
> 40. "Lord! dismiss us with thy blessing"
> 62. "When I survey the wondrous cross"
> 75. "Come, Holy Spirit, Heavenly Dove"
> 129. "Hasten, sinner, to be wise"
> 131. "The Spirit, in our hearts"
> 137. "O that my load of sin were gone!"
> 143. "Jesus, Saviour [*normally* Lover] of my soul"
> 147. "When I can read my title clear"

175. "Jesus! and shall it ever be"
177. "Guide me, O thou great Jehovah"
180. "Awake, my soul, stretch every nerve."

Six of these have lived through the hymnal revisions of 1871, 1874, 1892, 1916, 1940, and 1982. Some of the additional hymns printed in some of these books made their way into the hymnal in 1865:

214. "There is a fountain, filled with blood"
228. "Alas! and did my Saviour bleed"
250. "Just as I am, without one plea"
255. "How sweet the name of Jesus sounds"
258. "All hail the power of Jesus' name"
268. "Sun of my soul!"
271. "Jerusalem, my happy home."

Still others came into the hymnal in 1871 and 1874, and some of these are still found in *The Hymnal 1982*. In addition to prayers for peace and for the sick, certain other prayers show up in a great many of these military prayer books, indicating the place they held in the popular piety of the period. Those found with the greatest frequency are the Collect for the Second Sunday in Advent ("Blessed Lord, who hast caused all holy Scriptures to be written for our learning...") and Jeremy Taylor's prayer "in behalf of all present" from the Visitation of the Sick ("O God, whose days are without end, and whose mercies cannot be numbered..."). Also generally included is a prayer from the Office of Institution ("O God, Holy Ghost, Sanctifier of the Faithful..."). Others frequently found include collects from among those printed after the Communion Service, the Collects for the First and Fourth Sundays of Advent, Ash Wednesday, Good Friday (the last Collect), Trinity Sunday, and the First Sunday after Trinity, the last prayer of the Burial Office, and the General Confession from the Communion Service. At least one of the prayers new to the 1892 revision of the Book of Common Prayer, "For the Unity of God's People," was a prayer from the English Accession Service that had been included in some of the Civil War military prayer books.

World War I

As early as 1914 many bishops authorized Occasional Prayers or Forms of Prayer for use in their dioceses.[35] Some of these contained prayers that would show up in the military prayer books of World War I.

In 1913 a Joint Commission was appointed by the General Convention to consider revision and enrichment of the Book of Common Prayer. Their report, published in 1915,[36] contained some new proposals and brought back into circulation some material from *The Book Annexed*,[37] a report prepared for the 1883 General Convention, which contained a substantial amount of material that did not make its way into the 1892 revision. The 1916 report served as a resource for compilers of military prayer books published after the United States entered the war. The 1916 General Convention also adopted a new hymnal which included several new hymns published in the military prayer books of World War I.

In April 1917 a twelve-page leaflet entitled *Forms of Prayer for Public and Private Worship in Time of War* was published. On the cover is this statement:

> Authorized for use by the Bishops of the following Dioceses: Albany, Bethlehem, Central New York, Delaware, Easton, Erie, Harrisburg, Long Island, Maryland, Newark, New Jersey, New York, Pennsylvania, Pittsburgh, and Washington.

It is possible that the contents had already been authorized and that the booklet was issued immediately after the United States entered the war. It provided a Collect (that for the Third Sunday in Lent), an Epistle (Jas 4:1-10), a Gospel (Mt 24:3-14), and an "Additional Collect." Along with prayers from the Prayer Book and other sources, and prayers new to this book, were two prayers from the 1916 report. One was a prayer associated with the Peace in the Roman Missal; the other was a prayer "For Our Country" which had been written for *The Book Annexed* by the Rev. George Lyman Locke,[38] but not incorporated in the 1892 Book of Common Prayer. A number of features of this booklet were included in subsequent military prayer books.

In August 1917 *Hymns and Prayers for the Use of the Army and Navy* was published by Houghton Mifflin Company of Boston and New York. *The Living Church* of 25 August, 1917, gave notice of its appearance and stated that it was compiled at the request of Bishop Lawrence, chairman of the War Commission, by Dean Rousmaniere of the Boston Cathedral, the Rev. John W. Suter, secretary of the Joint Commission on the Prayer Book, and the Rev. George Hodges, D.D., Dean of the Episcopal Theological School. The first pages are devoted to fifty hymns, thirty-seven of which are found in the 1892 hymnal and forty-three in the *Mission Hymnal* which had been authorized by the General Convention of 1913. The four not in either book are: "God of our fathers, known of old"; "Mine eyes have seen the glory"; "Oh, say, can you see"; and "O beautiful for spacious skies." The first three of these had been approved for the 1916 hymnal. A volume containing the music was also published at that time.[39] The next pages of the prayer book are devoted to Prayer Book versions of psalms and canticles.[40] The next section is entitled "Readings from the Bible." The first two pages are selections of one, two, or three verses; these are followed by twenty-two longer selections. Following these pages is a section of prayers. Some of these had been included in *A Book of Offices and Prayers for Priest and People Compiled by Two Presbyters of the Church*, which had been edited in 1896 by J.W. Suter and C.M. Addison.[41] Others came from various sources, including *The Book Annexed* and the 1916 report, and some were probably written especially for this book. The next three pages are devoted to "A Form of Service." The order begins with a hymn; this opening hymn is followed by responsive Opening Sentences, the first and third of the Versicles and Responses from Morning Prayer, another hymn, a Psalm ("To be read responsively"), a Lesson, another hymn, and prayers ending with the Lord's Prayer and the Grace. Printed for permissive use before the Lord's Prayer is a short Penitential Order consisting of a brief general confession followed by the Collect for the Twenty-First Sunday after Trinity. Though the rubrics specify "Chaplain," there is no reason why this service could not be conducted by a lay person. The next four pages are given over to a wartime litany which is introduced by William Bright's collect "For the Spirit of Prayer,"[42] which had been included in *The Book Annexed* and the 1916 report. On the last page is printed four stanzas of "St. Patrick's Breastplate," a hymn new to the 1916 hymnal.

The *Living Church* for 18 August, 1917, contained a notice that the Bishop White Prayer Book Society had published *A Prayer Book for the Public and Private Use of our Soldiers and Sailors with Bible Readings and Hymns*. This book went through at least ten editions, totaling 197,000 copies.[43] The book is prefaced with a quotation from President Wilson under the title "The Motives and Objects of the War." Unlike the book compiled at the request of Bishop Lawrence, this book includes the full texts of Morning and Evening Prayer, the Litany (with additional petitions), and Holy Communion. Along with additional prayers from the Prayer Book and other sources, it includes several from the 1916 report, some of which go back to *The Book Annexed*. It is significant that among these "Special Prayers" are prayers for the enemy, prayers for the departed, and prayers of social concern.

Instructions are then given for use "if called upon to give Christian burial to a comrade." After a prayer "Before Bible Readings" ("Blessed Lord, who hast caused all holy Scripture to be written for our learning ...") come selections from the psalms,[44] "New Testament Readings," mostly familiar passages but some evidently chosen with the particular situation of the soldier in mind,[45] and "Hymns." Of the sixty-two hymns, thirty-seven were from the 1892 hymnal, nine from *The Mission Hymnal*, and five (all songs of a patriotic nature)[46] authorized by the General Convention of 1916 for inclusion in the new revision. The remaining eleven are all national anthems or patriotic songs. In 1918 the Bishop White Prayer Book Society issued a hymnal for use with the hymns and canticles included in this book.[47] This hymnal is "pitched within the singing range of the average man" and "scored for military bands by a Government Commission." The prayer book was designed for use at regular services conducted by a chaplain who had access to additional books, for private devotional use, and for use in one emergency situation, burial of the dead.

In October 1917 the Church Literature Press of New York published a similar though somewhat smaller book, *Soldiers and Sailors Prayer Book Compiled from the Book of Common Prayer and other sources*. The Foreword states that it is sent forth "with the hope that it may be a companion, and source of comfort, both in weary night watches and arduous day duties, when you are far from home and kin."

In addition to these, other military prayer books were edited by individuals. The Rev. Milo Hudson Gates, later Dean of the New York Cathedral, edited the *Campaign Prayer Book*.[48] The numbered pages provide the complete form for the four "regular services," the propers for the Church Year, and the psalms. The unnumbered pages at the beginning and end of the book include "certain prayers, chosen from various sources approved by our bishops, which this time of warfare has already tested and proved helpful."

Another book, privately printed by the Rev. John Montgomery Rich, and "Presented to American Heroes at the Front by Col. Edwin A. Stevens," was entitled *The Lord's Service and Popular Tune Book*. This book, which came out in two editions, the "All-American Gospel Edition" and the "Wilson and Lafayette Edition" was "Dedicated to President Wilson: For the Rights of Humanity: Gospel Reading Christianity: Liberty Enlightening the World." The contents consisted of forty-seven hymns from the 1892 hymnal, missionary Vespers" (Evening Prayer through the "Fixed Collects"), and "The

Lord's Service" (the Prayer Book eucharistic rite with supplementary material and with communions "at the mid-day choral Lord's Service" discouraged). The "Wilson and Lafayette Edition" differed from the other in that it included full-page pictures of Wilson, Lafayette, the U.S. Capitol, and the Statue of Liberty.

In contrast to the military prayer books of the Civil War period, those of World War I, with one exception, included the eucharistic rite. The editors anticipated the 1928 revision of the Book of Common Prayer in including prayers for the dead. These books certainly played a part in bringing into use many of the prayers in the 1916 report. At least two of the prayers included in the book in which Suter had a hand lie behind other new prayers that would be included in the 1928 book.[49] The area of concern indicated in the prayers is broader than in those of the Civil War books. There are fewer long prayers and more in collect form. The penitential and eschatological elements are not as prominent. Pietistic and evangelical hymns still occupy a very prominent place. Aside from the patriotic songs, the hymns that are consistently found in these books are the following:

"Abide with me"
"Fight the good fight"
"Go forward, Christian soldier"
"He leadeth me"
"Holy, Holy, Holy! Lord God Almighty"
"In the Cross of Christ I glory"
"Jesus, Lover of my soul"
"Lead, kindly Light"
"My faith looks up to Thee"
"Nearer, my God, to Thee"
"O God, our help in ages past"
"Onward, Christian soldiers"
"Rock of Ages, cleft for me"
"Soldiers of Christ, arise"
"Stand up, stand up, for Jesus"
"Sun of my soul, Thou Saviour dear."

World War II

The Living Church for 19 February, 1941, contained this news item:

A new special service book called the Prayer Book for Soldiers and Sailors has been completed by the special committee appointed by the Army and Navy Chaplains' Commission. The committee consists of the Rev. Dr. James Thayer Addison, the Rev. John W. Suter jr. [sic], and Chaplain J. Burt Webster, U.S.A.

Suter was the son of a member of the committee which had edited *Hymns and Prayers for the Use of the Army and Navy* in World War I. Addison was the son of the man who had collaborated with Dr. Suter, Sr. in the editing of a book of prayers and of a book of offices.[50] *The Living Church* for 2 April, 1941, announced that the book had been published by the Church Pension Fund. The ninety-six page book obviously took as its starting point *Hymns and Prayers for the Use of the Army and Navy*. The principal addition is the printing in full (with the exception of all but two of the Offertory Sentences) of "The Order for The Administration of the Lord's Supper or Holy Communion" from the Book of Common Prayer. The principal source for the prayers not retained from the 1917 book was a small booklet, *Prayers New and Old*, which had been published by Forward Movement Publications under the editorship of the Rev. Canon Gilbert P. Symons in 1937 and circulated widely throughout the church since that time. Thirteen psalms from the King James Version were printed.[51] The biblical readings were given headings. Several passages included in the 1917 book were dropped out, and four new ones were added. At the end of the book thirty-eight hymns were printed. Twenty-three of these were carried over from the 1917 book. Rather than printing a separate tune book, the editors suggested use of *The Wayside Hymnal*, which had been compiled by Canon Symons and published by Forward Movement Publications the previous year, which was available at five cents per copy. All of the texts were included in the 1916 hymnal except for four.[52]

The Korean Conflict

At the time of the Korean Conflict a revision of the World War II book was published by the Church Pension Fund under the title *The Armed Forces Prayer Book*, "for The Armed Forces Division of the Protestant Episcopal Church." The person chiefly responsible for this book was the Rev. Percy G. Hall, S.T.D., who was at that time Executive Secretary of the Armed Forces Division of the National Council of the Episcopal Church. This is not a new book but an enlarged and revised version of that of 1941. Immediately after the eucharistic rite some important new additions are printed, including a section not found in previous military prayer books and entitled

"Spiritual Communion." It consists of directions and forms for use when "on any Sunday or other Day of Obligation . . . you are prevented from making your Communion." There is a relationship between this and an "Act of Spiritual Communion" in the Forward Movement booklet *Be of Good Cheer,* which is acknowledged as the source of other material in this book.[53] The next new feature of the 1951 book is the inclusion of the Order for Holy Baptism from the Book of Common Prayer. This is followed by a form for "Baptism in Extremis" from a Forward publication, *Manual for Servicemen,* which had been compiled by Canon Symons and printed earlier that year. Another new feature is "The Way of Penitence." The source is acknowledged as the Forward Movement publication *Be of Good Cheer.* Among the "Prayers" all but three of those in the 1941 book were retained. Several of the new prayers had been printed in Forward Movement booklets. Canon Symon's *War-Time Prayers* or his *God Be With You,* or Francis J. Moore's *Prayers for All Occasions.* All of the psalms, the "Bible Readings," and the hymns of the 1941 book were retained, and additional ones were added in each of these sections.

The Vietnam Conflict

In the spring of 1967 the Seabury Press published "for the Bishop for the Armed Forces" *A Prayer Book for the Armed Forces 1967.* Immediately after the title page are instructions, "How to Use This Book," which state that it is intended to help "both in your private prayers and in public worship." The contents of the book represent an attempt to deal seriously with a need that had not been faced as realistically in the books that preceded it.

> For public use there are short services arranged for worship and the administration of the sacraments in the field, at sea, in the air, or in other circumstances when the services of the Church cannot be carried out in the usual manner. The Book of Common Prayer, the Bible, and hymnals are always useful, but this book alone contains enough material for complete services under these conditions. The directions in the last section of this book make it possible for a lay person to lead a service of worship without difficulty.

A statement by the Bishop for the Armed Forces, Arnold M. Lewis, gives credit for the "general editing" to the Rev. H. Boone Porter, Jr., D.Phil., Professor of Liturgics at the General Theological Seminary.

The first section of the book is devoted to "Personal Prayers." It includes "Daily Prayers for the Morning," short prayers for use at certain times "During the Day," and "Daily Prayers for the Evening." These are followed by "Various Prayers for Private Use." Several of these were carried over from the 1951 book. Others are from the Book of Common Prayer or *The Hymnal 1940* ("God be in my head"). New to this book is a brief prayer "For One's Sweetheart, Wife, or Husband," and a very striking addition, "A Prayer to Our Lord," which is from *The Abiding Presence*.[54] The section of "Personal Prayers" ends with a page of "Short Prayers" that "The prayerful Christian will find it helpful to know by heart." Included are several scripture verses, the *Trisagion*, the Anthem from the Visitation Office, and a brief invocation to the Holy Spirit.

"A Service of Worship," which is very similar to "A Form of Service" or "An Order of Worship" of the 1917, 1941, and 1951 books, follows the section of prayers. Two very important changes have been made in this service: it can be led by a lay person, and the preaching of the word comes immediately after the reading.

The next section is entitled "The Holy Communion." This section is introduced by instructions for "Preparation for Holy Communion" and "Thanksgiving after Holy Communion." "A Short Service of Holy Communion" is provided "to enable Military Chaplains of the Episcopal Church to celebrate the Holy Eucharist under conditions which make it not feasible to use the full service as set forth in the Book of Common Prayer." The section designated "The Ministry of the Word" may begin with a hymn, followed by the Salutation and the Collect for Purity "or some other." A passage of Scripture is to be read "as the Epistle."[55] A psalm or a hymn may follow. A passage is to be read "as the Gospel."[56] The readings may be followed by an explanation or a brief sermon. The Apostles' Creed may then be said, and a short litany may follow. The section headed "The Ministry of the Sacrament" begins with the short confession and absolution from the Visitation Office. "When convenient" the bread and wine are to be brought to the priest "by representatives of the congregation." At this time a hymn or psalm may be sung or said. Immediately after the presentation of the offerings comes the eucharistic prayer (the final paragraph has been abbreviated), the Lord's Prayer, and the breaking of the bread. The people may say or sing the *Agnus Dei*. After the people have received, the priest and people are to say the postcommunion prayer in the revised form of *Prayer Book Studies*

XVII,[57] which had been published by the Standing Liturgical Commission the previous year. The priest is then to dismiss the people with a blessing.

The "General Directions" which follow allow for use of the Communion of the Sick from the Book of Common Prayer instead of the form provided, indicate permissible propers, allow for a lay person to lead the litany, and point out that "It is appropriate for the Epistle to be read by a lay person." These directions indicate times when it is possible for "The Ministry of the Word" and "The Ministry of the Sacrament" to be used separately, provide for reservation for the sick, and point out that the Sacrament "is not to be administered to persons who have not first received Holy Baptism." This rite is based on many of the principles exhibited in the proposal of *Prayer Book Studies XVII*: greater flexibility, more lay participation, a litany form for the intercessions, juxtaposition of bible readings and sermon, restoration of the breaking of the bread, and a return to the "Four-Fold Shape of the Liturgy." Instructions are provided for "When Holy Communion Is Not Available." And recommendations are made in regard to the conditions under which a person might receive communion in another Christian body; additionally, devotions are suggested for use when a public service is unavailable.

The Order for Holy Baptism from the Book of Common Prayer is printed in full except for parts not used at the baptism of an adult. The provisions for "Emergency Baptism" from the 1951 book have been reworked somewhat, chiefly in providing for use of a greater portion of the regular rite by a lay person "if time permits."

Under the heading "Penitence and Confession" are instructions concerning confession and a form for private confession. The instructions are much fuller than those of the 1951 book. The form is much the same except for the addition of a list of psalms which constitute suitable penances. The Ten Commandments and the Summary of the Law are printed on the page that follows.

New to the book is a section "For the Sick or Wounded," which opens with instructions on the use of such times as "opportunities for spiritual growth" and instructions on the church's ministry for the sick. Under the heading "The Ministry of Healing" are forms from the Visitation Office and an abbreviated version of a traditional prayer[58] which may be used "by a priest at any time to bless oil for the sick."

In a section "For the Dying" are instructions on preparing for one's own death and on attending a dying comrade. The dying, after appropriate prayers, are to commend themselves to God in the words of our Lord, "Father, into thy hands I commend my spirit." One attending a dying Christian is to use the Prayer Book Commendation. Another form is provided for use with "one who does not profess the Christian faith." The section "Burial of the Dead and Memorial Services" contains a short form for "emergency burial" and references to other materials in the book which could be used to construct a fuller form or for a "Memorial Service."

The next section is devoted to psalms and canticles. "A Guide to the Psalms" is provided to point to those particularly appropriate to various days or seasons of the church year and "For Particular Needs." A short instruction on the psalms and their use is provided. Twenty-six psalms, or portions of psalms, are printed under appropriate titles.[59] After a brief instruction on canticles, the *Venite*, *Te Deum*, *Gloria in excelsis*, *Magnificat*, and *Nunc dimittis* are printed, and a reference is given for the *Jubilate Deo*.

The next section, "Bible Passages," is introduced by a guide to appropriate passages for the church year and for particular needs. Instruction is given on how to use the passages, and the collect for "Bible Sunday" is printed as "A Prayer for Understanding Holy Scripture." Nine passages are printed under the heading "Short Passages."[60] Twenty-six longer passages are printed under the appropriate headings.[61] All passages are quoted from the Revised Standard Version. Only two of the short passages and four of the longer ones had been included in the 1951 book.

The next section, "Prayers for Public and Private Use," opens with "A Guide to Prayers and Collects" for the church year and for particular needs. Many of the collects and prayers have been retained from the 1951 book, and others are drawn from the Book of Common Prayer. A new prayer for the Coast Guard was written by the Rev. Canon Peter Chase. Prayers "For Those Witnessing to Christ," "For Our Allies and for Other Nations," and "For Christian Race Relations" were drawn from *A Calendar of Prayers for Missions, 1961-1962*, published by the National Council of the Protestant Episcopal Church. The prayer "For the Impoverished" was written by Miss Karen Eagle for a young people's competition and published in *The Living Church*, 24 April, 1966. The last of the "Closing Prayers and Blessings" is the dismissal from the recently published *Prayer Book Studies XVII: The Liturgy of the Lord's Supper*.

The section devoted to "Hymns" begins with a guide for the selection of hymns for the church year and for particular needs. The melody line of each hymn is printed above the text. For accompaniments, the reader is referred to the *Armed Forces Hymnal,* published by the Armed Forces Chaplains Board, which contained all but two of the hymns, and to *The Hymnal 1940,* which contained all except for the verses for the Marine Corps and for Airmen which have been appended to "The Navy Hymn." Merbecke's setting for the *Sanctus* and the *Agnus Dei* have also been included. Of the twenty-eight hymns (not including the *Sanctus* and *Agnus Dei*), fourteen had been included in the 1951 book. Only eight hymns have been retained throughout this line of 1917, 1941, 1951, and 1967 books:

"All hail the power of Jesus' Name"
"Eternal Father, strong to save"
"Holy, Holy, Holy! Lord God Almighty!"
"In the cross of Christ I glory"
"My country, 'tis of thee"
"O God, our help in ages past"
"Onward, Christian Soldiers"
"The Church's one foundation."

Many of the more individualistic and pietistic texts, so heavily represented in earlier books, have been replaced by hymns associated with the church year and the eucharist.

The hymns are followed by a brief instruction on the church year, a table of moveable holy days, and a table of epistles and gospels for the church year, which was repeated from the 1951 book. Suitable epistles and gospels are also suggested for several minor holy days, for national holidays, and for weddings and memorial services. Four pages of instructions are provided to help an inexperienced person plan and lead a service of worship.

This book attempts to meet a number of needs that were not dealt with in earlier military prayer books. It deals more realistically with situations in which time or equipment are minimal or when a chaplain is not available. The selections of psalms, bible passages, prayers, and hymns have been enriched. Provisions allow for a more adequate celebration of the church year. The insights of recent scholarship are brought to bear on the structure of the eucharistic rite. Provisions are made for increased lay participation in the eucharistic rite and for lay leading of other services of worship. Direction is given concerning private devotions, and substantial material is provided for such use.

A Prayer Book for the Armed Forces 1967 may have introduced some people to some forms not in the 1928 Prayer Book which would be included in the Book of Common Prayer 1979: for example, the noonday prayer "Blessed Saviour, who at this hour didst hang upon the cross," the compline antiphon, the mealtime grace "Blessed art thou, O Lord, our God," the *Trisagion*, and the *Agnus Dei*. It also anticipated the Book of Common Prayer 1979 in including a form for private confession and a prayer for blessing oil for the sick.

The Latest Revision

The adoption of a new Book of Common Prayer in 1979 and a new hymnal in 1982 made revision of *A Prayer Book for the Armed Forces 1967* necessary. The preface of *A Prayer Book for the Armed Forces 1988* expresses gratitude to "Howard E. Galley who, with the Rev. Dr. Donald W. Beers, compiled and edited this book." Though the book was brought into conformity to the new Prayer Book and new Hymnal, the outline of the book and much of the contents stem from the 1967 edition.

Much of the material new to that book was retained. In the eucharistic rite two forms for the Prayers of the People are printed. One of these is Form IV from the Book of Common Prayer; the other is the litany from the eucharistic rite of the 1967 book. Much of the material introducing the various sections and the different rites has been retained, as has the section "When Holy Communion Is Not Available" and the form for the commendation of a dying person who does not profess the Christian faith.

The sections of psalms, of readings, and of hymns are introduced by revised versions of the guides for the church year and for particular needs that had been introduced in the 1967 book. Of the twenty-three psalms, fifteen were retained from the 1967 book.[62] Headings had been introduced for the psalms in that book and they are provided in the 1988 revision. Of the forty-one readings, fourteen were retained from the 1967 book. The collects for the principal seasons and days of the church year of the 1967 book were retained.[63] Eleven of the thirty hymns were also retained from the 1967 book.

* * * * * * * * * *

Boone Porter's *A Prayer Book for the Armed Forces 1967* was an important stage in the development of military prayer books. It provided an outline and a great deal of material that have stood up well enough to be retained in the later revision. This book certainly introduced some people to some of the insights of the Liturgical Movement and helped prepare them to deal with the forthcoming

Services for Trial Use and the Book of Common Prayer 1979. Though it is not as well-known as many of his other works, Boone Porter made an important contribution to worship in the Episcopal Church in editing *A Prayer Book for the Armed Forces 1967*.

Notes

1. *Miscellaneous Writings and Letters of Thomas Cranmer, Archbishop of Canterbury, Martyr 1556*, ed. J.E. Cox (Cambridge: Cambridge University Press, 1846) 494.

2. *Private Prayers, Put forth by Authority during the Reign of Queen Elizabeth*, ed. W.K. Clay (Cambridge: Cambridge University Press, 1851) 567.

3. Ibid. 570-576.

4. F.E. Brightman, *The English Rite: Being a Synopsis of the Sources and Revisions of the Book of Common Prayer with an Introduction and an Appendix*, 2 vols. (London: Rivingtons, 1915) lvii-lxviii.

5. *Luther's Works: American Edition*, vol. 53, *Liturgy and Hymns* (Philadelphia: Fortress Press, 1965) 153-170.

6. A number of the forms from the Elizabethan era are printed in *Liturgical Services: Liturgies and Occasions Forms of Prayer set forth in the Reign of Queen Elizabeth*, ed. W.K. Clay (Cambridge: Cambridge University Press, 1847) 457-695.

7. Ibid. 626-631; see also 470.

8. Psalms 5:2; 22:16b, 11, 13; 3:3; 7:1; 10:16; 7:2 and 22:21; 74:20; 59:1; 7:18; 22:22-23.

9. *Liturgical Services* 543-544, 610-611.

10. Ibid. 632-646.

11. Ibid. 647-651.

12. See Harold R. Willoughby, *Soldiers' Bible through Three Centuries* (Chicago: University of Chicago Press, 1944) for a facsimile reproduction and an account of reprints of this work and of other "Soldiers' Bibles."

13. See Edward Almack, *The Cavalier Soldier's Vade-Mecum* (London: Blades, East & Blades, 1900) for a facsimile reproduction, with introduction and notes.

14. Psalms 27:1, 3; 46:1, 2, 3, 7; 44:5, 6, 7, 8; 55:1, 2, 19, 20; 62:4; 35:22, 23; 144:7; 18:50, 51; 56:10, 11; and *Gloria Patri*.

15. Marion J. Hatchett, *The Making of the First American Book of Common Prayer 1776-1789* (New York: Seabury Press, 1981) 53, 57-58, 83.

16. Ibid. 92-93.

17. See, for example, for a reference to the authorization of this form by Bishop Hobart, *An Exposition of the Memorial of Sundry Presbyters of the Protestant Episcopal Church: presented to the House of Bishops, during the General Convention of Said Church, 1853. By One of the Memorialists* (New York, 1854).

18. *Family and Private Prayers*, 2d ed. (New York: T. and J. Swords, 1823).

19. See William McGarvey, *Liturgiae Americanae: or the Book of Common Prayer As Used in the United States of America Compared with the Proposed Book of 1786 and with the Prayer Book of the Church of England, and an Historical Account and Documents* (Philadelphia: Philadelphia Church Publishing Company, 1907) xxxvii-xxxix.

20. See, for example, *An Order for a Second Evening Service, in the Churches, in the Diocese of New Jersey: set forth by the Bishop* (New York, 1857).

21. Psalm selections 32, 38, 48, 82, and 29 (Part I), which are metrical paraphrases of portions of Psalms 38, 43, 62, 104, and 34, and Hymns 75, 129, 103, 131, 179, 180, and 40 in what is probably the first edition and the briefest of *Mission Service*. A fuller edition included eleven selections from the metrical psalter and thirty-seven hymns.

22. Hymns 17, 131, 133, 147, 179, 88, 175, 62, 60, 176, and 177 and Psalm 70 (Part II), which is a version of the last portion of Psalm 91.

23. These are not the same as the Selections of the Prayer Book, though many of the same psalms are included in both Selections. Included are Psalms 1, 15, 19; 32, 42; 46, 50:1-15; 51, 67; 92:1-4; 103, 121; 139; 145:1-19, 150.

24. *Journal of the Proceedings of the General Council of The Protestant Episcopal Church in the Confederate States of America* (1862) (Augusta, GA: Press of Chronicle & Sentinel, 1862) 182-183.

25. *Stephen Elliott Letter Book*, a manuscript in the Southern Historical Collection, University of North Carolina Library, as quoted in Lawrence F. London, "The Literature of the Church in the Confederate States," *Historical Magazine of the Protestant Episcopal Church* 17 (1948) 347.

26. *Journal of the Diocese of Virginia* (1864) 37.

27. Ibid.

28. Ibid. 23.

29. *Selections from the Book of Common Prayer, in use in the Protestant Episcopal Church, in the Confederate States of America. Containing the Order for Daily Morning and Evening Prayer, the Litany, and Occasional Collects* (Charlottesville: James Alexander, 1861).

30. *The Confederate Soldier's Prayer Book: a manual of devotions compiled mainly from the Book of Common Prayer and arranged for public and private use in camps and hospitals* (Petersburg: St. Paul's Congregation, 186?).

31. *Church Intelligencer* (21 November 1862).

32. Ibid. (27 March 1863).

33. A.H. Noll, *Doctor Quintard* (Sewanee, TN, 1905) 97-98.

34. Published in Columbia, SC, by Evans and Cogswell in 1864.

35. See "The Evening Prayer Leaflet" for 4 October, 1914, "The Order for Evening Prayer for the Special Day of Intercession Proclaimed by the President of the United States," which contains this note: "The Special Features of this Leaflet are taken from the Form set forth by the Bishop of New York and Licensed also for use in the Dioceses of—."

36. *Report of the Joint Commission on The Book of Common Prayer Appointed by The General Convention of 1913.*

37. *The Book Annexed to the Report of the Joint Committee on the Book of Common Prayer Appointed by the General Convention of MDCCCLXXX* (Worcester, MA: Stone, 1883).

38. J.A. Muller, *Who Wrote the New Prayers in the Prayer Book?* (Philadelphia: Church Historical Society, 1949) 15.

39. *Hymns with Tunes to Accompany Hymns and Prayers for the use of the Army and Navy* (Boston, 1917).

40. Psalms 15, 23, 46, 51, 67, 91, 100, 103, 121, 145, and *Venite, Magnificat,* and *Nunc Dimittis.*

41. The publisher was E.S. Gorham of New York; the book was revised in 1902; the "Eleventh Edition" was published in 1914.

42. William Bright, *Ancient Collects and Other Prayers, Selected for Devotional Use from Various Rituals,* 3rd ed. (Oxford and London: J.H. & J. Parker, 1864) 233.

43. Correspondence with the Rev. W. Roulston McKean, D.D., Secretary of The Bishop White Prayer Book Society, 4 January, 1968.

44. Psalms 1, 7, 15, 19, 23, 24, 34, 51, 62, 64, 73, 80, 90, 91, 97, 99, 103, 116, 130, 139.

45. Mt 5:1-16; 6:5-15; Lk 8:4-15; 10:23-37; 15:11-32; Jn 1:1-14; 3:1-21; 14:1-21; 15:12-27; Acts 10:34-48; Rom 8:14-39; 1 Cor 6:9-20; 10:1-15; 13:1-13; 15:20-58; Eph 6:10-18; 1 Thes 4:13-5:12; Heb 11:32-12:2; Jas 1:12-27; 1 Pt 4:1-19; Rv 7:9-17; 21:1-8, 10, 22-22:5.

46. "Once to every man and nation"; "Oh! say, can you see"; "Mine eyes have seen the glory of the coming of the Lord"; "God of our fathers, known of old"; and "Lord God of Hosts, whose mighty hand."

47. *Hymnal for the Public and Private Use of Our Soldiers and Sailors.*

48. This book was published by Thomas Nelson and Sons of New York. No date is given on the title page. The only date is the Custodian's Certificate, August, 1897. The selections included on the unnumbered pages indicate that the book belongs to the period of World War I.

49. Compare "For Those We Love" and "For Those who have given their Lives in the Service of Our Country" with the prayers "For Those We Love" and "Memorial Days" in the 1928 Book of Common Prayer.

50. *A Book of Offices and Prayers* (cited above) and *Offices for Special Occasions Compiled by Two Presbyters of the Church* (New York: E.S. Gorham, 1904).

51. Psalms 15, 23, 46, 91, 100, 103, and 121 were retained from the 1917 book, and Psalms 1, 19, 43, 95, 96, and 130 were added.

52. "I need thee every hour," "We gather together," "O beautiful for spacious skies," and "Be still, my soul." The first two of these had already been approved for inclusion in *The Hymnal 1940.*

53. This form had previously been published in 1944 in another Forward Movement booklet edited by Canon Symons, *Hope and Courage* 81.

54. *The Abiding Presence and Other Meditations and Intercessions* (London: SCM, 1923).

55. 1 Cor 10:15-17 is printed.

56. Lk 7:1-10 (the Gospel for Trinity XXI) is printed.

57. *Prayer Book Studies XVII: The Liturgy of the Lord's Supper* (New York: Church Pension Fund, 1966).

58. See *Prayer Book Studies III: The Order for the Ministration to the Sick* (New York: Church Pension Fund, 1951) 37-38.

59. Psalms 1, 12, 43, 51, 84, 91, 100, 103, 119 (Part II), 121, 124, 130, and 150 were retained from the 1951 book, and Psalms 8, 31:1-6, 63, 67, 93, 122, 123, 127, 128, 134, 139, 143, and 146 have been added.

60. Mt 11:28-30, Is 41:10; 45:22; Mt 19:18-19; Lk 9:23; Jn 3:16-17; 11:25; Rv 3:30; and Eph 4:4-6.

61. Jn 1:1-14; Is 42:1-8; Lk 5:29-32; Mt 8:23-27; 9:18-26; Mk 10:6-9; 10:13-16; Jn 6:35, 54-58; 10:9-16; Lk 15:11-32; Mt 25:34-40; 1 Cor 11:23-26; Jn 14:1-6; Is 53:1-6; Jn 20:19-23; Heb 4:14-16; Rom 8:14-17; 8:34-39; 1 Cor 13; Gal 3:26-29; 5:19-24; Eph 2:18-22; Jas 5:13-16; Dt 8:6-10; Rv 12:1-12; 21:1-5.

62. Psalms 22:1-11, 14-18; 24; 46; 65; 85:8-13; 98; 114; and 118:1-6, 19-24 replace Psalms 8; 31:1-6; 43; 91, 93; 119 (Part II); 123; 124; 127; 128; 134; and 143.

63. Though in two instances, Ascension and Pentecost, an alternative collect, new to the Book of Common Prayer in the 1979 revision, was substituted for the collect printed in the 1967 book.

Lex Credendi:
Creation, Theology, and Liturgy

7

"Invigorated Chaos": In Pursuit of a Doctrine of Creation for Ecologically Minded Anglicans

Charles P. Price

IT HAS BEEN TWENTY-FIVE YEARS SINCE LYNN WHITE WROTE HIS SEMINAL article, "The Historic Roots of Our Ecologic Crisis."[1] Its criticism of the negative contribution of Jewish and Christian teaching about creation to sound environmental attitudes was biting, if only half true. White objected chiefly to the language of transcendence and dominion in Genesis 1. It has, he argued, become an invitation to environmental exploitation, especially after the technological revolution. Ever since then, theologians have sought to emphasize human responsibility for creation as well as control over it, and to find ways to underline God's immanence in nature as well as God's transcendence over it, thinking thereby to produce more careful and responsible attitudes among the human species to God's great handiwork.

Jürgen Moltmann, for example, near the beginning of *God in Creation*, the second volume of his systematic theology, remarks:

> . . . [a]n ecological doctrine of creation implies a new kind of thinking about God. The centre of this thinking is no longer the distinction between God and the world. The centre is the recognition of the presence of God *in* the world and the presence of the world *in* God.[2]

In the end, Moltmann settles for a Trinitarian doctrine of creation, with a strong emphasis on the Cosmic Christ, who is the agent of creation, and the Cosmic Spirit, the Creator Spirit, who indwells creation.

> This doctrine views creation as a dynamic web of interconnected processes. The Spirit differentiates and binds together. The Spirit preserves and leads living things and their communities beyond themselves. This indwelling Creator Spirit is fundamental for the community of creation.[3]

I contend in this study that an understanding of nature as the work of the indwelling Spirit, serving as the agent of a transcendent Father, has run through Anglican theology at least from the time of Hooker. This understanding almost disappeared during the ascendancy of deist theology, somewhat ironically as we shall see; but the doctrine has come around to full and mature expression in the thought of Charles Raven and Arthur Peacocke. It has had a long and variegated history in the Anglican tradition; but for us Moltmann's proposed new thinking about God in creation is not new. It is the reaffirmation of a sometimes submerged but now strongly re-emergent thread of Anglican natural theology. It has been part of the fabric of our thought for four hundred years, and over the last century has become increasingly prominent. It should serve us well as we try to provide a theology of creation for the ecological crisis.

Dogmatic and Natural Theology Traditions of Creation Doctrine

We begin with an unfamiliar but useful distinction. I want to separate the dogmatic tradition of the doctrine of *creation* from the natural theology tradition of the *genesis of nature*. The former approach to understanding God's relation to the world carries us to biblical and particularly creedal affirmations of the creative activities of God. In this material, the focus is on the divine omnipotence, the transcendence of deity, and on the distinction between the infinite and unconditional character of the God of Christian revelation on the one hand, and the finite conditioned character of the created order on the other.

The second tradition of understanding the creative activity of God begins with an awareness of the world around us with "its atoms, world, and galaxies, and the infinite complexity of living creatures."[4]

Here the focus is on nature, on the wonder of the universe and the immanent activity of God within the structure of things, although God's transcendent power has regularly been in its purview as well.

From patristic times dogmatic theology has schematically appropriated the creative work of God to the Father, the first Person of the Trinity. The immanent work of the Spirit, although always assumed, was rarely emphasized, particularly in liturgical formulations so potent in shaping the mind of the church. In dogmatic and liturgical traditions, creation has come to be associated almost exclusively with the transcendence of God.

In the seventeenth and eighteenth centuries, moreover, the response among natural theologians to the heady discoveries of science, particularly astronomy, was some form of deism. Deism also emphasized God's transcendence, though in quite a different way from the dogmatic tradition. The immanent work of the Spirit was forgotten. The creative act was conceived in mechanistic terms, the work of a clock-maker who set the machinery in motion and retired to watch what happened. Only since the appearance of *Lux Mundi* in 1881 has God once again been considered to be creatively immanent in nature, and the work of the Holy Spirit been seen to operate within natural processes. The significance of this recaptured emphasis on the work of the Spirit for an ecologically responsible doctrine of creation can scarcely be overstated.

The Dogmatic Tradition:
James Ussher (1581-1656),
John Pearson (1613-1686), and Beyond

English theology in the sixteenth and seventeenth centuries was not centrally concerned with the doctrine of creation. Formative English theologians struggled on soteriological and ecclesiological fronts. As far as sixteenth-century formularies are concerned, the word *creation* does not appear in the *Articles of Religion*. Article I refers to the "one living and true God . . . the Maker and Preserver of all things both visible and invisible,"[5] an echo of the Nicene Creed. Article VIII establishes the authority of the three creeds, all of which, to be sure, include a clause on creation. The homilies listed in Article XXXV do not cite creation as a topic. Jewel's *Apology* contains no more than a passing reference.[6]

In the seventeenth century biblical and creedal theologians continued to treat the doctrine of creation in the old patristic way, with somewhat more detail than in the sixteenth. Typical and widely accepted versions of the doctrine appeared in the writings of James Ussher and John Pearson.

A passage from Ussher's *Annales Veteris Testamenti a Prima Mundi Origine Deducta* (1650), for example, provides the sole entry under the heading of "Creation" in More and Cross' standard anthology of seventeenth-century Anglican thought.[7] That very fact gives it some claim to be regarded as representative. What is more, this passage is one of a handful of Latin entries in the anthology, perhaps a further indication of the paucity of references in this literature.

The cited paragraphs from Ussher's work comprise a brief commentary on the first chapters of Genesis. Ussher purports to establish the date of the creation of the world in the week of 23 October in the year 710 "of the Julian era." He specifies the work God performed on each day of that week, adding little to the biblical account of the first five days except for the creation of angels on the first. For the sixth day, Ussher conflated the accounts of creation in Genesis 1 and Genesis 2. Adam, Ussher observed, was made in the image of God, "consisting chiefly of divine intelligence of mind and genuine holiness of will"[8] (translation mine). He and his helpmate, Eve, were granted "lordship over living things" (*dominium in animantia*).[9] One notices the emphasis on the transcendence of God, and the consequent dominance of humankind, made in God's image, over the rest of creation. Claim for domination here, however, is balanced by concern for holiness, a fact which ecological critics of Christian doctrine tend to overlook when it occurs.

Perhaps even more typical of dogmatic work in the seventeenth century is Pearson's *Exposition of the Creed* (1659),[10] a work which went through eleven editions before 1753 and was reissued in a new edition as recently as 1890. Pearson's comments on the article, "Maker of heaven and earth," extend for thirty-two pages. In its entire length, however, there is only one passing mention of the role of the Spirit immanent in creation:

> It is true indeed, some ancient accounts there are which would persuade us to imagine a strange antiquity of the World, far beyond the annals of Moses, and account of the same Spirit which made it.[11]

That is all. Pearson's energy is spent in establishing God as creating *ex nihilo*, in rejecting any theory of emanation, and in justifying the appropriation of the work of creation to God, the Father of our Lord Jesus Christ. For all intents and purposes, Pearson envisages creation as the act of an exterior workman, an architect making a building. The mechanistic analogy for creation predominates.

Other creedal commentaries point in the same direction. E.A. Litton in his early twentieth-century *Introduction to Dogmatic Theology*[12] made a suggestive distinction between *creatio ex nihilo*, to account for God's initial creative act, and secondary or *mediate* creation, to account for the successive acts by which the world was "prepared to be the abode of man" (p. 73), but he did not develop it. Oliver Quick's *Doctrines of the Creed*[13] a generation later contrasted the work of God as craftsman and as artist (pp. 39 and 43). His treatment of the image of the artist begins to deal with some of our contemporary problems. Nevertheless, both craftsman and artist remain images of workers *ab extra*, despite the potential of the second to bear different freight.

It would not be unfair to conclude that if the only Anglican approach to a doctrine of creation lay through this dogmatic work and creedal exposition, Anglicans too would need the new kind of thinking which Moltmann proposed.

The Natural Theology Tradition of Creation Doctrine Begins: Richard Hooker (1554-1600)

The point of this essay, however, is to say that a second approach to creation has been available virtually from the beginning of Anglican thought. It appears as early as Hooker, thus receiving its initial formulation before the rise of modern experimental science.

Hooker, like his contemporaries, was not primarily concerned with the doctrine of creation in the usual dogmatic sense. In *Ecclesiastical Polity* he did not deal with creation directly or in any systematic way. Moreover, issues raised by the new science could not yet have been in his mind. His discussion of creation, or as it will be more useful to call it now in this context, nature, emerges indirectly in the course of his elaboration of law in Book I.[14] Here Hooker makes his sweeping survey of the place of law in the cosmos, aiming to show how the laws governing church and state fit into "one great scheme of things entire." In the beginning God set himself a law "to do all things by,"[15] and along the way Hooker is moved to consider '[t]he lawe which naturall agents have given them to observe, and their necessary manner of keeping it."[16] The reader will note here a subtle change in emphasis from the approach to creation in the dogmatic tradition. Hooker brings into focus here not God's relation to the world traditionally expressed in terms of *ex nihilo* doctrine. He is rather interested in the way *nature behaves*. He remarks:

> Those things which nature is said to do, are by divine arte performed, using nature as an instrument: nor is there any such arte or knowledge in nature herself working, but in the guide of nature's work.[17]

Furthermore, it is the Spirit who puts the laws to work, immediately carrying into effect through nature's instrumentalities the purposes laid up in the mind and heart of God, to which the Spirit is privy.

> That law, the performance whereof we behold in things natural, is as it were, authentical or an original draft written in the bosom of God himselfe; whose spirite being to execute the same, useth everie particular nature, everie meere naturall agent only as an instrument created at the beginning . . . Nature therefore is nothing else but God's instrument . . .[18]

The Spirit has a "go-between" role, in other words, indwelling both God and the world. This feature of his thought keeps Hooker from representing God's relation to the world purely and simply as that of an architect and absentee observer. The Spirit makes the triune God a "hands-on" operator. This aspect of *Ecclesiastical Polity* is not a major one. It is not elaborated, for the character of this relationship was not a major question of the day. Yet an emphasis different from that found in purely creedal and dogmatic exposition has been struck.

The Natural Law Tradition Assumed:
John Donne (1571-1631) and George Bull (1634-1710)

There is evidence to suggest that some seventeenth-century theologians acknowledged the creative work of an indwelling Spirit rather as a matter of course. This possibility is raised in a Pentecost Sermon of John Donne and a Discourse by George Bull.

Donne preached the Pentecost sermon at St. Paul's in 1629. The text was Genesis 1:2: ". . . and the Spirit of God moved upon the face of the waters."[19] Donne argued that it was the Spirit of God who acted in creation, not merely a Power of God. ". . . there is more of God in this Creation, then the Instrument of God, Nature, or the Vice-roy of God, Providence."[20] The Spirit of God who moved upon the face of the waters at creation was none other than the Holy Spirit, whom Christians worship as the Third Person of the Trinity. What the Spirit created by hovering over the water was nature itself.

> ". . . no power infused into the waters, or earth there, could have enabled that earth then to have produced Trees with ripe fruit in an instant, nor the waters to have brought forth whales, in their growth, in an instant. The Spirit of God produced them then, and established and conserves ever since, that seminall power which we call nature, to produce all creatures (then first made by himself) in a perpetual succession.[21]

For Donne the agent of creation was the Spirit, as it was for Hooker. But Donne made explicit his view that the act of the Spirit in creation involved all the *Personae* of the Trinity: "This is the person, without whom there is no Father, no Son of God to me, the Holy Ghoste."[22]

The Spirit in this exposition creates Nature full blown, like Minerva from the head of Zeus; and thereafter the Spirit sustains Nature in the continual production of the profusion of things in the world.

This two-stage process, Donne goes on to say, is analogous to the operation of the Spirit in a person's *conversio ad deum*.

> So in the first act of man's conversion . . . men cannot be conceived to do anything, in the rest he may; not that in the rest God does not all; but that God finds maturity and mellowing to concurre with this notion in that man . . .[23]

Donne sees that the agent of creation and new creation alike is the indwelling Holy Spirit, who works in these two stages in each case. Donne assumes the operation of the Spirit in the creation of the world as the more familiar case; it prepares the way for his discussion of the second, the work of the indwelling Spirit in the creation of a new human being. The Spirit is immanent and works through natural processes in each case.

A brief paragraph in George Bull's *Discourse Concerning the Spirit of God in the Faithful*[24] makes the same point. As the title of the Discourse suggests, it is not primarily about the creation of the world at all. Bull intended to describe how the Holy Spirit operates within the human spirit, as Donne did in the Pentecost Sermon. Moreover, Bull pointed out—as Donne did before him—that the working of the Spirit within the human spirit is analogous to the working of the Holy

Spirit upon the waters of chaos. Like Donne, Bull provides for a two-stage process, although Bull's two steps in the human person are not the same as Donne's. Bull holds that the Spirit first produces in the Christian person the "blessed graces and fruits which he works in us,"[25] and then enlightens our minds so that we can comprehend what God has done for us.

At this point Bull draws his analogy with the creation of the world:

> That Spirit of God, which in the first beginning of things moved upon the face of the great deep, and *invigorated the chaos*, or dark and confused heap of things, and caused light to shine out of the darkness, can with greatest ease, when he pleases cause the light of divine creation to arise . . .[26]

This allusion to creation is not developed. As in Donne's Sermon, the Discourse assumes the biblical allusion as familiar. Bull used it as a reference which would be illuminating and helpful. One may infer that it would have been taken for granted by his readers. If the role of the indwelling Spirit in creation, "invigorating the chaos," were questionable, the analogy would lose its force.

Hooker, Donne, and Bull all articulated the immanent action of the Spirit in creation. They represent a theological tradition reaching from the end of sixteenth century to the beginning of the eighteenth. None of them elaborates this aspect of his thought. They seem to regard these basic ideas as readily accessible to their readers. Yet this tradition, the natural law tradition of creation doctrine, covers a significantly different range of topics from what we are calling the dogmatic tradition of creation doctrine. This second tradition emphasizes the indwelling action of the Spirit, although it also includes the action of the transcendent God. In Hooker's case, the Spirit was a "go-between" between the Father and nature. The dogmatic tradition, because its focus is on God, emphasizes the transcendence and omnipotence of the Father, though, to be sure, allowing for the work of the Spirit. The natural law tradition, because its focus is on the world, has ample room for consideration of immanence. It uses organic images of growth and fruitfulness. The language of the dogmatic tradition, on the other hand, impresses the figures of architect and maker. The natural law tradition includes the interiority of God in the creative process; the dogmatic tradition stresses God's exteriority. Not unexpectedly, though after a tortuous history, the natural law tradition has opened the way to a full Trinitarian doctrine of creation.

The Rise of Empirical Science and the New Philosophy: The Eclipse of the Indwelling Spirit in Creation Doctrine

Francis Bacon (1561-1626) and René Descartes (1596-1650)

One should not press the contrast between the dogmatic tradition and the natural theology tradition to the point of contradiction. The language of transcendence appears in both. Hooker, it may be recalled, used imagery of both transcendence and immanence, and Donne's understanding of creation was explicitly Trinitarian. An adequate doctrine of the Trinity would encompass both aspects of God's creative activity. However, a wedge was inserted between God's transcendence and God's immanence by the New Philosophy which took its rise in the seventeenth century and by the natural theology which was forged to deal with the scientific discoveries which so transformed the use and understanding of reason in these years.

The rise of experimental science is associated with the name of Francis Bacon. He had no particular religious or theological interest. His contribution was the development of a method for arriving at truth by observation and induction. An observer was to examine the natural world by the use of the senses, through microscopes and telescopes as it turned out. One studied the human body. One collected data, arranged them in suggestive and repetitive patterns, drew conclusions, and tested the conclusions. Empirical science was born.

By this method have come most of the inventions and most of the knowledge which characterize the modern world. A theologian must not be unappreciative of the tremendous advances in understanding the cosmos made possible by this new method. Yet this method invites the reification of nature. The observer makes the world an object. The experimenter is put in a position of control, even domination; and as someone has said, one is hesitant to do experiments on "Mother" Nature. To affirm that the same Spirit of God which illumines our minds has also invigorated the chaos, and that therefore there is some kind of kinship between humankind and the rest of the natural world did not prove to be a congenial idea for experimental science.

This divorce between humankind and the natural world was deepened by the implications of the reflections which occurred to René Descartes on that famous day in the stove, the day which

William Temple called "the most disastrous moment in the history of Europe.."[27] In his *Meditations* Descartes provided a stance for approaching everything in the universe with the aim of understanding it. He made his well-known distinction between mind (*res cogitans*) and matter (*res extensa*).[28] He thought that mind was in touch with God. By the ontological argument the mind could establish the existence of God. But God the Spirit was related *only* to human beings as spirits. There was no place for the Spirit of God in the natural order. Matter was devoid of any divine aspect or presence. The Holy Spirit did not use matter as an instrument except through the instrumentality of the human spirit. Descartes could speak of human beings as "masters and possessors of nature,"[29] and this relationship involved no kinship to nature and in the end no responsibility for it. Subsequently, adventurous thinkers were emboldened to objectify the subhuman realm completely. The way lay open not only to observation and experiment but also to exploitation and abuse. Pearson in the *Exposition of the Creed* held that humanity should be humbled by the power of God to create *ex nihilo*. Followers of the Cartesian school operated under no such strictures. God no longer spoke out of a flaming bush but emerged at the end of a logical proof devised by the human mind.

Modern philosophy, including currently prevalent attitudes toward nature, is ordinarily regarded to have taken its rise in the thought of René Descartes.

Isaac Newton (1642-1727) and William Paly (1743-1805)

Isaac Newton was both a mathematical genius and something of a theologian. His great work, *Principia Mathematica* (1687), has been called one of the half-dozen most famous books of science ever written. Charles Raven, twentieth-century English theologian and scientist, speaks of the theory of gravity which Newton formulated in that book as "the first great integrative principle to be formulated by the New Philosophy."[30] It would be hard to overstate its influence on the subsequent development of science. Its success assured the dominance of a mechanical model of the universe for the next two hundred years.

Newton was a devout Christian. (He wrote a considerably less famous commentary on *Revelation*.) He himself saw no danger in the materialism of the New Philosophy, and indeed no contradiction between a mechanical model for inanimate nature and a firm belief in both divine purpose and human responsibility for the creation. Like Kepler, Newton considered that he "but thought God's thoughts after him."[31] Most of his thoughtful contemporaries would have said the same. Pope's couplet is famous:

> Nature and nature's laws lay hid in night;
> God said, "Let Newton be," and all was light.[32]

Machines, after all, were the creations of finite minds. They were invented to carry out the purpose of their fabricators and wholly under their control. Why should not the mechanism of the cosmos be similarly related to God? Such a line of reasoning brought Newton, like all deists, to reject any thought of the immanent activity of the Spirit in the world.

> This Being [God] governs all things, not as the soul of the world but as Lord over all. And on account of His dominion, He is wont to be called Lord God, *pantokrator*, or Universal Ruler . . . Deity is the dominion of God, not over His own body, as those who imagine who fancy God to be the soul of the world, but over servants . . . And from His true dominion it follows that the true God is a living, intelligent, and powerful Being . . .[33]

This kind of language, of course, was afforded to Newton by the dogmatic tradition. But Newton does not use it to discuss the classical set of problems. It appears here in an entirely different context, used by a natural theologian, who specifically rejects the second kind of imagery we have been tracing, involving the immanence of the Holy Spirit in the world, the language which Hooker, Donne, and Bull used to good effect. Such was the deistic solution to the theological questions about creation posed by the rise of science in the seventeenth century. It lies at the heart of the ideas which spurred the development of the industrial and technological society which emerged first in Western Europe and America, and now embraces the world.

The classical exponent of this deistic theology was Archdeacon William Paley, whose *Natural Theology*[34] made the figure of God as the divine watchmaker, who set the world's machinery in motion and returns only occasionally to repair flaws, to be a famous, vivid, and influential expression of God's relation to the world. By a supreme irony it was the *natural theologians* who carried the transcendence of God and the mechanical model for the universe to a logical extreme. Some of the language of the dogmatic tradition was employed, but it

was shorn of the elements of balance and humility which characterized the ancient theology. The language of immanence was set aside.
The Spirit was "quenched."

Reaction: The Cambridge Platonists

While Newton was engaged in his epoch-making studies at Trinity
College, Cambridge, Ralph Cudworth was at work next door at Clare
on *The True Intellectual System of the Universe*, a vast, sprawling, and
difficult treatise which represents a first reaction against the New
Philosophy of Descartes and his successors.

Cudworth was one of the Cambridge Platonists, that remarkable
group of mid-seventeenth-century philosopher-theologians who, in
opposition to a fiercely intolerant Calvinism on the one hand and
what they came to conceive as the arid materialism of the New
Philosophy on the other, sought to find a way between them based on
a luminous interpretation of the Christian faith different from either.
In doing so, they laid down pioneering positions on religious tolera-
tion and the revelation of God through nature, although their work
is marked by the awkwardness and obscurity which often accompa-
nies the breaking of new intellectual ground.

One of the Cambridge Platonists, John Smith, is said to have
introduced the study of Descartes to Cambridge. Another member of
the group, Henry More, corresponded with Descartes.

> Cartesianism seemed to provide exactly the kind of foundation
> which the intellectual life of the new age demanded. It saw the
> material world as subject to the strict rule of mechanical laws, yet
> at the same time it acknowledged the reality of the spiritual
> world.[35]

The dualism which Descartes' view of the world entailed did not
at first disturb the Cambridge Platonists, since they were used to
dualism in another form through the Platonic and neo-Platonic
thought which influenced them so greatly.

Cudworth and More, however, eventually had to part company
with Cartesianism. They came to realize, particularly as they faced
the intractable and uncongenial results of the development of Cartesian thought by Hobbes, that the tendencies of the New Philosophy
ran to atheism and materialism. Cudworth saw even more clearly
than his colleagues that if "nature was in some sense a coherent and
intelligible system, then it could not be explained either in terms of
the random movements of matter in space . . . or of the arbitrary and

incalculable acts of God and other supernatural and demonic agents."[36] He elaborated a comprehensive alternative in his *magnum opus* entitled *The True Intellectual System.*

In it Cudworth staked out a territory between Cartesianism and Calvinism.

> This Cartesian Philosophy is highly obnoxious to Censure upon some Accounts, the Chief of which is this: that . . . it derives the whole System of the Corporeal Universe from the Necessary Motion of Matter . . . without the guidance or direction of any understanding Nature."[37]

The version of Calvinism regnant at the time, on the other hand, required that "God himself doth all immediately and, as it were with his own hands, form the body of every gnat and fly, insect and mite . . .[38]

On the way to his alternative view, Cudworth put forward the idea of a "plastic nature." *Plastic* here, of course, means not "artificial" or even "capable of being moulded," but rather "formative," "creative," *capable of moulding*, its first dictionary definition.[39] According to Cudworth, plastic nature is "an inferior instrument" under God which "doth drudgingly execute that part of his providence which consists in the regular and orderly motion of matter."[40] This plastic nature is thus kin to the "nature" which in the earlier natural theology tradition, represented by Donne and Bull, was the first creation of the Spirit of God and in turn the shaper of the individual things in the world. This concept allowed Cudworth to say, for example, that "all things are disposed and ordered by deity without any care or distractious Providence."[41] Plastic nature is a form of life, the lowest form to be sure. It suggests the "invigorated chaos" of Bull, or to reach further (and later), Hegel's *This*, the initial form of the Absolute Spirit after it had turned itself into matter by "diremption." In the Hegelian dialectic, the *This* then evolves into the human spirit, able to enter into communion with Absolute Spirit. Cudworth's plastic nature evolves into the cosmos through divine "art" (*pace* Hooker) or purpose.

It would be foolish to claim too much prescience for Cudworth. As Raven observes in *Science and Religion*, Cudworth was not "a thinker of first rank or the author of a completely coherent philosophy," but "from his conscious emphasis on an organic interpretation of nature and from his many and suggestive foreshadowings of future ideas, we can dismiss the belief that science has always and necessarily been mechanistic."[42]

Nevertheless, the Cartesian philosophy and deistic theology held the field in the seventeenth and eighteenth centuries. The work of

Cudworth and the Cambridge Platonists was virtually ignored at the time, and the immanent work of the Spirit in creation forgotten in both the dogmatic and natural theology traditions of creation doctrine.

The Challenge of Evolution: "*Lux Mundi*" (1881)

God's immanent activity in creation was recognized in a more powerful and permanent way two hundred years later in the work of a group of late nineteenth-century Anglican theologians who rose to meet the challenge of Darwin's theory of evolution. Under the leadership of Charles Gore, they published that decisive collection of essays, *Lux Mundi: A Series of Studies in the Religion of the Incarnation.*[43]

These authors came to terms with evolution by arguing that evolution was the *way* God created, and that the incarnation of the Divine Son as Jesus of Nazareth was the definitive and finally revealing case in point. To use the language of this essay, though not of *Lux Mundi* itself, evolution was God's means for bring creation to perfection. The perfection of creation required God's immanent activity. The effort to understand God's action toward the world solely in external terms, as the deists had tried to do, had resulted in making God's relation to the world wholly unintelligible (as the Cambridge Platonists had predicted it would!). Aubrey Moore put it this way in his essay on *The Doctrine of God*:

> The one absolutely impossible conception of God in the present day is that which represents him as an occasional visitor. Science had pushed the deists' God farther and farther away, and at the moment when it seemed he would be thrust out altogether, Darwinism appeared, and under the disguise of a foe did the work of a friend. It has conferred upon philosophy and religion an inestimable benefit, by showing us that we must choose between two alternatives. Either God is everywhere present or he is nowhere.[44]

These theologians use evolution to interpret God's immanence in nature, precisely the point which the Cartesian-Newtonian form of natural theology could not recognize and which the Cambridge Platonists had labored in vain to restore. The development was possible because after Darwin biological, organic images became as accessible and as powerful for expressing God's relation to the world as mechanical ones had been before.

The elaboration of this point is connected in a number of subsequent authors influenced by *Lux Mundi* with an understanding of the stages of being as old as Aristotle, who classified things found in nature as inanimate, vegetable, animal, and human. To this classification is now added the idea that the immanent God, God the Spirit, pushes the whole process along from within. (A contemporary theologian might want to add here that God also draws the process along, luring it from without.) This idea is developed in the work of Gore himself, Lionel Thornton, William Temple, and Charles Raven. Temple's exposition is eminently succinct: "We see," he concludes at the end of his explanation, "each grade dependent for its existence on the grade below and dependent for its own full actualization on the grade above."[45] The whole, he goes on to say, is explicable only on the basis of a Will which intends or purposes the whole.

> ... to seek the explanation of the universe in a Purpose grounded in a Will is Theism; it is the acceptance, provisionally at least, of the doctrine of God as Creator.[46]

The affinities between the operation of both Will and Spirit as Love are well-known. Both are immanent as well as transcendent. It seems reasonable to conclude that Anglican thought has been working for over a century to restore an understanding of God's action in creation as immanent as well as transcendent. From this point of view, the process comes to its fruition in the Incarnation, and this resultant new focus on the Incarnation accounts for the frequent assertion that Anglican theology is peculiarly a theology of Incarnation. It is doubtful whether such a statement could be sustained for earlier Anglican thought.

Recent Anglican Thought about Creation: Charles Raven and Arthur Peacocke

This account of the natural theology tradition of creation doctrine in Anglican theology comes into the present by mention of two important expositions of the subject: Charles Raven's Gifford Lectures, *Natural Religion and Christian Theology*[47] (1953) and Arthur Peacocke's *Creation and the World of Science*[48] (1978). Raven was an ornithologist and Peacocke a practicing chemist. Both assert and develop in fruitful ways the immanental understanding of God in the world.

Raven's work culminates in two eloquent chapters on "The World and the Spirit" and "The Spirit and the Community." He argues:

> The fact is that if we are to see the creative process as a whole and culminating for us in Christ, we shall regard it as at every level

reflecting in its own measure something of the quality of deity: from atom and molecule to mammal and man each by its appropriate order and function expresses the design inherent in it . . . If Christ crucified be the one perfect manifestation of the Godhead to us, then we shall expect to find foreshadowings of it at every preliminary stage of the creative process . . .[49]

Raven's work is especially suggestive when it cites extraordinary examples in subhuman nature, occurrences which defy ordinary explanation, like the sequence of events which permits the survival of cuckoos hatched in the nest of hedge-sparrows.

The odds against the random occurrence of such a series of coincidences are . . . astronomical. Nor could a single accidental performance of it should it happen establish any guarantee of its fixation and repetition.[50]

Raven presents an impressive array of evidence to show that nature is instinct with some kind of life, of Spirit.

We have already argued that if God is to be conceivable and revealed to us, there must be, alongside the Godhead who is beyond existence—the universal subject—the Godhead mani- fest and operative in the creation . . . the "germinal Logos," the "Inner Light" . . . the Spirit of God, the Spirit of Christ, the Spirit the Holy One."[51]

Raven is the heir to the tradition we have been seeking to trace through Hooker, Donne, Bull, and the Cambridge Platonists. Shades of "invigorated chaos!"

Toward the end of *Creation and the World of Science*, Peacocke summarizes his work in language which readers of this essay will find familiar, though he is reaching for a new dimension of under- standing.

Thus the understanding of God's relation to the world, of the doctrine of creation, that we have been developing in the light of the sciences, is congruent with an understanding of hope that is grounded on the character of Love of the transcendent God who is immanently active in all events, most notably in the personal, and uniquely transparently in Jesus the Christ. The immediacy of God's creativity in and through the actual events of the hierarchical complexities of the stuff of the world is what consti- tutes the dimension along which hope is generated in man as he apprehends that loving, urgent, and fulfilling Presence."[52]

In that hope we seek to care for and preserve the environment, indeed the world and the whole cosmos, which God has graciously bestowed upon us.

Notes

1. Lynn White Jr., "The Historic Roots of Our Ecologic Crisis, *Science* 155 (1967) 1203-1207.

2. Jürgen Moltmann, *God in Creation*, trans. Margaret Kohl (San Francisco: Harper SanFrancisco, 1991) 13.

3. Ibid. 103.

4. Book of Common Prayer 827.

5. Ibid. 867.

6. John Jewel, *An Apology of the Church of England*, ed. J.E. Booty (Charlottesville: University Press of Virginia, 1974) 22.

7. James Ussher, *Annales Veteris Testamenti a Prima Mundi Origine Deducta*, edited in *Anglicanism*, ed. P.E. More and F.L. Cross (Milwaukee: Morehouse, 1935) 257-258.

8. Ibid. 257.

9. Ibid. 258.

10. John Pearson, *An Exposition of the Creed*, rev. W.S. Dobson (Appleton, Milwaukee, 1859) 71-103.

11. Ibid. 88-89.

12. E.A. Litton, *Introduction to Dogmatic Theology on the Basis of the Thirty-Nine Articles* (London: Robert Scott, 1912) 71-74.

13. Oliver C. Quick, *Doctrines of the Creed* (London: Nisbet and Co., 1938/46) 34-46.

14. Richard Hooker, *Of the Laws of Ecclesiastical Polity*, 4 vols., Speed W. Hill, gen. ed. (Cambridge: Harvard University Press, 1977), vol. I, book I, pp. 55-142.

15. Ibid. I.2.1, p. 58.

16. Ibid. I, 3, pp. 63-69.

17. Ibid. I.3.4, p. 67.

18. Ibid. I.3.4, p. 68.

19. John Donne, *The Sermons of John Donne*, 10 vols., ed. Evelyn M. Simpson and George R. Potter (Berkeley: University of California Press, 1958), vol. 9, pp. 92-108.

20. Ibid. 97.

21. Ibid. 99-100.

22. Ibid. 101.

23. Ibid. 103.

24. George Bull, *The Works of George Bull, D.C.*, 6 vols., col. and rev. Edward Burton (Oxford, 1846), vol. 1, pp. 31-51.

25. Ibid. 39.

26. Ibid. 39. Italics mine. This passage is the source of the title of the present essay.

27. William Temple, *Nature, Man and God* (London: Macmillan, 1951) 57.

28. René Descartes, *Discourse on Method and the Meditations*, trans. F.E. Sutcliffe (Penguin Books, 1968). In the second Meditation the human being is identified as a "thing that thinks" (*res cogitans*) (p. 100), and substance as "what has extension" (*res extensa*) (p. 109). See also the sixth Meditation, p. 156.

29. Ibid., Discourse 6, p. 78.

30. Charles Raven, *Natural Religion and Christian Theology*, 2 vols., *Science and Religion* (Cambridge: Cambridge University Press, 1953), vol. 1, p. 134.

31. Johannes Kepler, *On Studying Astronomy*.

32. Alexander Pope, *Epitaph Intended for Sir Isaac Newton*, cited in *Bartlett's Familiar Quotations*, 13th ed. (Boston: Little Brown and Co., 1955) 321a,

33. Isaac Newton, *Philosophia Naturalis Principia Mathematica*, in Moore and Cross, *Anglicanism* 230.

34. William Paley, *Natural Theology, or Evidences of the Existence and Attributes of the Deity Collected from the Appearances of Nature* (New York: Jonathan Leavitt, 1831) esp. 9-13.

35. Gerald Cragg, ed., *The Cambridge Platonists* (Oxford: Oxford University Press, 1968) 12.

36. Raven, *Natural Religion* 112.

37. R. Cudworth, *The True Intellectual System of the Universe (1678) (New York and London: Garland Publishing Inc., 1978)* 175.

38. Cragg, The Cambridge Platonists 236.

39. See *Oxford English Dictionary*, vol. 7, p. 959.

40. Cragg, *The Cambridge Platonists* 239.

41. Ibid. 240.

42. Raven, *Natural Religion* 117.

43. Charles Gore, ed., *Lux Mundi: A Series of Studies in the Religion of the Incarnation*, 15th ed. (London: John Murray, 1921).

44. Ibid. 73.

45. William Temple, *Christus Veritas* (London: Macmillan, 1954) 6.

46. Ibid. 9.

47. Raven, *Natural Religion*, vol. 2, p. 139.

48. Peacocke, Arthur R. *Creation and the World of Science* (Oxford: Clarendon Press, 1978).

49. Raven, *Natural Religion*, vol. 2, p. 139.

50. Ibid. 139.

51. Ibid. 163.

52. Peacocke, *Creation* 355.

8

The Theme of Creation in the Liturgical Theology of Alexander Schmemann

Byron David Stuhlman

WE ORDINARILY APPROACH THE DOCTRINE OF CREATION FROM THE PERSPECTIVE of systematic theology rather than from that of liturgical theology. In this essay, I want to explore what insight the perspective of liturgical theology can bring to our more systematic inquiries. To do so, I will explore the approach of Alexander Schmemann. But before we begin our exploration, two questions arise: (1) Who was Alexander Schmemann, and what approach did he take to the task of liturgical theology? (2) How does the theme of creation fit into his treatment of liturgical theology? It is to these questions that I now turn.

Alexander Schmemann, former dean and professor of liturgical theology at St. Vladimir's Seminary outside New York City, was perhaps the most persuasive interpreter of Orthodoxy to both Orthodox and non-Orthodox in the third quarter of this century.[1] His well-known presentation of liturgical theology, *For the Life of the World: Sacraments and Orthodoxy*,[2] was written as a study guide for a conference of the Student Christian Movement and achieved enormous popularity in English and a host of foreign languages.[3] Schmemann's popular style can be misleading, however; behind his deceptively simple eloquence lay a profound grasp of the theological and liturgical traditions of Orthodoxy. His liturgical theology is not just a theology of the liturgy; it is a theological interpretation of Christian life done in the context of the life of the church as a worshiping community. He writes:

> [L]iturgy is . . . the *locus theologicus par excellence* because it is its very function, its *leitourgia* in the original meaning of that word, to manifest and to fulfill the Church's faith and to manifest it not partially, not "discursively," but as living totality and catholic experience. It is because liturgy is that living totality and that catholic experience by the Church of her own faith that it is the very *source* of theology, the condition that makes it *possible*.[4]

Schmemann's approach to liturgical theology appears at first glance closely akin to the western theology of the paschal mystery which scholars such as Louis Bouyer did so much to appropriate for the church in the liturgical movement in the twentieth century. Schmemann was educated in the Orthodox Theological Institute of Paris (known as St. Sergius) at the very time when western scholars like Bouyer were associated with the Institut Catholique in the same city. John Meyendorff goes so far as to say, "It was from that existing milieu that Fr Schmemann really learned 'liturgical theology,' a 'philosophy of time,' and the true meaning of the 'paschal mystery.'"[5]

A closer look at Schmemann's theology, however, reveals that he did not work from this perspective at all, however much he may have been influenced by it. His liturgical theology is a theology of the *pascha*, not the paschal mystery. It would appear that he avoided mystery as a starting point for his theology—perhaps for two reasons. First, like other critics of Dom Odo Casel, the pioneer in formulating the theology of the paschal mystery, he believed that Casel had assimilated the Christian mystery of salvation far too closely to pagan mystery religions.[6] Second, he saw in what he called "mysteriological piety" too great an accommodation of the church to an unredeemed world.[7] And he saw that mysteriological piety given shape in the strand of liturgical commentary derived from Dionysius the Areopagite, in whose works mystery was a key concept.[8] Schmemann's theology of liturgy as *pascha* approaches liturgy in a very different way from this strand of the Byzantine tradition.

Creation is not a theme which Schmemann treats as a separate topic in his liturgical theology. It is, nonetheless, a theme which plays a significant role in his interpretation of liturgical tradition and in his understanding of the theological tradition of Orthodoxy. The theme of creation figures in three different ways in his work.

1. Creation, Redemption, and *Eschaton* (or World, Church, and Kingdom) are the three "dimensions" of Christian life and the church's liturgical experience in Schmemann's theology. Schmemann is working with an *eschatological symbolism*, where the liturgical life of the church is "symbolical" because it "holds together" these three dimensions in the proper tension.

2. This understanding of creation is *ontologically grounded*, for the symbolical structure of creation serves, in Schmemann's account, to manifest God's *presence* in the world. Schmemann contrasts this patristic view of the created world as sacrament to the later western perspective, where a symbol represents what is absent.

3. Creation figures in both a *positive* and a *negative* way in Schmemann's narrative account of the Christian life: *positively* as endowed with the potential for realizing God's eschatological *telos* for humanity and for the world in the kingdom; *negatively* as short-circuited by human sin and so distorted into an end in itself instead of a means to communion with God.

We shall now look at these three strands in Schmemann's account of creation and conclude by assessing how they contribute to a more adequate view of creation than is customarily found in western theological traditions.

Schmemann's Eschatological Symbolism:
World, Church, and Kingdom as Dimensions of Reality

Schmemann drew, as I have argued elsewhere,[9] on the typological strand in the Christian tradition. The categories with which he worked were world (creation), church (redemption), and kingdom (*eschaton*). He saw liturgy as the *passover of the church from the world to God's kingdom*. This becomes the *leitmotif* both of his interpretation of the church's liturgy and of his theology. The church's liturgy for Schmemann is understood in terms of its eschatological symbolism. Working with a view of symbol as that which "holds together" or "brings together," he writes:

> In the [doctrine and understanding of the early church], sacra-
> ment was not only "open" to, it truly "held together" the three
> dimensions or levels of the Christian vision of reality: those of
> the Church, the world, and the Kingdom. And "holding" them
> together it made them *known* in the deepest patristic sense of the
> word as both understanding and participation. It was the source

of theology—knowledge *about* God in His relation to the world, the Church, and the Kingdom—because it was knowledge *of* God and, in Him, of all reality. Having its beginning, content and end in Christ, it at the same time revealed Christ as the beginning, the content and the end of all that which exists, as its Creator, Redeemer, and fulfillment.[10]

He goes on to say that

> . . . the proper function of the "leitourgia" has always been to *bring together*, within one symbol, the three levels of the Christian faith and life: the Church, the world, and the Kingdom; that the Church herself is thus the sacrament in which the broken, yet still "symbolical" life of "this world" is brought, in Christ and by Christ, into the dimension of the Kingdom of God, becoming itself the sacrament of the "world to come," or that which God has from all eternity prepared for those who love Him, and where all that which is human can be transfigured by grace so that all things may be consummated in God; and that finally it is here and only here—in the "mysterion" of God's presence and action—that the Church always becomes that which she is: the Body of Christ and the Temple of the Holy Spirit, the unique *Symbol* "bringing together"—by bringing to God—the world for the life of which He gave His Son.[11]

Schmemann's categories of world, church, and kingdom might be understood as his transposition of the categories of shadow, type, and reality in the typological tradition. In this tradition, which represents one approach to understanding the meaning of the biblical text and of liturgical rites, the created order foreshadows the truth which will be revealed eschatologically and which is even now present proleptically in the life of the church as a type of the life of the kingdom. Schmemann has taken these categories of interpretation and redeployed them as dimensions of the Christian existence, linking them with his understanding of liturgy as a *pascha*, a rite of passage. In the liturgical life of the church we *pass over* with Christ to the kingdom. In this way Schmemann has given a new dynamic to the older tradition of interpretation. He understands the church, then, both in cosmological terms and in eschatological terms: it is the sacrament, for him, of both the world and the kingdom. Or, we might say, the church is the world on pilgrimage to the kingdom by way of the cross, and in its liturgical life it participates proleptically in the goal of its pilgrimage.

Schmemann's treatment of the eucharist in these terms is familiar. In the eucharist the *church* is called out of the *world* and proleptically passes over to the *kingdom*. Schmemann's treatment of Easter as a sacrament of time provides another example. The *pascha* begins as a feast of *creation*—the offering of the firstfruits. What Schmemann calls the "mystery of *natural* time" found its fulfilment in "the mystery of time as *history*" in the Jewish *pascha*. But this in turn is transformed into "the mystery of eschatological time"—the means by which we move toward fulfilment in God's kingdom. Christ fulfills all the meanings of the feast in his passage to the Father—"the whole movement of time in all its dimensions." Western theology has tended to be embarrassed about the ultimate origins of Easter in the celebration of the rebirth of nature in spring, but Schmemann incorporates this natural dimension into his account.[12]

In western theology we have tended to work with only two of these dimensions, instead of all three. We speak of the order of *creation* and the order of *redemption*, of the world and the church. We divide reality into nature and supernature and make supernature the redemptive contravention of the natural. What is missing from this picture is this third dimension, the *eschatological* dimension.[13] We have lost sight of the *eschaton*, of the kingdom. We have also lost sight of the role of the Holy Spirit. But for Schmemann it is only from the perspective of the kingdom can we understand either the world or the church properly. For the Gospel is the proclamation of the kingdom of God, and in the life of the church that kingdom is revealed as proleptically present in this world. Schmemann argues that when we fail to relate these dimensions properly, we fall into heresy. Unless we work from an eschatological perspective, we stand in danger either of exalting the church at the expense of the world and falling into ecclesiastical triumphalism (as if the church were the kingdom), or of exalting the world at the expense of the church and falling into secularism (as if the cult sanctified the world *as it is in its fallenness*). In other words, we fall into heresy whenever we lose the eschatological tension between total rejection of the world and total acceptance of the world.

The World as Sacrament: Schmemann's Ontological Basis

Schmemann grounds this view of reality in the symbolic structure of creation—a symbolic structure that is a means not only of cognition, but also of participation:

If, for the Fathers, symbol is a key to sacrament it is because sacrament is in continuity with the symbolic structure of the world in which "omnes ... creaturae sensibiles sunt signa rerum sacrarum" [a citation from Thomas Aquinas]. And the world is symbolical—"signum rei sacrae"—in virtue of its being created by God; to be "symbolical" belongs thus to its ontology, the symbol being not only the way to perceive and understand reality, a means of cognition, but also a means of *participation*. It is then the "natural" symbolism of the world—one can almost say its "sacramentality"—that makes the sacrament possible and constitutes the key to its understanding. If the Christian sacrament is *unique*, it is not in the sense of being a miraculous exception to the natural order of things created by God and "proclaiming his glory." Its absolute newness is not in its ontology but in the specific "res" which it "symbolizes," i.e., reveals, manifests, and communicates which is Christ and His Kingdom. But even this absolute newness is to be understood in terms not of total discontinuity but in those of fulfillment. The "mysterion" of Christ reveals and fulfills the ultimate meaning and destiny of the world itself. Therefore, the institution of sacraments by Christ ... is not the creation *ex nihilo* of the "sacramentality" itself, of the sacrament as means of cognition and participation. In the words of Christ, "do *this* in remembrance of me," the *this* (meal, thanksgiving, breaking of bread) is already "sacramental." The institution means that by being referred to Christ, filled with Christ, the symbol is fulfilled and becomes sacrament.[14]

It is this insistence that sacramental symbolism is *intrinsic*, not *extrinsic*, that distinguishes him from the theological tradition of the west, which tended to forget this truth. For this reason, the symbol came to be understood in the west as something which pointed to an *absent* reality, or re-presented an *absent* reality. It is this failure to grasp the intrinsic character of sacramental symbolism by western theologians that made a doctrine of the symbolic presence of Christ in the eucharistic elements seem inadequate to western theologians.[15] From their perspective, what is *symbolic* is not *real*. Yet this makes the sacraments arbitrary institutions of Christ. It loses sight of the deeper truth that by referring already highly-charged ritual actions to Christ, by making them his *anamnesis*, the church in its *eucharistia* restores them to the purpose which God intended.

The World as God's Good Creation Fallen and Redeemed

The perspective from which Schmemann works is basically that of Irenaeus, for whom the goodness of creation, its original perfection, is understood as a potential for the realization of God's purposes rather than as the accomplished realization of those purposes. The fall is thus a failure to realize the *telos* of creation, rather than a loss of a *telos* already realized. And the *oikonomia* of Christ is a restoration of the created potential of creation for its original *telos*, which is proleptically revealed in him as the firstfruits of the new humanity. Christ is what Adam was meant to *become*. This aspect of Schmemann's theology is found more frequently in his narrative treatment of the eucharist than in his systematic exposition of theological themes. We find it, for example, in his exposition of the eucharist in *For the Life of the World*.

That narrative begins with an account of God's initial purposes for humanity and for the world: with the world as God intended it at creation. He writes:

> The unique position of man in the universe is that he alone is to *bless* God for the food and the life he receives from Him. He alone is to respond to God's blessing with his blessing. The significant fact about the life in the Garden is that man is to *name* things . . . To name a thing is to manifest the meaning and value God gave it, to know it as coming from God and to know its place and function within the cosmos created by God.

> To name a thing, in other words, is to bless God for it and in it . . . The first, the basic definition of man is that he is *the priest*. He stands in the center of the world and unifies it by his act of blessing God, of both receiving the world from God and offering it to God—and by filling it with this eucharist, he transforms his life, the one that he receives from the world, into life in God, into communion with Him. The world was created as the "matter," the material of one all-embracing eucharist, and man was created as the priest of the cosmic sacrament.[16]

This is Schmemann's account of the world as God intended it, and of the destiny for which God created humanity.

But we failed to fulfil this destiny. From his account of the creation, Schmemann moves on to the fall:

> [The forbidden fruit] is the image of the world loved for itself, and eating it is the image of life understood as an end in itself.

> To love is not easy, and mankind has chosen not to return God's love. Man has loved the world, but as an end in itself and not as transparent to God . . . It seems natural for man to experience the world as opaque, and not shot through with the presence of God. It seems natural not to live a life of thanksgiving for God's gift of a world. It seems natural not to be eucharistic . . .

> The natural dependence of man upon the world was intended to be transformed constantly into communion with God in whom is all life. Man was meant to be the priest of a eucharist, offering the world to God, and in this gift he was to receive the gift of life. But in the fallen world man does not have the power to do this. His dependence on the world becomes a closed circuit, and his love is deviated from its true direction. He still loves, he is still hungry. He knows he is dependent on that which is beyond him. But his love and his dependence refer only to the world in itself . . .

> When we see the world as an end in itself, everything becomes itself a value and consequently loses all value, because only in God is found the meaning (value) of everything, and the world is meaningful only when it is the "sacrament" of God's presence. Things treated merely as things in themselves destroy themselves because only in God have they any life. The world of nature, cut off from the source of life, is a dying world. For one who thinks food in itself is the source of life, eating is communion with death.[17]

Sin has short-circuited creation, so that neither humanity nor the world is capable of realizing the purposes for which God created them.

The work of Christ is the restoration of the human race and the world to the purposes for which God created them, so that they may attain the goal for which God destined them—the kingdom of God. The eucharist is the proleptic realization of that goal, which was achieved in Christ.

> The Church fulfills itself in heaven in that *new eon* which Christ has inaugurated in His death, resurrection, and ascension, and which was given to the Church on the day of Pentecost as its life, as the "end" toward which it moves. In this world Christ is crucified, His body broken, and His blood shed. And we must go out of this world, we must ascend to heaven in Christ in order to become partakers of the world to come.

But this in not an "other" world, different from the one God has created and given to us. It is our same world, *already* perfected in Christ, but *not yet* in us. It is our same world, redeemed and restored, in which Christ "fills all things with Himself." And since God has created the world as food for us and has given us food as means of communion with Him, of life in Him, the new food of the new life which we receive from God in His Kingdom *is Christ Himself*. He is our bread—because from the very beginning all our hunger was a hunger for Him and all our bread was but a symbol of Him, a symbol that had to become reality . . .

> We offered the bread in remembrance of Christ because we know that Christ is Life, and all food, therefore, must lead us to Him. And now when we receive this bread from His hands, we know that he has taken up all life, filled it with Himself, made it what it was meant to be: communion with God, sacrament of His presence and love . . .[18]

We in our humanity are restored through Christ as the priests of creation. Creation is restored as the material of the offering which we offer as the priests of creation.

Schmemann returns frequently to this theme of the sacramental purpose of creation. We find it in his treatment of the offertory at the eucharist,[19] and in his treatment of what is offered.

> Only bread and wine: very ordinary things. And in all liturgies, ancient and modern, a brief great moment comes when those very ordinary things are being offered to God while still retaining their ordinary character. We take two things out of our daily and secular world, and place them apart on the altar.

> Consider the bread and wine for a moment. What are they there for? We can, of course, look on them as mere raw material, mere instruments for the coming of grace. In that case, their particular character and origin will be unimportant. But we shall miss the point if we think along those lines . . .

> A great Russian poet—not a church-goer—once said: "Every time the priest celebrates the Eucharist, he holds in his hands the whole world, like an apple." This is not only symbolic, it is hard rational fact . . . When we offer bread and wine and place them on the altar, not only is our act relevant to Christ's offering two thousand years ago, but we are also relating that offering to the facts, the physical basis of our human condition as it has existed from the very beginning . . . The world was God's gift to us, existing not for its own sake, but in order to be transformed, to become life, and so to be offered back to God as man's gift.[20]

A similar treatment of water in baptism is found in *Of Water and the Holy Spirit: A Liturgical Study of Baptism*:

> In the Christian worldview, *matter is never neutral*. If it is not "referred to God," i.e. viewed and used as means of communion

with Him, of life in Him, it becomes the very bearer and *locus* of the demonic . . . Only the bible and the Christian faith reveal and experience matter on the one hand as essentially *good*, yet on the other hand as the very vehicle of man's fall and enslavement to death and sin, as the means by which Satan has stolen the world from God. Only in Christ and by His power can matter be *liberated* and become again the symbol of God's glory and presence, the sacrament of His action and communion with man . . . The holy water in baptism, the bread and wine in the Eucharist, stand for, i.e. *represent* the whole of creation, but creation as it will be at the end, when it will be consummated in God, when He will fill all things with Himself . . . Thus *consecration* is always the manifestation, the epiphany of that End, of that ultimate Reality for which the world was created, which was fulfilled by Christ through His Incarnation, Death, Resurrection, and Ascension, which the Holy Spirit reveals today in the Church and which will be consummated in the Kingdom "to come."[21]

Matter is sacramental, but the sacramental purpose for which God created it, as a link of life and love between God and humankind, is realized only when it is referred to Christ, when it becomes his *anamnesis*.

Evaluating Schmemann's Contribution

We have looked at Schmemann's doctrine of creation from three different angles: (1) from his eschatological symbolism, which works with world, church, and kingdom as the three dimensions of Christian existence; (2) from the ontological basis in which he grounds this symbolism, where the symbolical structure of the world is understood as a means of both cognition and participation; and (3) from the narrative interpretation which he gives to the Christian story. Does this yield a coherent picture of creation for us? Does it provide a necessary corrective to the western theological tradition?

Schmemann's Witness to the Eschatological Telos of Creation

What lies behind the perspective which Schmemann brings to his theology, I would argue, is the creative encounter of the biblical tradition and Greek philosophy which is characteristic of the eastern patristic synthesis. The translation of the biblical tradition into Greek modes of thought was the risky but imperative task which faced the church in the early centuries of its life. The danger was that the dynamism of the biblical narrative would be lost in the translation into the thought patterns of the eclectic Platonism of late antiquity. Put another way, what has been called the horizontal eschatology of the biblical witness might be lost in the vertical eschatology of the Platonic contrast between God's being and our becoming, between the spiritual (or rational) and the material.

Something very much like this did happen in the east in the neo-Platonic synthesis of Dionysius the Areopagite. But the dominant strand of eastern thought was the far more creative synthesis of the Cappadocians, whose theology rejected the negative assessment of becoming characteristic of neo-Platonism and developed the positive assessment which we find in Gregory of Nyssa.[22] These theologians safeguarded the eschatological tension which is characteristic of the New Testament witness to Christ. It is this eschatological tension that is characteristic of Schmemann's theology.

The western tradition developed differently. Here the dominant treatment of eschatology was individualized and verticalized. The predominant interest eventually fell on the destiny of the individual: the commentaries on "the last things" in theological treatises focussed their attention on what each Christian faced at his or her death. The corporate eschatology of the biblical witness was theoretically affirmed but in reality relegated to a somewhat embarrassed reference to the second coming of Christ. This neglect led from time to time to outbreaks of apocalyptic fervor on the fringes of the church, but the dominant theological traditions no longer integrated the eschatological perspective into their work, but relegated it to an appendix. This is what led to the tendency to treat only the order of creation and the order of redemption, without reference to the eschatological dimension. Neither world nor church is put in its proper perspective when this happens: the true eschatological tension between the two is lost because the eschatological *telos* is lost sight of.

The rediscovery of the eschatological witness of the New Testament at the beginning of the twentieth century by scholars such as Johannes Weiss and Albert Schweitzer therefore sent shock waves through the dominant theological traditions. No one knew quite how to integrate the discovery into theology. It is only in recent decades that western theology has begun to come to terms with the eschatological dimension of Christian existence. Those who have dealt with it most creatively are probably Jürgen Moltmann and

Wolfhart Pannenberg. With Moltmann in particular we might note how long this integration has taken. His early theology of hope is so strongly eschatological that his system is out of balance; his most recent work, *Christology on the Way*, reflects a more mature appropriation of eschatological themes into his theological system.

Schmemann was there ahead of these western theologians, however, because the liturgical witness of the Byzantine rite had preserved this eschatological perspective for those with the insight to understand its message. In the liturgy the biblical witness remained a living reality, at a time when theology fell prey to other influences. As a consequence, eschatology does not seem an alien body in Schmemann's system, but from the first is integrated into a carefully-balanced framework. His theology is eschatological through and through, but the cosmological and the ecclesiological dimensions are never lost sight in his emphasis on eschatology.

Schmemann's Witness to the Goodness of Created Matter

Although the theological tradition of Dionysius made of material reality nothing more than the stuff of a kind of ladder of contemplation by which the rational soul ascended to God, Orthodoxy never suffered from the false rationalism and spiritualism which tended to disincarnate Christian worship and Christian existence in the west. In the west the dominant strand of Protestant tradition after the Reformation in the end followed the lead of Luther's emphasis on the preached word and Calvin's theological iconoclasm, rather than the fervent sacramental piety of both reformers. The rationalism which despoiled worship after the age of the enlightenment and the emotional pietism which constituted the reaction to it both were largely verbal in their approach to worship. One discounted the material character of Christian existence for the sake of human "rationality"; the other discounted it for the sake of the "spiritual" character of the human relationship to God. Schmemann, for whom material reality is the link of life and love between God and humanity, falls into neither trap.

Schmemann's Witness to God's Continuing Creativity

The biblical literalism which was the ironic result of the enlightenment also led to a seriously impoverished doctrine of creation. The great interpreters of Scripture in the early church were no less passionately convinced than the modern advocate of the literal interpretation of Scripture and biblical inerrancy that the Bible was inspired by the Holy Spirit. But they were not under the delusion that the inspired authors were capable of writing nothing but historical prose. The treatment of Genesis 1 and 2 by such authors as Basil of Caesarea, Augustine, and others strikes us as highly fanciful at times. But it does not result in a doctrine of creation which limits God's creative activity to an initial series of discrete acts at the beginning of time. The orthodox tradition never lost sight of God's continuing creativity, which will reach its *telos* and fulfilment at the *eschaton*. It did not fall prey to the modern biblicist reduction of creation to an initial series of special acts of creation. The deist and the fundamentalist are closer to each other in this regard than either would like to admit, for the deist like the fundamentalist locates creation as an initial act. The difference is that the fundamentalist argues for God's intervention in an already completed creation and the deist argues against it.

A doctrine of creation like that of Alexander Schmemann, which works from the broad perspectives of the patristic witness and which holds in balance the *cosmological, ecclesiological,* and *eschatological* dimensions of the world provides a perspective on creation that avoids these multiple traps: it views creation and redemption from the perspective of their eschatological *telos;* it avoids the individualizing of eschatology; it affirms the goodness of created matter without making of it an idol; it affirms the continuing creativity of God. We have much to learn from it.

Notes

1. For biographical data, see John Meyendorff, "A Life Worth Living," in Thomas Fisch, ed., *Liturgy and Tradition: Theological Reflections of Alexander Schmemann* (Crestwood, NY: St. Vladimir's Seminary Press, 1990) 145-154, and Fisch's own introduction to the book, 1-10.

2. This is the title of the present edition (Crestwood, NY: St. Vladimir's Seminary Press, 1988). It was first published in 1963 and has also appeared in English under the present subtitle as its title and under the title *The World as Sacrament.*

3. *Pour la vie du monde* (1969); *Il mondo come sacramento* (1969); *Gia na zese ho kosmos* (1970); *Aus der Freude Leben: Ein Glaubensbuch der Orthodoxen Christen* (1974); *För världens liv* (1976); *samizdat* edition in Russian, *Za zhizn' mira* (1973). See Paul Garret, compiler, "Fr. Alexander Schmemann: A Chronological Bibliography (excluding book reviews)," *St. Vladimir's Theological Quarterly* 28:1 (1984) 11-26, for these editions.

4. Schmemann, "Liturgical Theology, Theology of the Liturgy, and Liturgical Reform," in Fisch, *Liturgy and Tradition* 40.

5. John Meyendorff, "A Life Worth Living," in Fisch, *Liturgy and Tradition* 149.

6. See his *Introduction to Liturgical Theology*, 3rd ed. (Crestwood, NY: St. Vladimir's Seminary Press, 1986) 103-110.

7. Ibid. 110-113.

8. Ibid. 129-131. Schmemann uses the term "mysteriological piety" to refer to an outlook which understood liturgical rites as sanctifying the world by their very performance, rather than as transforming the world by articulating the eschatological faith of the Christian community. In such an outlook, liturgy stands in danger of being used to sanctify the world in its fallen state, rather than judging and redeeming the world by reference to God's kingdom.

9. See my 1991 dissertation for the graduate department of religion at Duke, "An Architecture of Time: A Critical Study of the Liturgical Theology of Alexander Schmemann," esp. chapters 2 -4.

10. Schmemann, *For the Life of the World* 144-145.

11. Ibid. 151.

12. See the treatment in *For the Life of the World* 56-57.

13. See his essay, "The World in Orthodox Thought and Experience," in his collection, *Church, World, Kingdom* (Crestwood, NY: St. Vladimir's Seminary Press, 1979) 67-84, here 73-77. Schmemann can talk of the world as created good, fallen, and redeemed, as the western perspective does, but the eschatological perspective transforms the meaning of these terms.

14. Schmemann, *For the Life of the World* 139-140.

15. Ibid. 138-139.

16. Ibid. 14-15.

17. Ibid. 16-17.

18. Ibid. 42-43.

19. See ibid. 33-36; a more extended treatment is found in *The Eucharist: Sacrament of the Kingdom* (Crestwood, NY: St. Vladimir's Seminary Press), 101-131 *passim*.

20. Alexander Schmemann, "The World as Sacrament," in his *Church, World, Mission: Reflections on Orthodoxy in the West* (Crestwood, NY: St. Vladimir's Seminary Press, 1979) 217-227, here 222-223 *passim*.

21. Alexander Schmemann, *Of Water and the Spirit: A Liturgical Study of Baptism*, revised edition (Crestwood, NY: St. Vladimir's Seminary Press, 1974), 48-50 passim; see also 37-40.

22. Gregory's positive vision is perhaps most easy accessible in his *Address on Religious Instruction* (also known as his *Great Catechetical Oration*). It is more fully developed in his ascetical works, such as his treatise *On Perfection*, and in works of philosophical theology such as his treatises *Against Eunomius*. The last of these has a highly-sophisticated treatment of

time, which carefully balances the horizontal and the vertical dimensions of eschatology. On Gregory's doctrine of perfection as perpetual progress see the Introduction by Jean Daniélou in *From Glory to Glory: Texts from Gregory of Nyssa's Mystical Writings*, Selected with an Introduction by Jean Daniélou, Translated and Edited by Herbert Musurillo (New York: Charles Scribner's Sons, 1961) 3-78, esp. 46-71.

9

Reclaiming the Larger Trinitarian Framework of Baptism

Louis Weil

ALTHOUGH THE EPISCOPAL CHURCH HAS LIVED FOR ALMOST TWO DECADES with the revised rite of Holy Baptism which was authorized in its present form in the Proposed Book of Common Prayer of 1976, initiatory norms and practice continue to be a source of pastoral tension in a variety of ways within the church. Even when the issues related to the rite of confirmation are removed from the picture, the practice of baptism itself remains problematic as adults continue to request the rite for their children or godchildren on the basis of long standing practice which the revised rite and its rubrical norms clearly contradict.

Even among clergy, who generally have had numerous opportunities to engage the theological and practical implications of the revised rite in clergy conferences and continuing education, the rite is often interpreted through a kind of filter of presuppositions which took root in a very different context. Although, for example, the rite affirms that "Holy Baptism is appropriately administered within the Eucharist as the chief service on a Sunday or other feast," (BCP, p. 298) the rite is still celebrated on occasion in quasi-private contexts according to the model which was common in an earlier era. In such a context, to speak only of this one issue, the ecclesial priorities of the rite become overshadowed by an entrenched theology which continues to interpret the rite in narrowly individualistic terms as a kind of private salvation contract. The fundamental problem in this interpretation is resolved only on the surface when the letter of the rubrical law is fulfilled, the baptism taking place at a public liturgy, but where the baptismal party are essentially strangers to the gathered assembly who are witnesses of the rite.

The underlying issue is that the rite of Holy Baptism as officially authorized in the 1979 Book of Common Prayer often stands in a kind of isolation from the theological framework upon which it is based, while another theology lingers on as a continuing source of its interpretation. Behind the latter there is a vigorous folk theology which has shaped the expectations of many church members when a child is born into the family, and this folk theology contradicts in significant ways the priorities of the renewed biblical and liturgical theology of initiation which has been a major fruit of recent decades of theological and pastoral reflection.

It is probably evident to most Episcopalians that there has been more attention given to baptism in teaching and in sermons since the 1960s than was true earlier. This attention has often been concerned with the dignity of every baptized person as a member of the Body of Christ, which has in turn contributed to a deepened awareness of the ministries of all baptized people rather than the earlier common identification of ministry with ordination. This issue itself points to the foundational recovery of the doctrine of the church as the society of faith created by baptism and reenacted and nurtured in the eucharistic celebration. This is why an individualized interpretation of baptism is so misleading theologically since it contradicts the fundamentally corporate meaning of baptism as membership in the Christian society and thus commitment to a way of living in regard to God and to other people, and not merely as a ritual veneer concerned primarily with the salvation of the individual.

The folk theology of baptism has been dominated by the idea of original sin and its power to separate the newborn child from the love of God if that sin is not removed by the waters of baptism. Certainly the whole Christian tradition has related baptism to the forgiveness of sin among a constellation of meanings connected to the initiatory rite, but it is the narrowed emphasis of the meaning of baptism upon this one aspect, and especially as seen in the context of the theory of original sin, which has dominated the theology of baptism and led to a theological imbalance with profound practical consequences.

Images of creation and birth offer a needed corrective to a too limited relation of baptismal meaning to the forgiveness of sin. A common phrase applied to baptism is "new birth" and yet this image has all too frequently been ignored in its implied linking of baptism to the mighty acts of God in creation and its suggestion that the primary context of the relation of humankind to God is one of awe and thanksgiving.

Similarly, at the popular level, Episcopalians have often failed to claim the charismatic aspect of baptism as an occasion in which the Holy Spirit is actively engaged at the heart of its sacramental meaning. At the prayer "Heavenly Father, we thank you," which immediately follows the water rite, although it is acknowledged that "by water and the Holy Spirit" the candidates have received the forgiveness of sins and been raised to the new life of grace, a lingering identification of confirmation with the activity of the Spirit seems to inhibit a genuine grasp of the place of the Spirit in our understanding of baptism.

As a consequence of this failure to claim the full Trinitarian meaning of baptism, the rite is interpreted predominately within a Christological context which focuses on the forgiveness of sins accomplished through the death of Jesus. This is, of course, a major facet of baptism's meaning, but if we look at the new rite without the filter of an inherited preoccupation with original sin, we find that much more is being proclaimed by the baptismal liturgy.

The modest goal of this study is to consider some of the liturgical texts of the rite of baptism for indications of the ways in which the rite has been interpreted by the community as it brought new members into its fellowship. We shall also observe the impact of the theory of original sin upon the evolution of the rites, leading eventually to the obscuring of primary images of baptism in its relation to creation and new birth, and the activity of the Spirit. In this time of increased baptismal consciousness, it is imperative that our attention not be narrowly textual. The rite of the 1979 Book of Common Prayer is genuinely representative of the church's larger store of baptismal images, yet there remains the work of effective attention to the wider pastoral context, the place where the baptismal identity is lived day to day. For that, the catechetical ministry of the church can fruitfully explore this wider range of baptismal meanings.

Cranmer's Prayers over the Water

The "Thanksgiving over the Water" in the baptismal rite of the 1979 Book of Common Prayer is by now so generally familiar that its dramatic contrast in content to the earlier forms of the blessing of the baptismal water in the Anglican Prayer Book tradition has probably faded from memory.[1] The prayer as initially shaped by Archbishop Thomas Cranmer in the Prayer Book of 1549 became the basic model for all subsequent forms for the blessing of water up to and including the American Prayer Book of 1928. There were, of course, some modifications of the text in successive revisions, and one significant shift in its theological stance, but from a literary point of view, the text as first published by Cranmer proved quite durable.

The 1549 Book of Common Prayer indicates that the water should be changed and blessed at least once per month. In other words, the water was not blessed at each baptism. The form for the blessing was printed as a kind of appendix to Cranmer's rite for private baptism "in time of necessity," and it appears there in a two-fold structure. The first part ("O most merciful God . . .") is a lengthy petitionary prayer which links the element of water to baptismal regeneration and to the descent of the Holy Spirit in the image of the action of the Spirit at the baptism of Jesus. It is in this context that the actual form for the blessing of the water appears:

> Sanctify + this fountain of baptism, thou that art the sanctifier of all things, that by the power of thy word, all those that shall be baptized therein, may be spiritually regenerated, and made the children of everlasting adoption. Amen.

In the revision of 1552, consistent with Cranmer's policy of removing all blessings of material elements, this petition for the sanctification of the water was eliminated.

The second part of the blessing of the font as it appears in 1549 became the source for the form of blessing in later editions of the Prayer Book. Since it is preceded by the petitions, including that quoted for the blessing of the water, the second element, preceded by a salutation and response, does not include any words of blessing over the water. The text of this prayer, which remained in the Anglican rite of baptism for over four centuries, reads as follows:

> Almighty and everliving God, whose most dearly beloved son Jesus Christ, for the forgiveness of our sins did shed out of his most precious side both water and blood, and gave commandment to his disciples that they should go teach all nations, and baptize them in the name of the Father, the Son, and the Holy Ghost: Regard, we beseech thee, the supplications of thy congre-

gation, and grant that all thy servants which shall be baptized in this water, prepared for the ministration of thy holy sacrament, may receive the fulness of thy grace, and ever remain in the number of thy faithful, and elect children, through Jesus Christ our Lord.

The 1552 revision incorporated these prayers over the water as a fixed part of each baptism, but shortened the petitions including, as we noted, the removal of the first paragraph with its prayer for the blessing of the water. This meant, consequently, that in this version the water is scarcely referred to at all. The phrase "prepared for the ministration of thy holy sacrament" was also removed because, from 1552 onwards, the prayer would be said at each baptism.

The removal of the actual petition for the blessing of the water, thoroughly consistent with Cranmer's principles in the 1552 revision, was not addressed for more than a century in Anglican practice. This is the significant theological shift (away from Cranmer's position) referred to above. In the Restoration Prayer Book of 1662, a petition for the blessing of the water reappeared within the authorized text, but now inserted into the second part of Cranmer's original prayers over the water. In the prayer "Almighty and everliving God" quoted above, after the phrase, "Regard we beseech thee, the supplications of thy Congregation," a new phrase is inserted: "sanctify this water to the mystical washing away of sin," and thus the rite first used by Anglicans on the American continent included a blessing of the baptismal water.

Substantial attention has been given here to the evolution of the Prayer Book form for the blessing of the water, first, because it was for centuries the liturgical form used by Anglicans, albeit with the modifications noted, but second, because the theological tone of these prayers reflects a shift of focus in the understanding of baptism which had occurred long before the Reformation and which thus shaped the context out of which these forms developed.

When we scrutinize the forms which we have quoted, and if we can keep in mind the content of the "Thanksgiving over the Water" (BCP 1979), we immediately see in this comparison a marked contrast in their respective theological foundations. In the Cranmerian texts, the focus of the meaning of baptism is predominately related to sin and the fall of humanity from grace. Although the theme of baptismal regeneration might be developed in terms of new birth and the gift of life in God's creation, the tone of the prayers does not move in that direction. The biblical image of Jesus' baptism in the Jordan is cited, but the only image which evokes an association with God's mighty acts in creation is a reference to "the old Adam" which is, of course, to Adam after the fall, the sinful Adam who had disobeyed God. Immediately following upon that image is, in the 1549 petitions, a prayer for the death of carnal affections in a context which seems to set human sexuality in opposition to what is spiritual. This opposition continues to be mirrored in the next petition which asks that the newly baptized may "forsake the devil and all his works."

The second part of Cranmer's text, the prayer "Almighty and everliving God," which became the primary text in later editions of the Prayer Book, continues to present a perspective to baptism almost univocally as the remedy for sin: the death of Christ was "for the forgiveness of our sins," although at its end the text does refer to the hope that the newly baptized will "ever remain in the number of thy faithful, and elect children," thus introducing at least a suggestion of what we might call an ecclesial and corporate aspect to the meaning of baptism.

This scrutiny of Cranmer's texts is not meant in any way to deny the relation of the practice of baptism in the church to the forgiveness of sins. That link is well grounded in Scripture, and is clearly attested by the liturgical tradition. My point is that baptism is this—and *more*. To see baptism narrowly defined in terms only of the forgiveness of sins is to fail to grasp the enormity of its meaning. How did baptism come to be seen so predominantly in this perspective, and how did this narrowed meaning take such a firm hold within the operational theology and practice of the church?

The Normative Model and Its Disintegration

From a theological point of view, an adult is always the normative candidate for baptism. When I say this in the classroom, someone will almost always respond that in our time and for most of the centuries of the church's history infants and small children have been presented in far greater numbers than adults as candidates for baptism. Yet being more numerous is not the same as being the norm. We are using the term *norm* in its theological sense which, as Aidan Kavanagh has said:

> has nothing to do with the number of times a thing is done, but
> . . . has everything to do with the standard according to which a
> thing is done. So long as the norm is in place both in practice and

in the awareness of those who are engaged in it, the situation is capable of being judged "normal" even though the norm must be departed from to some extent, even frequently, due to exigencies of time, place, pastoral considerations, physical inabilities, or whatever. Yet to the extent possible, the norm must always be achieved to some extent lest it slip imperceptibly into the status of a mere "ideal" all wish for but are under no obligation to realize.[2]

Concerning the rites of Christian initiation, Kavanagh goes on to say that:

The norm of baptism . . . [is a] solemn sacramental initiation done especially at the paschal vigil and preceded by a catechumenate of serious content and considerable duration. This implies strongly, even if it does not require, that the initiate be an adult or at least a child well advanced in years.[3]

It is important for us to reclaim this idea of norm within the Episcopal Church and to bring it to bear upon our pastoral model for the celebration of baptism, both in regard to the complete text of the rite and to the practical directions authorized and published with the rite. It is this ritual whole— not merely the text but also the context— which constitute the norm. As Kavanagh warns, when the church loses a sense of the norm in its full meaning, it becomes merely an ideal which is never realized in experience. As was certainly the case in baptismal theology, the continuous experience of a deprived model, a model which seems almost a caricature of the norm, will in the long run reshape the theological understanding of the rite itself.

In the fourth century, as the church moved from a situation of persecution toward what we may call "the Christendom model," the source of adult converts within a given, usually urban, society gradually dried up as the society as a whole found itself baptized, as, in other words, the general society and the Christian society came to be the same thing. Since the baptism of the infants and children of converts had apparently been customary from the earliest times,[4] it was this derived practice (i.e., infant baptism based upon the faith profession and baptism of the parents) which endured when adults were, on the whole, already baptized. This situation led to a dramatic shift in the whole liturgical and social context in which baptism took place, but although infant candidates came to dominate in number, their baptism continued to be, theologically, based upon the faith and practice of the adult community.

If we may use the text of the *Apostolic Tradition* as a least an example of an early pattern of Christian initiation, the whole description of baptism indicates the normative character of the adult candidates. Further, Hipplolytus' description makes an important link between the baptismal profession of faith at the time of the immersion of a candidate, and the pattern of eucharistic proclamation in which the newly baptized will participate not only as the fulfillment of the initiatory process but as they share in the assembly of all the baptized on Sundays for the remainder of their lives. As Hippolytus describes the rite of baptism, the actual immersions took place in the context of the candidates' affirmation of the creed, the summary of Trinitarian faith which the neophytes would share with the Christian community into which they were being incorporated. According to the evidence available to us, whether in the text of the *Apostolic Tradition* or elsewhere, this profession of the creed was a baptismal rite only and did not find a place in the eucharistic liturgy until centuries later, and then in its conciliar Nicene form.

What then was the link in the ongoing life of the baptized between their baptismal profession and their weekly assembly on Sundays? If we look at the model text of a eucharistic prayer presented by Hippolytus, we find that it closely corresponds in structure and content to the baptismal creed; it is, as it were, the creed fleshed out. In other words, as the members of the Sunday assembly heard the eucharistic prayer, it echoed with the creedal phrases which each had proclaimed at baptism. The meaning of baptism was thus affirmed and reaffirmed within the full scope of Trinitarian faith. Christian initiation as mirrored in the text of the *Apostolic Tradition* and in a large body of patristic literature[5] was an integrative event in which within an intense liturgical focus a whole constellation of images associated with the church's faith were brought together and thus became the foundational event from which weekly occasions of common prayer, especially and primarily on Sunday, drew their meaning. It is for this reason that Easter emerged as the preferred season for baptism because of the close correlation between the faith-event of the resurrection of Christ and the primacy of that event in the church's understanding of baptism. The rite of baptism offered a unified symbol which held together all the fundamental images of the Christian profession of faith.

The disintegration of this unified symbol has been well documented elsewhere.[6] Suffice it in this context to say that, given the emergence of Christendom after the liberation of the church by Constantine in the fourth century, the increased frequency of infants as the usual candidates for baptism led to a profound shift in the way the rite was understood. Within the normative model described earlier, it was evident that infants and children were baptized on the basis of the professed faith of their parents, who were often being baptized at the same time. In the increasing absence of adult candidates, and the consequent marginalization of preparatory catechetical rites which for their integrity required adult candidates, the focus shifted to the infants in themselves as the larger context of mature profession was obscured and eventually lost. It was in this new situation that the theological foundations of baptism narrowed to a preoccupation with sin.

Impact of the Theory of Original Sin

The German biblical scholar Herbert Haag has challenged the folk theology of the relation of baptism to original sin in a study entitled *Is Original Sin in Scripture?*[7] Haag sums up his research on this question as follows:

> Baptism does not bring about the removal of "original sin", but rather rebirth as a child of God; it makes man a member of Christ. Through it he participates in Christ's life; he is taken up into the community of salvation, into the People of God, into the church. But participation in the life of Christ cannot be reconciled with sin. Consequently, baptism also becomes, for those who personally have committed sins, a sacrament which takes away sins.[8]

Haag's study of the scriptural evidence thus leads him to deny an idea which has, unfortunately, dominated the folk theology which has attached itself to infant baptism and led to a preoccupation in practice with sin as the primary reason for which baptism exists. Having rejected the notion that there is a scriptural basis for the idea of original sin, Haag is able to reaffirm the foundational meaning of baptism from which all its associated meanings flow: baptism is incorporation into the community of the church, with all that such incorporation implies.

How did this idea of original sin come to exercise such a dominating role for the practice of baptism? The idea originated as an explanation of how sin, associated with the disobedience of Adam, was handed down from generation to generation from our earliest human ancestors to our own time. St. Augustine (354-430) speculated that through intercourse the semen of the father led to the conception not only of the physical body but also of a defective soul passed on from Adam to all subsequent generations. Another theory suggested that the body bears a genetic flaw inherited from Adam, and although the soul is directly created by God, it becomes tainted through being contained by a corrupt body.[9]

These theories are problematic because of their apparent rejection of a theology of creation which sees the whole physical universe as originally good because it is the work of God. This negative view of human physicality was carried even further by Augustine in his debate with Pelagius where he espoused the theory that human nature is marked by original sin because conception always involves sexual passion which is by its nature inordinate and sinful. Although the debate actually grew out of Augustine's conviction that human salvation depended always and only upon the grace of God, his opposition to Pelagius' rather optimistic view of human nature led Augustine to an ever greater emphasis upon the fallen state of mankind: before human beings commit actual sins, they already share the defect integral to human nature which is the sin of Adam in which all share the guilt. We are thus born for damnation.[10]

Baptism, Augustine taught, cleanses mankind from that original guilt, but, indicative of Augustine's profound negativity about human sexuality, even after baptism the tendency to sin remains, and is most apparent in the sexual passions, in what Augustine calls "concupiscence." Such negative views about human sexuality are not found only in Augustine. The ascetic St. Jerome (342-420), writing in the same era, said that "in view of the purity of the body of Christ, all sexual intercourse is unclean."[11] In due course the impact of such teaching with its tendency to identify sin in some primary way with sexual acts was to fuse these attitudes with the biological theory of original sin so that not only were sexual acts sinful, even within marriage, but original sin, the human race's identification with Adam and Eve as the original sinners, was extended throughout all generations by the ejaculation of semen in sexual intercourse. Is this view not echoed in Cranmer's phrase, "Grant that all carnal affections may die in them"?

An ironic aspect of Augustine's debate with Pelagius is that at this same time the social context of the church's life was shifting as it took an increasingly dominant role within society as a whole. By the end of Augustine's life the decline in the number of adult candidates for baptism was dramatic. By the close of the fifth century, many of the preparatory rites of initiation were done in private because most of the candidates were now infants who were unable to receive the pre-baptismal catechetical instructions.[12] As a consequence, the adult community ceased to be witnesses and hearers of this process and thus the catechumenal ministry of the church collapsed, and the rite of baptism was left suspended and isolated from the context which had sustained its full meaning. Baptism was left as a minimalized sacramental rite increasingly attached to infants at the time of birth. It can be no surprise that in the context of this development, Augustine could defend his theory of original sin in connection with the practice of infant baptism. If original sin were not a reality, he asked, why would the church baptize infants? The social context had obscured the fundamental meaning of baptism as participation in the life of Christ through membership in the people of God. The meaning was now narrowly focused on sin.[13]

The 1979 Rite and Its Implications

Given this dramatic shift of focus in the understanding of the meaning of baptism, we may now observe in conclusion how profoundly the baptismal rite of the 1979 Book of Common Prayer represents a radical recovery of the church's larger understanding of baptism. Once the rite came to be seen as individually linked to an infant's salvation from original sin, the classical model with its sensitively integrated signs was doomed. In due course, as baptism was linked to birth in the face of fear of infant death with the taint of original sin, the theological relation between baptism and the paschal celebration was lost.[14] With the increasing infrequency of lay adult communion, eventually limited annually to Easter (in 1215), the link between baptism and communion was undermined and eventually broken.[15] Finally, geographical factors contributed to a diminished participation of bishops in the rites of initiation and eventually to the development of a separated rite of the laying-on-of-hands which was often delayed until several years after the baptism, if it was performed at all.[16]

Although Archbishop Cranmer achieved a certain reintegration of these shattered elements, for a variety of reasons much was left unresolved. It was, for example, inconceivable to restore communion to its appropriate relation to baptism when infants continued the most numerous candidates and when reform-minded leaders were committed to the need for rudimentary catechetical teaching prior to reception of the sacrament. Further, the theology of original sin and its relation to baptism continued as an unquestioned part of the common religious understanding. The rite thus continued to be individualistically focused on the forgiveness of sins, with only a hint of awareness of other aspects of baptismal meaning.

The rite of Holy Baptism in the 1979 American Book of Common Prayer has on the whole accomplished the reintegration which Cranmer began in regard both to the text and its larger contextual implications. The introductory rubrical directions (p. 298) indicate the context: the rite "is appropriately administered within the Eucharist as the chief service on a Sunday or other feast." By this simple phrase a revolution is effected: baptism is restored to its eucharistic context at major occasions of public worship. The underlying theological premise is that baptism pertains to the life of the entire Christian community. It is an ecclesial act, not one narrowly centered on the individual and some quasi-private sense of salvation. The rubric also implies, although it does not explicitly state, the early Christian understanding that baptism finds its completion in communion, for infants as well as for adults. In recent years that idea has gained an increasing observance with the Episcopal Church.[17]

The rubrical directions at the beginning of the rite establish the fundamental theological principle that "Holy Baptism is full initiation by water and the Holy Spirit into Christ's Body the Church." Here we see the theological foundation of baptism affirmed: the purpose of baptism is first of all incorporation into Christ; other meanings, including the forgiveness of sins, derive from that. The role of the Holy Spirit in baptism is inherent in this theological understanding, and is reinforced by the inclusion of the prayer for the gifts of the Spirit immediately following the water rite, having been removed from its ambivalent place in the rite of confirmation in the 1979 Book of Common Prayer.

One other significant contextual matter is established in the directions, in the set which are printed after the rite (p. 312), where it is stated that "Holy Baptism is especially appropriate at the Easter Vigil, on the Day of Pentecost, on All Saints' Day or the Sunday after All Saints' Day, and on the Feast of the Baptism of our Lord (the First Sunday after the Epiphany)." It is important to note the primacy of place which is given to the paschal season, with the Vigil as the principal occasion, in this list of baptismal feasts. They may be called baptismal feasts because the meaning of these days is grounded in the theology of baptism; they lift up aspects of its meaning. This rubric is not a theoretical ideal dreamed up by liturgists. Rather, it points to the primary concern of this essay that an indifference to the wider framework of a baptism, the full context as well as the text, ultimately robs baptism of its depth of meaning, minimalizes its sign, and leaves it an individualized salvation contract.

This larger perspective must, of course, be applied to the rite itself. Baptism is not essentially a sacramental formula set within a framework of secondary and ultimately disposable elements. Our awareness of Emergency Baptism (BCP, p. 313) has contributed to the idea that in the end only the Trinitarian formula really matters. That is a minimalist view which it may be appropriate to invoke for real emergency situations, but it cannot be the foundation for an adequate baptismal model.

When we consider the rite as a whole, we find that it begins with a full liturgy of the word including a sermon. After the Presentation and Examination of the Candidates, there is the affirmation of The Baptismal Covenant, which is made up of the baptismal creed and five questions related to the Christian lifestyle. In previous American versions of the Prayer Book, the creed had been replaced by the phrase, "Dost thou believe all the Articles of the Christian Faith, as contained in the Apostles Creed?" This was at variance with the English tradition in which the minister recited the creed, and the candidates affirmed belief. In the 1979 Book of Common Prayer, the form of creedal affirmation is in a dialogue form with the celebrant. Its inclusion is an important indication of the larger framework of Trinitarian faith within which the water rite is performed.[18]

The affirmation of faith leads to the ceremonies at the font, including the Thanksgiving over the Water. As we saw earlier in this essay, the Cranmerian materials dealing with this aspect of the rite were very much influenced by concerns of the Reformers in regard to blessing and by the persistence of the linking of baptism primarily to the forgiveness of sins. The 1979 rite offers us a prayer which emerges from a very different set of concerns. Its structure parallels the form of a eucharistic prayer, and using water as a unifying image, it proclaims a summary of salvation history: creation, the Exodus, the baptism of Jesus by John, its link with the death and resurrection of Jesus and our incorporation within his paschal victory through our own baptism. The second paragraph of the prayer develops this latter theological image as the foundation of the church's continued practice of baptism. It is in that context that the sanctification of the water is proclaimed in the third paragraph.[19]

Finally, as noted earlier, immediately after the water rite, the prayer for the gifts of the Holy Spirit is said. In the Anglican Prayer Book tradition, this prayer had always been placed within the rite of confirmation, thus contributing to an abiding ambivalence among Anglicans as to the full initiatory meaning of baptism.[20] Now being placed after the water rite in the American Book of Common Prayer, a clear stand has been taken that baptism is a full initiation, but also that it is itself the primary pneumatic event in the life of a Christian, the sacrament in which the gifts of the Holy Spirit are given.

If we interpret this rite through the filter of the mentality which dominated the earlier Anglican rites, and before that much of the medieval understanding of baptism, we shall, in effect, betray the texts we use and the encompassing faith which they proclaim. The rite challenges the church to an intentional reclaiming of the larger context of Christian faith. The paschal context which the rite lifts up is much more than an impracticable ideal. It is an imperative if we are to reclaim that larger awareness of our baptismal union with God which reaches out to the whole of our lives as it forms us to be the People of God in the world.

> We thank you, Father, for the water of Baptism.
> In it we are buried with Christ in his death.
> By it we share in his resurrection.
> Through it we are reborn by the Holy Spirit.

Notes

1. Comparative charts of Cranmer's two versions and their sources, plus the version of the 1662 Boof of Common Prayer may be found in F.E. Brightman, *The English Rite*, vol. 2 (London: Rivingtons, 1915) 724-761. The sequence of authorized texts for the American BCP are similarly set out, and compared to the English 1662, in Paul V. Marshall, *Prayer Book Parallels*, vol. 1 (New York: Church Hymnal Corp., 1989) 232-309.

2. *Aidan Kavanagh, The Shape of Baptism* (New York: Pueblo Publishing Co., 1978) 108.

3. Ibid. 109.

4. Joachim Jeremias, *Infant Baptism in The First Four Centuries* (Philadelphia: Westminster Press, 1960); see especially Jeremias' discussion of the significance of Hippolytus' *Apostolic Tradition* (par. 21) 73-75.

5. Abundant comparative evidence is set forth in H.M. Riley, *Christian Initiation* (Washington, D.C., The Catholic University of America, 1974). See also the analysis of homiletical evidence in E. Yarnold, *The Awe-Inspiring Rites of Initiation* (Slough, England: St. Paul Publications, 1972).

6. See J.D.C. Fisher, *Christian Initiation: Baptism in the Medieval West* (London: S.P.C.K., 1965).

7. Herbert Haag, *Is Original Sin in Scripture?* (New York: Sheed and Ward, 1969). Haag's concern is not primarily with baptism but rather with a careful examination of the biblical material which has been used as a foundation for the theory of original sin. It is only in his conclusions that Haag is concerned about the implications of his study for baptism.

8. Ibid. 107-108.

9. See the discussion of the development of the doctrine of original sin in the patristic period in Edward Yarnold, *The Theology of Original Sin* (Notre Dame: University of Notre Dame Press, 1971) 51-65.

10. An interesting discussion of Augustine's debate with Pelagius and related issues is found in Elaine Pagels, *Adam, Eve, and the Serpent* (New York: Random House, 1988) 127-150. For a summary of Augustine's teaching, see B. Neunheuser, *Baptism and Confirmation* (New York: Herder and Herder, 1964) 115-134.

11. Jerome, *Adversus Jovinianum* I, 20.

12. Fisher, *Christian Initiation* 5-7.

13. Ibid. 112.

14. Ibid. 109-119.

15. Ibid. 101-108.

16. Ibid. 120-140. See the discussion of these developments in Nathan D. Mitchell, "Dissolution of the Rite of Christian Initiation", in *Made, Not Born* (Notre Dame: University of Notre Dame Press, 1976) 50-82.

17. See my articles, "The Practice of Infant Communion," in *Liturgy* 4:1 (Washington, DC, 1983) 69-73, and "Disputed Aspects of Infant Communion," in *Gratias Agamus*, ed. W. Vos (Rotterdam, 1987) 256-263; also R.A. Meyers, "Infant Communion: Reflections on the Case from Tradition," in *Anglican and Episcopal History*, vol. 57 (1988) 159-175, and L.L. Mitchell, "The Communion of Infants and Children," *Anglican Theological Reivew* 61 (1989) 63-78.

18. For a discussion of the liturgical use of creedal formulas, see my "Proclamation of Faith in the Eucharist." in *Time and Community*, ed. J. Neil Alexander (Washington, D.C.: The Pastoral Press, 1990) 279-290.

19. See L.L. Mitchell, "The Thanksgiving over the Water in the Baptismal Rites of the West," *Worship: Initiation and the Churches* (Washington, D.C.: The Pastoral Press, 1991) 177-194; see also M.J. Hatchett, *Commentary on the American Prayer Book* (New York: Seabury Press, 1980) 274-275.

20. A discussion of this issue may be found in E.C. Whitaker, *Sacramental Initiation Complete in Baptism* (Bramcote, Notts: Grove Books, 1975).

10

The Redemption of Creation:
A Liturgical Theology

Ralph N. McMichael, Jr.

An increasing dimension of the liturgical movement is what is known as liturgical theology.[1] Liturgical theology is not a theology of the liturgy *per se*, but theology which arises from the liturgy, and hence is to be considered *theologia prima* or first-order theology. That is, the doing of theology—saying something about God—should begin where the Christian community has its primary encounter with God in its worship. *Theologia secunda* is our reflection on this primary experience of God in word and sacrament which issues in a systematic and/or sacramental theology.[2] This means that the task of theology is not primarily to be considered as a disembodied (outside the worshiping Body of Christ) intellectual striving toward coherence of understanding. It has often been the case that theology has been conceived without due regard for the way in which the community prays. For example, one might read a learned treatise on the presence of Christ in the eucharist without any reference to the eucharistic liturgy itself. The question arises regarding the relationship between the church's prayer and its belief. Does belief grow from the fecund ground of prayer, or is prayer simply the seasonal bloom on the doctrinal tree?

The liturgical movement is characterized by a *retour aux sources* which means that we continually view our liturgies in broader perspectives. Sources do not serve as authoritative schema for new liturgies, but they do help us to fill in the gaps in our corporate memory which serves to give the worshiping community a keener awareness of its identity. A part of this awareness is that theology in the patristic church grew out of the church's ongoing life which included its liturgy. Much of patristic theology comes to us as commentaries on the liturgy, and as homilies preached within a liturgical context. Contemporary discussions of liturgical theology inevitably turn to the patristic phrase *lex orandi, lex credendi* as a basis for doing theology. That is, the essence of liturgical theology is the premise that the law of prayer establishes the law of belief. Once again, the primary encounter with God in worship is the foundation for all subsequent reflection. This is not to say that theology is only appropriate when it is liturgical, nor is *lex orandi, lex credendi* to relegate disciplined thinking to the pietistic realm. It is to affirm what Anglicanism has customarily asserted: our doctrine resides with our worship.

The task of liturgical theology, and its understanding and proclamation of *lex orandi, lex credendi*, are not without their problems and harsh realities. At times it seems that the call for *theologia prima* to be rooted in our worship goes largely ignored. I am concerned that the phrase *lex orandi, lex credendi* is becoming simply a mantra chanted by the cult of liturgical scholars, and like all highly cultic sayings it is irrelevant outside the cult itself. In other words, the contention that the law of prayer establishes the law of belief is often repeated within the confines of professional liturgical scholars, but it goes to a great extent unheeded in the larger church. This can be done by the effort to establish a *lex credendi* which seeks or creates its own *lex orandi*, or the formulation of doctrine that simply takes no notice of the church's prayer. Often the result of belief floating above prayer is a liturgical/doctrinal schizophrenia whereby a community or individual can believe one thing but pray another. However, there is another dimension to whether a community believes what it prays or not, and that is whether the community acts on its belief. *Lex orandi, lex credendi* is to always include *lex vivendi*. Does a community take notice of its liturgical prayer; does it believe what it prays; and does it act on this belief?

The continuum *lex orandi, lex credendi,* and *lex vivendi* and a theology of creation comprise the theme of this essay. It is acknowledged that the relationship between prayer, belief, and living is a dynamic one with extensive interplay so that they are not to be considered as independent self-enclosed realities. Therefore, this study will have some interplay between its presentation of corporate prayer which establishes belief that issues in a certain life style.

It was stated above that the phrase *lex orandi, lex credendi* is largely ignored in the church, and I would like to offer an example having to do with a possible theology of creation. The Standing Commission on Human Affairs of the Episcopal Church presented a report on the environment to the 1991 General Convention in which it sought to deal with the growing ecological crisis.[3] The report refers to and supports a document called "The Episcopal Church in Communion with Creation: Policy and Action Plan for the Environment and Sustainable Development," which was promulgated by a consultation formed by the Presiding Bishop in September, 1990. The second point of this document's call to action states "that a theology responsive to the revelation of Christ in creation today must be formulated and proclaimed." One may ask what are the sources for the formulation of this theology of creation? The report makes reference to Colossians 1:17 and Romans 8:20-24 to explicate what it calls an interconnectedness between God and creation. The report also appeals to science, mysticism, and feminism as sources for a development of theology responsive to an ever-deepening threat to the environment. When it comes to the liturgy, the *lex orandi*, as a source for a theology of creation, the *lex credendi*, the report says very little. There is mention of baptism as the sacrament which connects us to God's creation and its growing appropriateness as a vocation to care for the earth. However, the liturgy of baptism and its central images such as water and anointing are not discussed. In fact, the report makes one explicit reference to the Book of Common Prayer when it quotes a phrase from Eucharistic Prayer C. The report reads: "and because we live in constant communion with creation we know more than ever, in the words of the Holy Eucharist, that 'this fragile earth' is truly 'our island home'."

What I propose to do in this essay is to begin to develop a liturgical theology of creation. The eucharistic liturgies of the Book of Common Prayer[4] will serve as a source for an exposition of a theology of creation that will speak to our current environmental crisis. In other words, I will work within the realm of *theologia prima* as I seek to explicate the continuum *lex orandi, lex credendi,* and *lex vivendi* with regard to creation and its redemption. This will be done in three sections corresponding to prayer, belief, and life style: what does our prayer say about creation; what are the theological dimensions presented by the liturgy; and how is the Christian community called to live out this theology.

Lex Orandi

An examination of the references made to creation in the eucharistic rites of the Episcopal Church yields four categories that would constitute a theology of creation. The first category, or grouping of creation imagery, is concerned with God's relationship to creation, and is to be found in the pre-*Sanctus*, preface, and *Sanctus* sections of the various eucharistic prayers. This is not surprising given the dominance of the West Syrian structure of the eucharistic prayer in the 1979 Book of Common Prayer. The West Syrian or Antiochene structure has traditionally included creation within the context of praise and blessing which often culminates with the *Sanctus*. The section prior to the preface in Prayers A and B of Rite II includes the phrase "Father Almighty, Creator of heaven and earth." Here the first person of the Trinity is named the creator, and it would follow that creation is an act proper to the Father. This is also born out by the proper preface "Of God and Father" which states: "For you are the source of light and life; you made us in your image and called us to new life in Jesus Christ our Lord." God is described as the creator in Prayer II of Rite I, "thou didst create heaven and earth"; and Prayer C names God as creator while recognizing the complexity of creation: "At your command all things came to be: the vast expanse of interstellar space, galaxies, suns, the planets in the courses, and this fragile earth our island home." As to the role of the Son and the Holy Spirit in the act of creation, one would detect this elsewhere in these eucharistic prayers. Since the Father has created both heaven and earth one could maintain that there is some continuity of existence between the heavenly and earthly realities. That is, somehow our structures of life within the created order are similar to the patterns that exist in the fullness of life with God. To propose that this is not the case would lead, in my opinion, to a form of dyotheletism within the Godhead. In other words, God has two wills by which heaven and earth were created. However, earth and heaven are not identical, and this is why our petition in the Lord's Prayer is that God's will be done on earth as it is in heaven. There is freedom within the structures of the created order which can issue in a distortion of God's will for the earth while at the same time there is the inherent possibility that the earth can be a place in which God's will can be enacted according to its complete expression in heaven. This possibility of fulfillment of God's will implies that heaven and earth are not diametrically opposed realities, but instead, creation is teleologically dependent upon heaven.

A recurring phrase in every eucharistic prayer of the Book of Common Prayer is found in the *Sanctus*: "heaven and earth are full of your glory." Creation is not only a place which has the potential to manifest God's heavenly will, but presently bears the mark of God's glory. It can also be said that the glory which fills the earth is the same glory that is in heaven. Otherwise, one would be forced to acknowledge that God exudes two distinct glories. This means that creation has the ability to and does manifest the transcendent glorious nature of God. This is not to say that creation has a coterminous relationship with the nature of God. It is not the same to say that the earth is full of God's glory as to say that the earth is God's glory. God's relationship to creation may be viewed according to the already-not yet dynamic of eschatology in that creation already is full of God's glory, but it does not yet fully glorify God. It is the vocation of creation to glorify God—to manifest the glory of God. The vocation of creation as arising from the fact that it is created by God is expressed in the pre-*Sanctus* section of Prayer D which reads:

> Fountain of life and source of all goodness, you made all things and fill them with your blessing; you created them to rejoice in the splendor of your radiance. Countless throngs of angels stand before you to serve you night and day; and beholding the glory of your presence, they offer you unceasing praise. Joining with them, and giving voice to every creature under heaven, we acclaim you, and glorify your Name as we sing [Sanctus].

The faithful response of God's people to the earth being filled with God's glory is to glorify God by rejoicing in the splendor of God's radiance, and by giving voice to all of creation. The church does this every time it celebrates the eucharist and when the people of God break forth into praise: "Holy, holy, holy Lord, God of power and might, heaven and earth are full of your glory."

The second category of a theology of creation which arises from the *lex orandi* of the eucharistic rites of the Book of Common Prayer has to do with humanity's relationship to creation. What does our eucharistic euchology say about the place and role of humanity within the created order? After the *Sanctus* and *Benedictus* Prayer B continues: "we give thanks to you, O God, for the goodness and love which you have made known to us in creation." The eucharistic community gives thanks to God for creation because its members have experienced the grace of God there. The people gather for the eucharist with the knowledge that they have received divine favor because they live in relationship with creation. Creation as revelatory of God's grace provides a context for subsequent movements of the eucharistic prayer such as thanksgiving for redemption, invocation of the Spirit, and the offering of the bread and wine. Therefore, the eucharist is never an escape from earthly existence, or an otherworldly haven, but a thanksgiving for our earthly existence which manifests the grace of God toward us. Our thanksgiving for the grace and love of God revealed to us in creation brings with it an accountability and responsibility. What is humankind's role within the created order?

Eucharistic Prayer C states that God has made humankind the ruler of creation: "you made us the rulers of creation." The prayer goes on to acknowledge that we have not been the rulers we were meant to be: "But we turned against you, and betrayed your trust; and we turned against one another." The vocation of humankind to be the rulers of creation can, through freedom of the will, become a distorted version of what God intended it to be in the action of creation. Prior to the sentence "you made us the rulers of creation," Prayer C uses the title "Ruler of the Universe" for God. Our role as rulers of creation is not lived out on our own terms, but is a participation in the life of God. God's own relationship to creation makes humankind's relationship to creation as rulers possible. Furthermore, our sovereignty over creation is to be faithful to God's own sovereignty in that we are to care for the earth as God does. God has ordained humankind as co-rulers of creation; God allows us to rule in God's stead. This mutuality between humankind's relationship to creation as rulers and God's sovereignty over creation is also expressed in Eucharistic Prayer D. It reads "you formed us in your image, giving the whole world into our care, so that, in obedience to you, our Creator, we might rule and serve all your creatures." This prayer includes "serve" along with "rule" (Prayer C) to characterize the way in which we are to treat creation. The vocation to rule and serve all of God's creation is to be faithful to humankind's own creation in the image of God. God has entrusted creation which is full of God's glory to those who themselves have been created as stewards of this creation. When we care for the earth, or exercise servant sovereignty, we are living out our own creaturehood which is characterized by the life of the creator.

The third way in which references to creation in the eucharistic rites may be assessed has to do with oblation, the offering of creation. Any discussion of oblation entails a consideration of what is being offered, by whom, and how is this possible. All of the eucharistic prayers of the Book of Common Prayer include offering language having to do with the bread and wine (gifts), and some of the prayers explicitly place the gifts within creation. References to this type of offering are as follows:

> . . . with these thy holy gifts, which we now offer unto thee, the memorial thy Son hath commanded us to make; having in remembrance his blessed passion and precious death, his mighty resurrection and glorious ascension; and looking for his coming again with power and great glory. [Prayer I and II, Rite I]

> . . . recalling his death, resurrection, and ascension we offer you these gifts . . . (Prayer A)

> . . . and we offer our sacrifice of praise and thanksgiving to you, O Lord of all; presenting to you, from your creation, this bread and this wine . . . (Prayer B)

> . . . and so, Father, we who have been redeemed by him, and made a new people by water and the spirit, now bring before you these gifts. (Prayer C)

> Recalling Christ's death and his descent among the dead, proclaiming his resurrection and ascension to your right hand, awaiting his coming in glory; and offering to you, from the gifts you have given us, this bread and this cup, we praise you and we bless you. (Prayer D)

I would now like to deal with the questions of what is offered, by whom, and how is offering possible with regard to the *lex orandi* just presented.

Bread and wine are offered within the eucharistic prayer, but the movement of offering is not isolated in terms of these elements. Bread and wine bring a whole array of significations to the ritual process in that they are a part of creation and a product of human labor. Bread and wine are not only a segment of creation, but in this context they represent creation: "presenting to you from your creation, this bread and wine" (Prayer B). The bread and wine are deemed gifts not because the eucharistic community gives them to God, but because God has given them; they are not our gifts to God, but God's gifts to us. Bread and wine are representative gifts of the giftedness of all creation; "and offering to you, from the gifts you have given us, this bread and this cup, we praise you and bless you" (Prayer D). The response of the people of God to the giftedness of life and creation is praise and blessing of the creator. The offering of the gifts of bread and wine is a dimension of the community's sacrifice of praise and thanksgiving: "and we offer our sacrifice of praise and thanksgiving to you, O Lord of all; presenting to you, from your creation, this bread and this wine" (Prayer B).

The offerers of the representative gifts of creation are all the baptized. Prayer C definitively articulates the identity of those who offer: "and so, Father, we who have been redeemed by him [Christ], and made a new people by water and the Spirit, now bring before you these gifts." Baptism is entry into the life of Christ Jesus our great high priest whereby one becomes a member of the royal priesthood. As a member of this priesthood one is to offer prayers to God on behalf of the church and the world, and one can offer the gifts that God has given. In this context all the baptized are priests of creation in that they offer the gift of creation to God, and this offering is a dimension of the redemption of creation. Not that the baptized redeem creation, but that through the offering of creation the baptized themselves are being redeemed. Of course, this means that the act of offering, exercising one's priesthood, has a claim on the lives of the baptized because to offer a gift is truly to offer oneself. Those who offer are themselves part of the giftedness of the created order in such a way as to be never completely separate from it. The redemption that is being wrought within the lives of the baptized community is the same redemption that is being worked out in creation. Therefore, how we handle creation says something not only about the redemption of creation, but about our own redemption. Baptism is participation in the death and resurrection of Jesus Christ, and this means that at the essence of redemption is the paschal mystery. It is the paschal mystery which makes redemption, and therefore offering, possible.

The transition from thanksgiving to supplication in the West Syrian structure of the eucharistic prayer has the customary phraseology of "remembering . . ., we offer." The content of the remembrance comprises various Christ events such as incarnation, crucifixion, resurrection, and ascension. This Christological context for offering is demonstrable in the above quoted sections of the eucharistic prayers of the 1979 Book of Common Prayer. It is the redemptive acts of God in Christ which make our redemption and that of creation possible. Keeping the memory of the way in which Christ has redeemed the world means that we became aware once again of our place in this redemption and how we are to live this out. Offering what has been given to us arises out of a renewed participation in the paschal mystery which is at the essence of our identity as baptized people who are the priests of creation.

The fourth way by which to categorize the *lex orandi* of the eucharistic rites of the Book of Common Prayer is in Christological terms. This Christological dimension to a theology of creation has already been touched upon with regard to the paschal mystery as that which makes the offering of creation possible. The explicit references to Christ's role in the redemption of creation are: "through Jesus Christ our Lord, the firstborn of all creation" (Prayer B), and "rising from the grave, destroyed death, and made the whole creation new" (Prayer D). The life, death, and resurrection of Jesus Christ comprise the all-encompassing salvific horizon for creation in that everything is to find its redemption in him. Creation is never to be viewed as isolated from God or as an independent reality untouched by the transforming event of the resurrection. Creation has its beginning and its end in Jesus Christ because all things were made through him, and all things will reach their fulfillment in his coming again in glory. In the incarnation Jesus became a part of the created order, and in the resurrection creation was ordered toward God as its source of redemption. In other words, God redeems creation from the inside out. Everyone who is baptized into the paschal mystery is called to be good stewards of creation because in so doing they participate in the resurrection. We are not called only to view or treat creation as it is, but as it can be. Does our treatment of creation allow it to manifest the abiding newness of the resurrection? Do we deal with creation more in terms of death than of life? This question will be taken up in the section below on *lex vivendi*. I would now like to turn to *lex credendi*, and a broader discussion of the theological issues raised by the elucidation of the *lex orandi*.

Lex Credendi

The discussion of the references to creation in the eucharistic rites of the Episcopal Church was categorized in four ways. Two of those ways had to do with relationship: God's relationship to creation, and humanity's relationship to creation. Fundamental to a theology of creation and to our understanding of these relationships is the area of systematic theology known as nature and grace. The systematic theological exposition of the relationship between nature (and by this term I mean the whole created order) and grace gives shape to all subsequent discussions involving the way in which God relates to, or abides with, the creation. Such theological issues as creation's ability to manifest the divine, and the two natures and the one person of Christ fall within the broader context of nature and grace. I would now like to explore the relationship between nature and grace as it arises from the *lex orandi* presented above. Sometimes the line of demarcation between *theologia prima* and *theologia secunda* is a hazy one, but roughly, I propose to delve into *theologia secunda* that is hopefully faithful to the *theologia prima*.

There are different ways to portray the relationship between nature and grace: compatible but separate; opposition; identification; and fusion. Nature and grace can be viewed as two separate realms which we sometimes deem the natural and the supernatural. These realms are compatible in that grace can be conveyed through nature but in episodic ways or sacramental events. This was the scholastic way of understanding nature and grace and is known as extrinsecism or a two-story view whereby grace occupies the second floor and nature the first. In this schema nature can be viewed on its own terms and according to its own end, and hence the scholastic concept of *natura pura*. Grace is superimposed on nature giving it divine qualities and a supernatural end, and nature is used to convey grace within the sacramental ritual. However, in this sacramental economy the inherent signification of the natural object can be lost due to the myopic concern for the supernatural. For example, instead of the signification of bread as a product of creation and human labor one fixates on the supernatural content ("substance") of the eucharistic body of Christ to the point where it is no longer necessary or desirable to use real bread when a cultic wafer will do. Creation is rendered a backdrop for the supernatural dimension which always subsists "above" the natural order.

Another way to view the relationship between nature and grace with the attendant theological ramifications is to characterize nature and grace in terms of opposition. This is done by a rigid bifurcation between what is spiritual and what is material. The spiritual realm exists separate from the material similar to the compatible (extrinsecistic) approach, but here nature is something that gets in the way of grace. One is to encounter the supernatural in proportion to one's divestment of the natural. This type of approach to the relationship between nature and grace can be articulated in a monophysite Christology and in a sacramental economy whereby the spiritual is never directly related to the material. Zwingli and his receptionist view of eucharistic presence would serve as an example of an appraisal of nature and grace which holds the created order as intrinsically alien to the divine.

The third way by which nature and grace can be related is identification. Nature and grace are viewed as the same reality in that creation is the same reality as God, and therefore there can be no distinction between the natural and the supernatural. This identification can take two forms: pantheism which declares that God and creation are identical; and panentheism which holds that creation is a part of God but that there is more to God. The classical theological tension between immanence and transcendence is collapsed within the immanent while the approach described as opposition collapses the tension within the transcendence. The identification of nature and grace robs grace of its essential quality of giftedness in that there is no longer the necessary polarity of giver to receiver of the gift. Gratuity ceases when it does not operate in the freedom of love. The identification of God with creation whether it be pantheistic or panentheistic disallows the possibility of grace and redemption because how can God freely give to God, or how can God redeem God?

The fourth approach to the relationship between nature and grace, and the one which I contend is reflected by the *lex orandi*, may be characterized as fusion. By this I mean that nature is infused with grace so that nature cannot be viewed as devoid of grace. However, nature is not the same as grace, but all nature is graced in the sense that God's self-communication of love has so deeply touched the created order that it cannot be considered as a distinct reality with its own *telos*. This is what is being proclaimed in the *Sanctus*: "heaven and earth are full of your glory." The belief that all nature is "graced" is also expressed by the following: "we give thanks to you, O God, for the goodness and love which you have made known to us in creation" (Prayer B); and "you made all things and fill them with your blessing; you created them to rejoice in the splendor of your radiance" (Prayer D). Since all of nature is grace-filled and has the vocation to glorify God, there is no pure nature in the sense that it is understood in the compatibility approach outlined above. Yet, there is freedom in the created order to respond to or faithfully reflect the gift of the creator's loving presence. Humanity is entrusted with this freedom while it too dwells within the realm of grace which is both gift and responsibility. In order for creation to fulfill its vocation of the glorification of God's presence, humanity must live into its own God-given calling as co-creators. In other words, "From the primal elements you brought forth the human race, and blessed us with memory, reason, and skill. You made us the rulers of creation" (Prayer C). The fusion of nature and grace is the context for a mutuality between humanity and creation in that the recognition and nurture of the grace-filled creation by humanity is itself to recognize and nurture its own graced existence. When we care for the earth as God's gift we increase in the knowledge of our own giftedness.

It is in the sacramental life that the mutual vocations of creation and humanity find their fullest expression. The baptized who lead the sacramental life are the priests of creation in that they incorporate and offer the material as both manifestation and realization of the spiritual. It has been asserted above that the *lex orandi* of the Book of Common Prayer presents a view of creation as a manifestation of God's gracious favor (all nature is graced) so that creation itself signifies the presence of God. This means that what is material in this world carries its own signification into the sacramental economy, and that this "natural" signification participates in the reality which is realized in the sacramental event. Therefore, the celebration of the sacraments is not nor should be ritualized as a cultic escape or total transcendence from materiality because to do so would be to distort the baptismal vocation to be offerers of creation, and the vocation of creation to be sacramental. Consequently, sacramental theology is not to be done in any "otherworldly" way, but it is to be worked out within the fundamental structure of human existence which includes all of creation. Of course, sacramental celebrations do not simply proclaim the inherent grace of materiality. They also bring the material into the fuller realization of what the world is called to be at the end of history when all will be in all. This is why the sacramental life is redemptive and eschatological. When we recognize that creation is a manifestation of the glory of God, and when this recognition leads to stewardship; we are celebrating the sacrament of creation which draws us and creation more deeply into our life in Christ (redemption), and we are presented with a vision of what we and creation will become (eschatology).

The relationship between nature and grace, and the sacramentality of creation are dimensions of God's salvific movement toward creation. Another dimension would be the incarnation. The significance of the incarnation regarding the theme of this essay has already been touched upon in the exposition of the *lex orandi*. Particular attention was drawn to the phrases: "through Jesus Christ our Lord, the firstborn of all creation" (Prayer B)" and "rising from the grave, destroyed death, and made the whole creation new" (Prayer D). The point I would like to make regarding the incarnation and the redemption of creation is twofold. First, the incarnation is God's movement within creation in that the second person of the Trinity became a full participant within the created order. This means that creation itself, and everyday human existence, becomes the context for divine presence so that we may state that creatureliness is affirmed as a dimension of divine order. However, and secondly, this affirmation of creation by the incarnation—"the first born of all creation"—is not a negation of the continuing need for redemption, but the foundation for it. That is, God's identification with creation in the incarnation is not to be viewed as the consummation of the redemption of creation, but the beginning. The enfleshment of God is not to be interpreted as a divine recognition that the flesh or creation is whole and good in and of itself, but a divine act whereby flesh and creation can be made whole and good—"rising from the grave, destroyed death, and made the whole creation new." The incarnation is part of the redemptive continuum which includes crucifixion, resurrection, and the second coming of Christ in glory. Therefore, creation is to be understood as a place of divine immanence (incarnation); as having a fallen nature (crucifixion); as being brought to new life (resurrection); and as being transcended by what is beyond itself (second coming of Christ).

Lex Vivendi

Earlier in this study a series of questions were asked regarding the continuum *lex orandi*, *lex credendi*, and *lex vivendi* within the life of the church or worshiping community. Does a community believe what it prays, and does this belief lead the community to action which is adequate to this belief? Of course, this continuum is never a linear progression whereby one can discursively formulate an equation of prayer plus belief equals action. Prayer, belief, and action are in dynamic and mutual relationship to each other and one dimension of this relationship will never comprehend another because our prayer, belief, and action can never fully comprehend the reality of God in our lives. However, this does not let us off the *lex vivendi* hook. The eucharistic community is always called to live into what has been proclaimed and invoked in its worship, and this vocation is ongoing and eschatological—already and not yet. How then is the community which prays the eucharistic rites of the 1979 Book of Common Prayer to live out the theology which issues from this prayer?

In order to explicate the *lex vivendi* regarding creation we must look once again at the *lex orandi* which has yet to be discussed in the previous exposition of the eucharistic rites of the Book of Common Prayer. The *lex orandi* to which I refer is found within the Prayers of the People which make an overt link between what a community prays for, and how it should act on this invocation. The Prayers of the People of the Holy Eucharist, Rite I (also known as The Prayer for the Whole State of Christ's Church and the World) includes the following precatory section: "Open, O Lord, the eyes of all people to behold thy gracious hand in all thy works, that, rejoicing in thy whole creation, they may honor thee with their substance, and be faithful stewards of thy bounty." Here the members of the community pray that they will recognize God's pervasive grace in creation, and in so doing they will be led to glorify the creator. The glorification of God is to be lived out in self-offering and in stewardship which is faithful to the giftedness of creation. The movement from praise of God as creator to a petition for responsible care for creation is found in the other forms of the Prayers of the People which include a reference to creation (Forms 2 and 3 have no such reference). Two of these references which are similar to the Rite I petition are: "For the good earth which God has given us, and for the wisdom and will to conserve it"(Form 1);" and "Give us all a reverence for the earth as your own creation, that we might use its resources rightly in the service of others and to your honor and glory" (Form 4). When the eucharistic community takes the stewardship of the earth seriously, and takes concrete action toward ameliorating our present ecological crisis, it is giving glory to God. Glorifying God by prayer and action is to recognize the abiding symbiosis between orthodoxy and orthopraxis. It is to uphold *lex vivendi* as an optic through which to view the authenticity of a community's *lex orandi* and *lex credendi*.

The remaining inclusions of creation within the Prayers of the People are more explicit regarding the ramifications of proper stewardship of the earth. They are: "For a blessing upon all human labor, and for the right use of the riches of creation, that the world may be freed from poverty, famine, and disaster" (Form 5); and "for the just and proper use of creation; for the victims of hunger, fear, injustice, and oppression" (Form 6). These petitions contain a strong ethical mandate that human activity within the created order is no benign exercise but something that has a horizon of accountability which is the state of the human condition. The eucharistic community's (or the church's) stewardship of creation is judged by how this stewardship heals the brokenness which exists within humankind. This brokenness stems not from an impoverished creation in itself—there is not enough to go around—but from the way in which the giftedness of creation has been mediated by human action or inaction in freedom.

There are two foci that are presented by a consideration of the Prayers of the People: first, the care of creation because it is a gift from God which manifests God's glory and grace; and secondly, whether the utilization and distribution of creation serves to help alleviate hunger, poverty, and injustice. Here there is a reiteration of what was explicated above regarding the offering of creation by the baptized who are the priests of creation. The offering of creation in the eucharist is to evoke within the community the dimensions and the possibilities of the redemption of creation and of itself. These dimensions and possibilities are literally fleshed out in human lives, and are hinted at in the Prayers of the People which themselves are within the movement of offering. A church which fervently seeks to heal the brokenness of creation—the ecological crisis—is a church which is exercising its priesthood to the end that not only will creation be brought into the fullness of redemption, but so will the church. Perhaps then the church can give an affirmative answer to the thematic query of this essay: do we believe what we pray, and if we do, will we live out this belief?

Notes

1. There is a growing body of literature on liturgical theology, but the reader would be well served by Aidan Kavanagh's *On Liturgical Theology* (New York: Pueblo Publishing Co., 1984). Also, for a good introduction to some of the major writers on liturgical theology and a select bibliography of

11

Thomas Traherne:
The Gift of Friendship

A. MacDonald Allchin

WHEN I BEGAN TO CONSIDER SUITABLE TOPICS FOR A CONTRIBUTION TO THIS volume, my mind went at once to the seventeenth century. My earliest memories of Boone Porter, which go back almost forty years, are of a man fired with enthusiasm for the Anglican writers of that period. To meet such a person was for me an event. Most of my contemporaries dismissed the seventeenth-century Anglicans as simply irrelevant to contemporary needs; some regarded them with a distant and dutiful respect. For Boone they were of urgent importance. I still have a picture in my mind of waiting in a long slow queue in a college canteen while Boone expounded Jeremy Taylor's theology of the eucharistic consecration with vehement emphasis. So Thomas Traherne at once seemed a suitable subject.

But Traherne commended himself for another reason too. One of the most lasting impressions of Boone is of a celebration of the Paschal Vigil at which he presided and preached. It was in the chapel of General Theological Seminary during the 1960s. The sermon linked creation and resurrection, Genesis and Easter Day, in an unforgettable way. It was the body and the world of which the body is a part which were being raised into newness of life. This too is an emphasis we find in the pages of Traherne, this amazing visionary writer, so much of whose work remains unknown and unexplored. May this study contribute to bringing to light some of the riches of his meditation on the wonders of creation and something of his understanding of the way in which that creation can enter into the church's prayer.

In this study I shall speak of Traherne and friendship. Being unmarried, Traherne knew how particularly precious this gift is. Friendship had a very special place in his own life and in his understanding of the Christian faith. For those who respond to him, it is difficult to understand how it could be possible to know his work without feeling in some way bound to him in friendship. Elizabeth Jennings puts this very well when she speaks of Traherne's writings as "an accessible art."

> The poetic prose of Traherne's Centuries of Meditations is an example of the art of sharing, of participation. It is an art wholly accessible, in no way private . . . Traherne wears no masks, casts no concealing shadow. He is in the deepest sense a man possessed. What possesses him is a sense of God and this he wishes to share, to distribute. He gives himself away to us in such a way that his work "becomes our property, part of our life."[1]

It is important to remember that not all Traherne's readers react to him in this way. In recent years he has found critics, and severe ones. Perhaps in reaction to over-easy claims for his status as a mystic some have been inclined to question his very honesty as a man of faith. They have found him garrulous, superficial, repetitive, in the end even insincere. I quote Louis Bouyer in his volume in *The History of Christian Spirituality*:

> This never-ending Benedicite . . . does not benefit from being so repeatedly pressed home . . . We wonder how the perceptive author of Christian Ethics could have managed so successfully to ignore sin and suffering. This voluntary blindness coming from wilful innocence makes us suspect either his sincerity or his perception.[2]

What are we to say to such accusations? Many things, but perhaps first of all to remark that Traherne is commonly known through only one of his many writings. It may well be that in the end we shall find that *Centuries of Meditations* is the most perfect of his works. But it is still too early to say for sure since so much of his writing remains unpublished. But unquestionably the *Centuries* has a very special quality to it, a kind of radiant happiness, which while it is characteristic of all Traherne's writings is in a exceptional degree to be found here. Is this, we may ask, because of the very special quality of the friend to whom and for whom Traherne wrote it, as at once a universal and highly personal affirmation of faith and Love?

But as Louis Bouyer allows in part, there are other aspects of Traherne. There is the argumentative controversialist who wrote *Roman Forgeries*. There is the liturgically minded priest expounding the significance of the church's year in *The Church's Year Book*. There is the man of tireless intellectual quest who is revealed in the *Commentaries of Heaven*. There is the exponent of the Christian way of virtue who composed *Christian Ethics*. There is the young and ardent but sometimes anxious pastor whom we discover in the *Select Meditations*. All these go to make up the total Traherne, a man who had packed into his thirty-seven years much thought, much prayer, much study, much writing, and much love. To most of those who read him, it seems clear that he was a man of rare and original visionary capacity who writes in a style altogether his own. Yet I see no reason to doubt his integrity when in the foreword to *Christian Ethics* he insists on the total orthodoxy of his intentions. His most startling assertions are, at least in intention, meant to fill out and develop the commonly held positions of the Christian faith.

> Perhaps you will meet some new notions; but yet when they are examined the author hopes that it will appear to the reader that it was the actual knowledge of true felicity that taught him to speak of virtue; and moreover, that there is not the least tittle pertaining to the catholic faith contradicted or altered in these pages. For he firmly retains all that was established in the ancient Councils, nay, and sees cause to do so, even in the highest and most transcendent mysteries; only he enriches all, by further opening the grandeur and glory of religion, with the interior depths and beauties of faith.[3]

As Elizabeth Jennings wisely remarks:

> However childlike, carefree and original the Centuries appear on a first reading, they are nevertheless profoundly orthodox, and always firmly attached to scripture and Christian dogma. It is *because* Traherne is so acquiescent to Christian teaching that he *can* be so original. He has discovered that "service" which is "perfect freedom" . . .[4]

The original vision in no way distances itself from the tradition of the Christian centuries taken as a whole.

In this study I shall concentrate my attention on one of the earlier of Traherne's unpublished writings, the *Select Meditations*, to be found at present in the library at Yale. I shall be happy if I can give at least some impression of the Traherne to be found in its pages, a younger less secure but no less ardent figure than that to be found in the works of his maturity. It is a work which dates at least in part from the very beginning of the 1660s, the moment of the restoration of the monarchy, and it shows some signs of having been composed at Credenhill in the Herefordshire countryside, not least in the reflections on the little church amidst trees, one of the few passages from it to have been so far published.

At the outset I should like to underline a point that is made by Julia Smith about the way in which Traherne's works have come down to us. It is a point which shows that friendship had an important part in the production of his works no less than in their contents. In her article in *Profitable Wonders* Julia Smith points out that "although most of them [i.e., Traherne's manuscripts] are written in Traherne's own small, neat and easily legible hand, almost all of them contain the handwriting of other people, too." She identifies at least three people "closely involved in the production of the manuscripts, either collaborating with Traherne in composition, or copying large quantities of texts at his direction. Writing was obviously not a solitary activity for Traherne." It is this last point that I should like to stress. His writings were produced for his friends; they were also produced with the intimate collaboration of his friends. Of the *Select Meditations* in particular, Julia Smith judges:

> There are fairly clear indications that it is a fair copy made from an earlier draft . . . Traherne probably did not make this copy of his work himself, but there are a few short passages apparently written in his characteristic hand, so that at least he seems to have been associated with the production of the manuscript.[5]

One only has to look at what Traherne has to say about friendship in *Centuries*, in *The Church's Year Book*, and in the *Select Meditations*, to see for him how intimate a co-inherence is believed to exist between those who are linked in spiritual friendship. They live in one another, feel in one another, rejoice in one another. We release powers and capacities in one another which would otherwise remain dormant. It seems that for him, writing was not only or even primarily a solitary activity. It was also a social one.

Who were these friends? There is a tantalizing reference to them by initials in the *Select Meditations*.

> And cannot I here so love my friends! O my TG, O my SH, O my brother! Ye wise and holy sages! . . . O how am I superabundantly exalted in your exaltation! Keep yourselves, O my friends, in the light of God's countenance, in the midland territories of his holy kingdom and be sensible of his love and delight in his glory.[6]

Are we right, as many earlier commentators have done, to assume that my SH must be Mrs. Susannah Hopton? I think we do better, at least at present, to remain agnostic on that point, where we have no certain proof. We do not know who the circle of Traherne's friends were. We can be sure that there was such a circle. It is not irrelevant to notice that in the decade before 1660 a rather famous circle of friends had formed itself a little further west in Wales around one of the foremost women writers of the time, Mrs. Katharine Phillips, "the Matchless Orinda." High ideals of spiritual friendship, linking men and women in a shared companionship, were something new and exceptional in the mid-seventeenth century. They were not altogether unknown, and they were becoming better known.

I have said that Traherne revealed in the *Select Meditations* is at least at times a more anxious, less secure person than the writer of *Centuries*. He felt as a newly ordained priest a great impulse to intercede for his people, but he was afraid that he would soon weary of this work.

> O my God, I could be quickly weary, quickly weary both of repenting and of interceding. But thy love is the encourager of mine, the soul and strength that animates mine . . . O pardon my weakness who am made in thine image. Make me great in patience and compassion, and love to thee.[7]

It is interesting that he combines repentance with intercession in this way. Should we see here an influence of Jeremy Taylor with his great emphasis on the intercessory role of the pastor and his detailed teaching of repentance? There are other places where the theme of penitence is found, revealing a sense of sin not always associated with Traherne but expressed in a way that is characteristic of him.

> A broken and contrite heart is made up of knowledge, sorrow and love; knowledge of our primitive felicity in Eden. Sorrow for our fall, love to God so gracious and redeeming. Knowledge of

our happiness in being redeemed, sorrow for sin against our Redeemer, love to God yet continuing favorable and gracious. Knowledge of the joys prepared for us, sorrow for our unworthiness in living beneath them, love to God for his goodness, magnified and exalted over us.[8]

In another much more personal passage, Traherne explores further into the depths of penitence and despair, speaking of the gift of tears as a source of new life and understanding.

That which refresheth and reviveth me is that I have light now, wherein I may see the odiousness of sin and feel and fear my soul was parched till I knew my God, confounded and desolate till I could apprehend his glory and reverence him. He is a mighty and terrible one unto me. And it is my joy that it is so. The giver of all treasures and the just exacter of all obedience. My soul was never a fountain of living waters till it was filled with fear and the tears of repentance. It was a dry and broken cistern, a parched well till he was known; till grief itself and mourning did revive it. When it toucheth the center of hell with despair, it reacheth unto the throne of God with the eye of hope, and is made what it ought [to be], wide and profound. I had rather roar by reason of the disquietness of my guilty heart, while I have God in my presence, than rejoice with kings, where sincerity and truth and God is absent.[9]

But if there are sign of Traherne the penitent in these pages, there are also frequent signs of Traherne the visionary. I quote three brief passages, two of which refer to the gospel narratives and one to the daily experience of life in a region where timber-framed houses are the rule. All three reveal Traherne's amazing power of seeing familiar things in an unfamiliar light. It is interesting that both gospel passages refer to the humility of Jesus. The first passage is:

O my soul, Jesus when he was upon earth washed feet. Little things are made infinitely rich by love alone. Snatch the occasion, become divine . . .[10]

The second passage:

There be many things wherein the modesty of man is an injurious counterfeit. Not modesty but ignorance, ingratitude, and thralldom, for such is that that is afraid to acknowledge the benefits of God and unwilling to perceive the good it hath received. Had I said that the Son of Man while we sit down will gird himself and come forth to serve us, I should have been accused by men to have spoken blasphemy. But now he has said it, it is believed; but hastily, passed over and not understood, yea, many read that take not notice he spake any such thing.[11]

And the third passage:

> O what a glorious place this must be; where God is so daily present. He is not more frequent among all the angels than he is with us. I do not see a carter on the road, nor a carpenter building a little cottage but in the light of heaven they are before mine eyes. Deep mysteries are beneath the surface of common works; this also cometh from the Lord of hosts who is wonderful in counsel and excellent in working.[12]

It is difficult to see in *Select Meditations* so clear a pattern of themes as in *Centuries*. The paragraphs are more uneven in length, in character, and in quality. If as the title suggests they are only selected from a larger collection, then it is possible that their writing may have extended over a period of years. However, two of the most striking and certainly from the theological point of view the most fascinating passages have to do with the recognition of the divine image within us. The first speaks of a personal experience of the light of God within, in a way as eloquent and powerful as anything to be found in Traherne's already published works. Here he speaks of the comprehension of the soul, a word that needs to be understood actively, of the power or capacity of the soul not only to understand but also to gather together into one and include the whole of God's creation within the littleness of a human life. This power is present in us solely because of our creation in the image and likeness of the infinite and eternal God.

> This endless comprehension of my immortal soul when I first saw it, so wholly ravished and transported my spirit, that for a fortnight after I could scarcely think or speak or write of any other thing. But like a man doting with delight and ecstasy, talk of it night and day as if all the joy of heaven and earth were shut up in it. For in very deed there I saw the divine image relucent and shining. There I saw the foundation of man's excellency and that which made him a son of God. Nor shall I ever be able to forget its glory. I can comprehend in my understanding the magnitude of a room, the wideness of the hemisphere and spaces extant above the stars. The heaven of heavens are not able to contain me, for my soul exceedeth all limitations. It is so like God almighty that it comprehendeth the heavens as the dust of a balance spanneth the world, seeth all ages as one day, sumounteth the heavens and searcheth further . . .[13]

In this passage Traherne speaks of a vision of the divine image shining out, relucent at the heart of the human person. He realizes vividly the presence and power of God within, mirrored in the human heart. And knowing himself to be so like God, to share in God's own power in gathering all together into one, he finds that he himself can contain the creation within himself.

The understanding of the unity and coherence of creation which this vision contains is not simply the recovery of a childhood vision of a transfigured world. It is strictly cosmo-theandric vision, which holds together God, humankind, and the whole creation. Traherne can comprehend the whole, gathered together into one, because he finds within himself a God-like capacity to know and love. In the beginning God saw all that he had made and behold it was very good. So when human persons learn to see with the eyes of God, they can see all things in the same original goodness and beauty of the divine creative act. This unity of God, world, and humankind, held together in a single focus, is basic to the whole of Traherne's understanding of life. It has been expressed through the Christian centuries in a variety of ways. One very striking expression of it is to be found in the *Dialogues* of Gregory the Great, where he is describing the life of St. Benedict. Here in the experience of Benedict the light of God is seen shining from above rather than from within but the content of the vision is strangely similar and all-inclusive.

> The man of God was standing at his window, where he watched and prayed while the rest were still asleep. In the dead of night he suddenly beheld a flood of light shining down from above more brilliant than the sun, and with it every trace of darkness cleared away . . . The whole world was gathered up before his eyes in what appeared to be a single ray of light.

Gregory comments:

> The light of holy contemplation enlarges and expands the mind in God until it stands above the world. In fact the soul that sees Him rises even above itself, and as it is drawn upwards in his light, all its inner powers unfold.[14]

It is interesting that this particular passage was to be quoted and expounded by the greatest theologian of the Byzantine Middle Ages, St. Gregory Palamas. It speaks of an experience central to east and west alike. This enlargement and expansion of the mind in God, this unfolding of the inner powers, is something of which Traherne is telling us, something of which he had almost overwhelming inner experience. In the light of God's creative and redemptive love all things hold together, the whole creation is seen as in a single ray of light. The human soul is drawn up into the very activity of God.

What is so striking in the vision of St. Benedict is that creation in its fullness is present within this vision of the divine light. We know God through his creation as well as beyond it. But we also know creation as a unity in and through the light of God. In both Benedict and Traherne all three elements in the complex term "cosmo-theandric" are held together in balance and harmony; but as we know in much western spirituality, both Catholic and Protestant, in more recent centuries, the element of creation seems to have been eclipsed, apparently left out. The present vogue for creation-centered spiritualities is a natural and not unexpected reaction to this situation in which the universe seems to have been set aside from the drama of the divine-human interchange with God. One of the great attractions of Traherne is that he speaks to this situation with such authority. He can help us restore our equilibrium, to find a God-centered spirituality in which humankind and all creation have their rightful place.

It is precisely of this fulfillment that Traherne speaks in another of the key passages in *Select Meditations*. This is one of the rare occasions when he directly criticizes the theological schools in which he had been brought up, and he criticizes them precisely because they have not taken seriously enough the abilities and capacities of the human person, our potential for free creativity in the pattern of God's creativity. Nor have they recognized how necessary it is that we should arrive at the gifts of creation which God himself has given us. By trying to go straight to the mystery of God in himself, without being willing to go through the mysteries of his creation, to go as the Greek Fathers would have put it, to *theologia* without going through *theoria physike*, they have arrived at their goal too soon, too suddenly. They apprehend things in too shallow a way.

But we will let Traherne speak for himself in a passage full of beautiful imagery whose interpretation I feel I have only begun to explore.

> To satisfy his nature he [God] would make his image; concerning which image the divines and schoolmen have apprehended too short and spoken superficially. They tread over a living river to the other side, and leave all that which should revive the grass and cherish the trees and make the shore to flourish, behind them. Bounty follows the nature of God, as light doth the sun, as a shadow its body. Being therefore infinitely bountiful, he is

infinitely willing to give all things, and that he may do so in the most perfect manner, creates his image to give it unto, which image they tell us consisteth in righteousness and true holiness, but for want of drinking that river I spoke of, diminish the beauty and glory of the shore by arriving at it too suddenly. They are silent in this, that man is made after God's image in respect of ability, capacity and power, and because I never had the happiness of seeing it, I knew not the glory of the divine image, nor the beauty of holiness nor the excellent nature of the righteousness unto which it was made. Nor did I see the reason of God's ways, nor the greatness of his love. Being infinite in bounty and willing to make his image, he made a creature like him, to behold all ages and to love the goodness of every being in all eternity, and of every excellence in every being, that by seeing it might receive, and enjoy by loving all the things in heaven and earth, and be as God himself who enjoyeth all by seeing and loving them. His works being made thus the image of God in similitude of power and infinitely beloved, God desireth his friend or son should use these powers, apply his mind to the beauty of all his ways and render all things a due esteem, loving the goodness which therein is seated.[15]

The river here recalls the river of the water of life which Ezekiel saw flowing out from under the threshold of the temple; the water of life which flows again in the Book of Revelation. It is a river which brings life to the grass and the trees on its banks and which nourishes the fish and living creatures within it. It is an image of the energy of God seen as his unbounded bounty, which follows directly on his nature. Creation and redemption alike flow out from the heart of God as the river flows out from the temple. A great preacher from the late eighteenth century in Wales, one of the foremost leaders of Welsh Methodism, Thomas Jones of Denbigh, also sees the bounty of God in terms of the river of life which flows out from the temple.

> Salvation in Christ is a feast and it is also a river, a river of virtue and strength. In it the frail believer has all the promises of God and all the properties of God, all that God has and all that God is as a living water to quench his thirst, and a strongly flowing stream which carries him on its current to the sea of his endless delight . . . Let your whole spirit unite with it, swim in it, drink from it, take it as your life and your nourishment.[16]

With Thomas Jones the thought is primarily that of our redemption in Christ, though the revelation of God in creation is by no means excluded as we can see from his eloquent meditations on that subject. With Traherne the primary emphasis is on the gift of God in creation, but gratitude for the work of redemption is never far from his mind. Both writers are insisting that we should immerse ourselves in the living stream of God's creative and redemptive bounty, and that we should allow the divine image to activate our own latent, unused powers and capacities. God gives all this bounty to the one whom he has made in his image and likeness, to his human creature who he has made to be his friend; gives it to his friend to enjoy, to esteem, to develop, to transform. He has put into humankind the image of his own ability, capacity, and power. Hence it is that human beings are to receive and enjoy all things in heaven and on earth, seeing and loving them as God sees and loves them. God desires that his friends, his sons and daughters, should use their powers actively, should apply their minds to the beauty of all his ways in creation and redemption alike. They should render to all things their due esteem, loving the goodness which is to be found within them all. Here indeed is Traherne's prescription for a full and happy human life on earth, the life which he himself lived with such energetic generosity. Here is the realization of the content of the image, the powers and capacities which bring us through the waters of the river whose streams make glad the city of God, to discover the true beauty of holiness, the fullness of the divine righteousness.

It is not surprising that one whose heart and mind was teeming with such thoughts and perceptions should at times have felt himself cut off from the daily concerns of the world around him. The one who is set on fire by the vision of God's love may, like the artist who is drunk with a vision of the world's beauty, sometimes finds it difficult to reconcile the demands of the inner life with the ordinary conventions of society. So Traherne exclaims:

> How happy thou hast made me, O God, in making me to love! A divine and spiritual lover is a wonderful great and unknown creature. A strange being here upon earth; an image of the deity in the wilderness, a disguised prince walking incognito among foreign people, unknown, unseen, incredible, exceeding great but very little, exceeding rich yet very poor, exceeding high yet very low, exceeding beautiful yet invisible, exceeding divine yet not valued.[17]

So as he walked about his parish and found that many of his parishioners were hardly able to respond to the intensity of his vision, he felt himself "a disguised prince walking incognito among a foreign people."

So all the more he valued those of his friends who could and did resonate to his vision of human life caught up into the very life of God.

> O my TG, O my SH, O my brother! Ye wise and holy sages! That see a little and understand your glory, ye are treasures unto me greater than the world, ye who are exalted in the glory of the Father and of his Son, Jesus Christ, by the love and ministry of all angels and all ages, and by the subservient ministry of all the world . . .[18]

At times one may feel that this was an over-exalted view of friendship, in which human persons are simply lost in a kind of Trinitarian exchange of love. "O give me more of the Spirit, whereby we strongly love and delight in each other, whereby we love in each other's soul and feel our joys and sorrows! . . . We are greater treasures than the world to each other. We are flames and lights and thrones to each other. In either the sun serveth us again; in either angels minister . . ." (there is a break in the manuscript here).[19] He wants only to love his friends in God and to love God in his friends. He prays: "with him let me walk as my eternal friend, and daily be engaged in those employments that will most delight him; my friends should relish me with a contiguous feeling . . ."[20] If indeed it was around Susannah Hopton that this group of ardent young disciples formed itself, it is moving to consider that more than forty years later, long after Traherne's death, they were still concerned to publish and make known his writings.

This understanding of friendship, though in one sense it was doubtless restricted to a few, was of course in principle, open to all. God is our friend, the friend of all his creatures, not only of those who are able to respond to him with a particular kind of directness. We can see signs of a further reflection on this theme of our co-inherence with one another in the Whitsun meditations in the *Church's Year Book*, where one of the greatest gifts of the Spirit to the church as a whole is seen in our being drawn together in mutual love in him.

> By communicating ourselves we fill others, by filling others we live in them, by living in them we feel in them, see and enjoy whatever they have and are. So dwelling in each other the Holy Ghost dwelleth in both, enjoying both and making both a benefit to the other.[21]

When we come to *Christian Ethics*, published in 1675, it seems as though the theme of friendship had become more commonly accepted and acknowledged than it was in the first years of the Restoration. "There is great talk of friendship" writes Traherne, as though it had become a common topic of conversation and inquiry.

> It is accounted the only pleasure in the world. Its offices are highly magnified of all; kindness of behaviour, a thorough and clear communion of souls, a secure reliance upon each other's fidelity, a perfect discovery of all our thoughts, intentions and resentments, an ardent willingness to impart lives and estate for the benefit of our friends . . . these are the *magnalia amicitiae et arcana mutuae benevolentiae*, the great and mighty effects for which friendship is admired.

But, Traherne says, these are only the externals of friendship, and he goes on to speak of an inner spiritual relationship almost in terms of the *Select Meditations*. But now he is ready to allow that such friendship is hardly to be found here below. "There are some slight aims and adumbrations of this friendship on earth, but the best and highest degree of it here beneath is but a rude and imperfect shadow. Only God is the sovereign friend."[22] It is in God that we must find our friends. It is in our friends that we are to find God.

Traherne then, we may conclude, was a man who was a profound lover of solitude and at the same time a profound lover of communion. The two things, far from being in conflict with one another, in fact supported and strengthened one another. The man who writes "in my close retirements I was some years as though nobody but I had been in the world . . . And I had nothing to do but walk with God as if there had been no one but he and I,"[23] is the same man who can say "Thou Lord hast made thy servant a sociable creature, for which I praise thy name; a lover of company, a delighter in equals. Replenish the inclination which thou thyself hast implanted."[24] That inclination to share himself freely with his friends was at the very center of his being. It is that which we meet in his writings and which makes them for us and for so many others an accessible art, a common possession.

Notes

1. Elizabeth Jennings, *Every Changing Shape* (London: Dent, 1961) 83-84.
2. Louis Bouyer, *Orthodox Spirituality and Protestant and Anglican Spirituality* (London: Sheed and Ward, 1969) 132-133.

3. Thomas Traherne, *The Way to Blessedness* (London: Faith Press, 1962) 19.

4. Jennings, *Every Changing Shape* 93.

5. Julia Smith, "Traherne in His Unpublished Manuscripts," in *Profitable Wonders: Aspects of Thomas Traherne* (Wilton, CT: Morehouse, 1989) 40.

6. *Select Meditations* II 38. Taken from the unpublished manuscript in the Beinecke Library at Yale University, by kind permission of the Curator of the Osborn Collection. I have modernized the spelling.

7. Ibid. I 84.

8. Ibid. I 93.

9. Ibid. III 21.

10. Ibid. III 56.

11. Ibid. II 67.

12. Ibid. III 20.

13. Ibid. IV 2.

14. Benedicta Ward, "Gregory the Great" in *The Study of Spirituality*, ed. C. Jones, G. Wainwright, and E. Yarnold (London: S.P.C.K., 1986) 279.

15. *Select Meditations* III 43.

16. Thomas Jones of Denbigh in *Trysorfa Ysprydol*, Book I, No. 5 (Hydref, 1800) 260; translated by the Rev. Paul Quinn.

17. *Select Meditations* II 64.

18. Ibid. II 38.

19. Ibid. II 72 and 73.

20. Ibid. II 99.

21. *The Church's Book*, Bodleian Library ms. Eng.th.c.51; see *Landscapes of Glory*, ed. A.M. Allchin (Wilton, CT: Morehouse, 1989) 38.

22. Ibid. 133.

23. *Select Meditations* III 69.

24. Allchin, *Landscapes of Glory* 40.

Lex Vivendi:
Creation and the Life
of the Church

12

The First Article
in the Eucharistic Lectionary

Reginald H. Fuller

ONE OF THE DELIGHTS OF *THE LIVING CHURCH* UNDER THE LEADERSHIP OF OUR honoree was his editorial essays on "The First Article"—that is, the first paragraph in the Creed, which affirms God as the creator of the universe and the source of all life. Like many others, Canon Porter has expressed dissatisfaction with the three-year eucharistic lectionary. It would seem to concentrate too exclusively on the second article, geared as it is to the gospel readings, not only during the festival seasons, but also in ordinary time. One aspect of this dissatisfaction is that the Hebrew Scriptures are never allowed to speak for themselves but, with the partial exception of the Sundays in Lent, treated as types of prophecies of the Christ event.

The *Common Lectionary* has been an attempt to meet some of these criticisms. During the season of ordinary time it provided minicourses on Old Testament themes, such as creation, wisdom, and divine providence. For a while the Episcopal Church permitted the experimental use of the first edition *Common Lectionary*, on a restricted basis, but later withdrew the permission. So we are left as we were before, with an apparently inadequate coverage of the First Article.

It may be worth enquiring what provision the Prayer Book lectionary actually does make to feature the theme of creation. Let us start with those occasions when the P story of creation (Gn 1:1-2:3) is read. It occurs twice in the eucharistic lectionary, at the Easter Vigil and on Trinity Sunday. On those occasions, however, other themes are predominant, the Easter event and the doctrine of the Trinity. It is unlikely that any homilist would preach a sermon on creation at either occasion. In addition, Genesis 1 is read in the office lectionary on Epiphany 1 in Year 2. But the office lectionary is rarely used in parishes on Sundays, and in any case the theme of the baptism of our Lord is the paramount concern of that day.

This is by no means a new problem, either in Anglicanism or in Western Christendom as a whole. There has never been any Sunday or season with the theme of creation as its primary concern. However, the 1662 Prayer Book did appoint Genesis 1 to be read at Morning Prayer on Septuagesima Sunday, and this provision colored the whole of that day. There is a reference to this in our present Prayer Book. In the section entitled "Historical Documents" (page 866) we read from Cranmer's Preface to the first English Prayer Book of 1549 the following words: "and in this sort the book of Isaiah was begun in Advent, and the book of Genesis in Septuagesima; but they were only begun, and never read through." Thus Cranmer, following earlier precedent, retained Genesis 1 and 2 for Septuagesina Sunday, and continued the reading of Genesis thereafter. Due to the fact that Mattins, Litany, and Ante-Communion were read as one service, the reading from Genesis provided the theme for the whole day. Thus John Keble's poem for the day in *The Christian Year* is a poem about the sacramental nature of the created order. At the top of the poem he quotes Romans 1:20: "The invisible things of Him from the creation of the world are clearly seen, being understood by the things which are made." The first two stanzas and the last are worth quoting:

> There is a book, who runs may read,
> Which heavenly truth imparts,
> And all the lore its scholars need,
> Pure eyes and Christian hearts.

> The works of God above, below,
> Within us and around,
> Are pages in that book, to shew
> How God Himself is found.

> ＊ ＊ ＊ ＊ ＊ ＊

> Thou, who has given me eyes to see
> And love this sight so fair,
> Give me a heart to find out Thee,
> And read Thee everywhere.

That poem, or most of its verses, set to the tune of St. Flavian, is very familiar in other Anglican churches. It was widely used on Septuagesima Sunday, which served as a celebration of God and his creation. In the twenties, when I sang as a boy in a Church of England choir, we always sang Keble's hymn, along with other hymns about creation, such as Joseph Addison's "The spacious firmament on high" (Hymnal 1982, #409), and Walter Chalmers Smith's "Immortal, invisible" (Hymnal 1982, #423). Our anthem at Evensong on Septuagesima Sunday would always be "The heavens are telling" from Haydn's *Creation*. When I came to the United States in the mid-fifties I found that all these associations of creation with Septuagesima were lacking. Genesis 1 had been shifted to Morning Prayer on the Monday after, and the themes of the Sunday itself were based exclusively on the eucharistic Propers. The Epistle of the day was 1 Corinthians 9:24ff. and the Gospel Matthew 20:1ff. The themes were those of running the race, working hard, and fighting the good fight. The hymns chosen reflected these themes, resulting in what I could only regard as an orgy of ecclesiastical militarism.

All this has now gone by the board in the new Prayer Books. The pre-Lent Sundays have disappeared. On the whole this is a gain. The Epiphany Season has been extended, and in the American Prayer Book culminates in a celebration of the Lord's Transfiguration, an admirable climax to the Epiphany, and a fine introduction to our Lenten pilgrimage up to Jerusalem. In the Alternative Service Book of the Church of England (1980) the Gesima Sundays have also disappeared, but provisions has been made for a new "Creation Sunday" on their "ninth Sunday before Christmas." In Year I the eucharistic lectionary appoints Genesis 1, Colossians 1:15-20, and John 1:1-14, while Year 2 has Genesis 2:4ff. and Revelation 4 (the gospel this time has a different focus, John 3:1-8). There is nothing like this in the three-year eucharistic lectionary of the 1979 Prayer Book.

What then is to be done about creation with the three-year lectionary? As we have seen, Genesis 1 gives us no help. One of the new features (actually it is a much older tradition revived) is the provision of three "eschatological" Sundays at the end of the Church Year. Together with the first Sunday of Advent, these Sundays feature the following themes: the Day of the Lord, the final Advent of God himself, the Parousia of Christ, the general resurrection and the last judgment. It used to be the tradition to preach during Advent on the so-called "Last Things": heaven, hell, death, and judgment. Some may be tempted to revive this kind of thematic preaching on the last three Sundays of the Church Year and the first Sunday of Advent. The trouble with this fourfold scheme of the Last Things is that, scriptural though they are, they were usually treated in a highly individualistic fashion. Heaven was the destiny of the individual after death, or its alternative, hell. It was the death of the individual, and the individual's judgment after death that was envisioned.

During this century, however, there has been a revolution in our understanding of eschatology. Johannes Weiss and Albert Schweitzer first showed that the whole of the New Testament is shot through with eschatology. It was not confined simply to the End but decisively determined the present. Rudolf Bultmann demythologized eschatology in existential terms. God's eschatological future confronts the individual again and again in the preaching of the word and demands a decision for authentic existence. This individualistic interpretation (it was often called "anthropological") proved to be a temporary detour. One of Bultmann's students, Ernst Käsemann, criticized Bultmann's existential and anthropological interpretation of eschatology precisely because of its individualism. Käsemann insisted on the historical and social dimensions of eschatology. The future was not just a reality constantly ahead of the individual. It involved the consummation of all human history and the final redemption of humanity. History is to come to an end in the Kingdom of God in which the redeemed share Christ's kingly rule. Käsemann's critique of Bultmann's individualism has been carried further by Jürgen Moltmann. For this younger scholar, the apocalyptic eschatology of the New Testament has a cosmic dimension, as well as a historical and social one. The Bible speaks not only of the consummation of human history in the Day of the Lord, or of the general resurrection of humankind. It speaks also of a new creation, a new heaven and a new earth.

I would suggest that it is here that we have the opportunity to preach about creation, and to do so in a way which is highly relevant to our present needs. There is one reading in the three-year lectionary which highlights the cosmic dimensions of eschatology in a remarkable way. This is Colossians 1:11-20, which is appointed for the last Sunday of Year C (Proper 29). This reading includes the great Christological hymn (vv. 15-18 unfortunately not printed as a hymn in NRSV). This hymn speaks of the second person of the Trinity as the firstborn, both of the original creation, and of the redeemed creation inaugurated through the Easter event. The hymn reads as follows:

> He is the image of the invisible God,
>> the firstborn of all creation;
> for in him all things in heaven and on earth were created,
>> things visible and invisible,
> whether thrones or dominions or rulers or powers—
>> all things have been created through him and for him.
> He himself is before all things,
>> and in him all things hold together.
> He is the head of the body, the church;
>> he is the beginning, the firstborn from the dead.

This hymn is an extension of an earlier hymn which presented wisdom as the agent of creation. God's created wisdom became incarnate in Jesus. He died the death to which all creation was subject (see Rom 8:18-25, the Old Testament reading for Proper 11A). His resurrection was not just an individual event. Nor was it merely the survival of his immortal soul. He was raised as the firstborn of all creation and therefore his resurrection was a resurrection of the body. It was not just a mere resuscitation of the body but its transformation and glorification. The crucial role played by the resurrection of Christ in the eschatological process is attested by the reading from the New Testament appointed for the last Sunday of Year A (Proper 29A) namely 1 Corinthians 15:20-28. This sets out four major stages in the eschatological process: (1) the resurrection of Christ as the firstfruits; (2) the parousia and the resurrection of those who belong to Christ; (3) the end, marked by the cosmic triumph of Christ and the subjection of all things to him; (4) the subjection of the Son to the Father, so that God will become "all in all"—i.e., the final achievement of his purpose in a new heaven and a new earth.

These two readings from Colossians 1 and 1 Corinthians 15 are pivotal to the last Sundays of the Church Year and to the first Sunday of Advent. They make it clear that the eschatological hope is not intended merely for the individual believer. It is a hope for the whole people of God, for the whole of humanity, and for the whole of creation, which is to be transformed and renewed in Christ. The Easter event, the bodily resurrection of Christ, is the sign and pledge of that transformation.

Recent study of biblical eschatology (see Moltmann, 1990) has further insisted that this future hope necessitates present praxis. The believing and hoping people of God is subject to "the pull of the future." The prospect of a new heaven and a new earth impels the community to erect signs in advance of that future hope. These signs occur in its struggles for social justice and for the reconciliation of peoples, and for the healing and the recovery of the created environment from ecological disaster.

The three-year lectionary certainly lacks a Sunday or season devoted to the theme of creation, such as the 1662 Prayer Book made possible through its office lectionary, or such as the Alternative Service Book of the Church of England provides for the ninth Sunday before Christmas in its Calendar. But the eschatological Sundays and the 1st Sunday of Advent provide a splendid opportunity to treat the theme of the new creation, thus the lectionary sets its concern for the first article, to which our honoree has devoted so much attention, but in the context of the second and third articles.

Bibliography

Ernst Käsemann, "On the Subject of Primitive Christian Apocalyptic" in *New Testament Questions of Today* (London: SCM, 1969) 108-137.

Jürgen Moltmann, *The Way of Jesus Christ: Christology in Messianic Dimensions* (New York: Harper-Collins, 1990).

13

Liturgy, Stewardship, and Creation

Nathan Wright

Foundations

Initial Definitions

THE TERM LITURGY, AS EMPLOYED IN THIS DISCUSSION, IS THE SHARED OR cooperative work of all creation, including—in a uniquely facilitating way—those who see themselves as "the people of God." In its more specialized sense, as in public worship, the term liturgy denotes the ongoing and re-energizing formal celebration by God's people of the collective work of all of life's creatures and created things.

Stewardship is literally the role of being a steward, that is, one who stands in for or who serves on behalf of the interests of another. Essentially stewardship is adverbial, in that it reflects or represents the manner in which—or the trust with which—we handle the work which is given to us to undertake in a vicarious or representative way. In this construction, since we must all give an account of the stewardship of our part in life's liturgy, stewardship and liturgy may be seen to be intertwined or interrelated in much the same sense as an adverb is to a verbal decree or command. Thus, when the Gospels tell us to "Go," that is a declarative statement or a proclamation of what our liturgy is, of what we are to do. As we hear in our spirits the repeated words "Well done!", we may sense that our stewardship proceeds with a growing, ripening trust.

If we may follow the pattern of *liturgy* as being the verbal declaration of *what* God wills for us in life and of *stewardship* as being the adverbial representation of *how* we respond to God's will, then the term *creation* would be seen as representing at least the *why* in this three-part equation. To what end or purpose are we to be engaged in liturgy,—i.e., to be seeking for and fulfilling the divine work which, according to the Scriptures, is assigned to us? A richly suggestive answer is afforded us in the reported dialogue between Jesus and Pilate.

> Jesus said, "My kingdom is not of this world . . . But now my kingdom is from another place."
> "You are a king, then!" said Pilate.
> Jesus answered, "You are right in saying I am a king. In fact, for this reason I was born, and for this I came into the world, to testify to the truth. Everyone on the side of the truth listens to me."
> "What is truth?" Pilate asked. With this he went out again to the Jews and said, "I find no basis for a charge against him." (Jn 18:36-38; New International Version)

Three elements of purpose are evident here which relate to the process of creation, enabling us to make the tentative definition which immediately follows. *Creation* is the fitting of life in the present for three ever-present and continually attainable experiences or conditions, in an infinite variety of forms and in every circumstance we may face in life.

Key Elements of Creation

In the above dialogue between Jesus and Pilate, the elements of (1) royalty or dominion, (2) the unfolding of, or growth into, truth, and (3) eternity, or life in its fullness or comprehensiveness on the eternal plane, are set forth, although not in this same order.

1. *Kingship and Dominion.* The attribution by Jesus, to himself, of royalty suggests that life in all its forms and in every circumstance is to be lived with a sense of victory and dominion, as—or since—all creation is an outworking or an evidence of that which is in essence eternally perfect and divine. Indeed, "for this reason [were we] born [or brought into being]." It would follow from what is stated here that life's highest purpose is to be enabled to reign and to find fulfillment

or, as we shall prefer, *dominion*. The ancient Greek philosopher Aristotle (384-322B.C.) who may be held, in some constructions, to be a kind of pre-Christian "saint" in regard to the breadth of beneficent vision and magnitude of intellect, pre-saged the thought of Jesus in this regard. In Aristotle's classic statement of the human purpose, he held that "What a thing *will be*, that it [already] *is*, whether a horse or a man." By this it is suggested that when we relate to any person, creature, or created thing, we are not to deal with such reality in terms of what we immediately see, i.e., existentially. Rather, we are to deal with all of creation's handiwork envisioning as best possible what may have been the purpose which its creator had in mind. We picture for all of life its highest and noblest state of being, and then in all of our relations with that life we work to facilitate the fulfillment of creation's envisioned plan. Such a process is what is meant by enablement or empowerment. We are to see in all of life God's life, mind, and hand. Then we are to help bring those aspects of divine life which we see into their fullest expression. Such is, in part at least, the process of creation—or of continual re-creation—which seeks to restore all things according to the Creator's pristine and perfect plan.

2. *Truth or Growth*. In his brief conversation with Pilate, Jesus speaks of himself as an exemplification and exponent of truth. Elsewhere Jesus says more plainly: "I am the Way, the Truth, and the Life. No one comes to the Father but by me" (Jn 14:6). Here Way, Truth, and Life are seen essentially as one, or at least as three personifications of one divine reality. Creation here may be inferred as knowing, or as ongoing growth into the unfolding will, realities, and mind of God. Pilate's unanswered question, "What is truth?" suggests the open-endedness of the reality of truth, which in the purely human experience is never fully known. Truth itself is experience, and ultimately it is to know God completely and to comprehend in their infinities the complex workings of God's universe. Small wonder that in Old Testament days God's face was always hidden! When truth comes to us, we know more of God and of God's inmost workings; indeed, we find ourselves standing on no less than holy ground.

My own father was strengthened immeasurably in his spiritual life by his working in the agricultural laboratory at Tuskegee Institute in Alabama with George Washington Carver. In practically all of the recountings of the work of famous scientists, there is evidence of a profound and reverential regard for the uncovering of life's truths.

With George Washington Carver, however, his science reached in the most remarkable way the level of piety brought to mind by Jesus when he attributed to himself the exemplification and revealed embodiment of truth. Dr. Carver's belief was in effect "God placed it there; God will show the way." To him scientific discovery was like the outworking of a prayer. It was like the opening of the diary of God's work. It was essentially an entering into the heartbeat and the handiwork of God.

In such a sense, creation's work is the relentless unfolding of God's mind and being; and in our successive experiences of entering into God's life and work we grow. The difference between the godly and the godless thus is that the ungodly seek to simply "go" through life while the godly seek to "grow." We come now to see creation as including the facilitation of growth into a fuller comprehension of God's truths—of discerning God's mind, heart, and presence in and through all persons, creatures, and created things.

Poetically, it may be put this way:

> We genuflect, or bow the knee,
>   At each God entity we see.

Eternity, Comprehensiveness (or an All-Inclusive-Consciousness)

In the brief conversation between Jesus and Pilate, Jesus states: "My kingdom is from another place." The King James version uses the term "realm" for place, implying or signifying a domain of power and influence, in this case being the eternal realm of spirit. This speech construction would probably have confounded Pilate, even as it would often tend to be sensed as somewhat esoteric today. With no results of any current survey of religious beliefs concerning the realm of the spirit before me, I state with some sense of dismay that in most of my own recent interim work experiences with bereaved families, there have been only scant evidences of anything other than the utter finality of life in every sense but memory, once physical death occurs. That this should be the case among Christians, even in a small degree, cuts at the heart of our common faith and experiences of God, for "To know thee, the only true God, and Jesus Christ whom thou has sent, this is eternal life" (Jn 17:3). Jesus thus positions himself as a representative and an embodiment of the eternal world, which is the spiritual atmosphere or area of life in which we as Christians are called to live and begin to make our never-ending home. The process of creation for Christians, even as it should come to be for the world at large, involves the patterning of our lives so that—as a popular song of the 1960s set forth—"on a clear day we can see forever."

The longest range view of life is the view of and into eternity. It is the only life scenario where all things are guaranteed to turn out well. It will take that kind of perspective to enable us, in every circumstance we may face, to "let patience have its perfect work" (Jas 1:4). Perhaps more importantly, our grasp of the oneness of creation, our understanding of the language of the constellations of the stars and the messages of the movements of the mountains and the seas, including what is in, above, and under them—and vice versa—does not represent a merely overnight experience. To be, in every sense, "in tune with the infinite" takes more than time. It takes an all-inclusive vision of reality, including the experience both of time (in all of its limited vastness) and of eternity (with its absolute unlimitedness) into which we must begin to enter at some present point or not at all. It is creation's goal to fit all of life for life's all-inclusive and longest lasting prize.

We may be helped at this point by a word concerning the ever-evolving language of our faith, and so also of our faith statements. The language of faith must always be, in some substantial degree, poetic. This condition is necessitated by our assessments of reality being bound or limited by the prevailing circumstances of the times in which we live. One example of this relates to our once-held view of heaven, which was seen to be a "place" in space set somewhere beyond the ceiling of the clouds or firmament. Today the language of faith must take an even bolder leap as it catches up with the teachings of St. Francis of Assisi concerning the spirit-hewn nature of even seemingly inanimate things which or who were called into their service of creation (i.e., their liturgies) to fill a vast pre-creation void. We hear the spirit of St. Francis in these words written some seven-hundred years ago:

> By sister water be [God] blessed
> Most humble, useful, precious chaste:
> Be praised by brother fire . . .
> Jocund is he, robust and bright
> And strong to lighten all the night . . .
> For death our sister, praised be,
> From whom no [one] alive can flee.
> Woe to the unprepared! . . .
> Let creatures all give thanks to thee,
> And serve in great humility.

For redemption to move apace, we must see far beyond what the human eye may comprehend, so that we join with all of the numberless hosts of creation.

What we have recently come to call "environmental stewardship"—which will be touched upon further along—has begun to open our minds to at least the faint possibility that there might be in the universe other agencies who have practiced with faithfulness—and long, long before us—their instinctive art of doing obediently God's will. This thought was recently set forth in what I have tentatively titled "God's Servants All."

> All nature in obedience
> Hymns praises with bright diligence;
> Through day and night in awe stands still,
> Nor veers from God's eternal will.
>
> Beneath the earth in caverns crawl
> God's creatures who, both large and small,
> Convert the wastes of time for good,
> Provide for life its daily food.
>
> And on the very ground we stand
> Are countless forms of life, like sand
> Upon a desert wilderness;
> In myriad forms our lives they bless.
>
> Within our bodies, too, they live;
> If we should learn from how they give,
> Our hearts might be like theirs, we
> May help perfect life's chemistry.
>
> Our teachers they who in the sky
> All wondrously forever fly;
> With inborn grace they show us ways
> To reach for glory all our days.
>
> So may we serve with all the rest
> Whom God has made to be as best;
> Not as above the others we
> Must sing with them eternally.

We are to comprehend or to include within our all-inclusive and everyday working view of reality, things of both time and eternity, of earth and heaven. We are also to see—and to serve with, as beloved co-partners—all of the earth's humans and all of her creatures and created things.

It is this essential spirit of comprehensiveness (or of all-inclusiveness) which Jesus' assertion that his domain is of another place represents. Where he is, there we are to be, helping to bring all of life with us there also.

Recapitulation - I

From what we have discussed thus far, we have sought to suggest how liturgy, stewardship, and creation, working together, comprise one redemptively-oriented whole. They represent or form a composite faith statement as to life's *What, How,* and *Why.* We shall now concentrate on the *Why* aspect of this triad, in order to surface its possibly crucial relevance in assessing and adjusting both the spirit and direction of the church's program life.

We have seen how liturgy, stewardship, and creation, taken together, represent one apparently credible faith statement (or song and scenario) concerning our part in the overall workings of God's world.

Liturgy, so we have noted, represents a beginning verb which states for us God's will. It perhaps most frequently tells us to "Go!"—to "Do ...!"—and to "Be!" *Stewardship,* in revealing the quality of our response, provides an index as to how well creation's wheels have been oiled and turned in order that life's growth, into becoming what God has willed, takes place. Again, liturgy sets forth our tasks and provides the impact or impetus of a shared celebration of what is to be a common task, indeed, life's all inclusive operations. In this same broadening light our sense of stewardship commands and impels us to mobilize all of the needed resources from ourselves, our fellow creatures and created things which will enable us to perform our life-unifying weekday labors, as well as our Sunday formal and ceremonial recommitments (or "liturgies") and re-directions. So also, we are pulled into life's movement toward the restoration of all things according to God's perfect plan, as we keep *creation's* end or purposes—the why's—in view. In such a way, liturgy inspires stewardship, and stewardship both summons and initiates the creative flow which leads life on to re-celebrate God's empowering word with such sufficiency that life, in endless fashion, further flourishes and grows. Our liturgy (reflecting the verb-subject of God's word), our stewardship (as adverbial modifier), and our latching onto creation's impetus toward life's fulfillment (as noun-like predicate) thus mark the immediately understandable, perpetually adjusting, and yet ever-lasting statement or language of our faith. So on and on through patient meanderings and detours, and through recurrent leaps and bounds, this triad's unstopping redemptive process flows.

Praxis

A Proving Ground

The testing of the relevance of our explorations comes in the process of their practical application, or in what technically as called *praxis*.

In this spirit, we may take the three basic principles relating to the "why's" of the Christian life, as we have just seen them expressed chiefly in the theme of creation and then apply them as tests of the efficacy or the practical or program side of the church's life. These principles, as just surfaced in this essay, are:

1. *Dominion*, i.e., does what we are engaged in, or propose to do, enable life (or lives) to reign and have dominion?

2. *Growth*, i.e., does what we do tend to encourage significant growth into the life of God?

3. *Inclusiveness*, i.e., does what we do reflect an inclusiveness of the whole (locally and in the wider universe, and in eternity—the time-less, spaceless cosmos—as well as in time)?

In our brief exploration we shall also be attentive to the degree in which what we do moves into the flow of liturgy, stewardship, and creation, as the ceaselessly redemptive song of life's ageless choir of all creatures and created things.

One of the simplest and yet most comprehensive models for a church congregation's program life is known as SWEEPS, an acronym for Stewardship, Worship, Evangelism, Education, Pastoral Care, and Service. It is this model as a working whole which we shall keep in mind while we focus on various aspects of stewardship, which may be thought of or defined, as we shall see, in a church's program life in at least several different ways. The importance of having such a model for the organization of a congregation (or of a larger church body) rests on the practical premise that every church member should be "active" in both a congregation's worship and program life. Only in such a way may the liturgy-stewardship-creation flow, as we have seen it thus far, begin to accomplish its ostensible work of facilitating the three test elements—or purposes of the Christian life—of (1) dominion, (2) growth, and (3) an inclusive-consciousness.

What Stewardship Is

While each of the six interrelated categories inevitably tends to overlap each other, this is nowhere more true than in the area of stewardship. For stewardship may be seen as the *how* (i.e., the *how well*) or the quality—of our involvement in every area of our witness or commitment. Thus, we are stewards in our worship and we are stewards in our evangelism and in each of the other program areas of a congregation's life. Indeed, for this reason stewardship has been defined increasingly of late as "the main work of the church." Christian people are called "stewards of the mysteries of God," reflecting our roles as trustees of God's grace in every area of life.

One especially logical and richly revealing explanation for the origin of the term "steward" is that it is derived from the words "sty" (as where pigs were kept) and "ward," meaning, in this case, a keeper of the sty. A Christian steward holds in trust what is of value to God, or in the divine ordering of life. That is what each Christian is called to be in everything which he or she may do. The SWEEPS model is designed, in this light, to be a framework or a platform for "learning by doing" within a congregation's life. As one of the age-old prayers or familiar collects of the church suggests, we engage in a life of "imperfect service" here on earth that we might be prepared for a life of "more perfect service" in the world to come. It would seem to be axiomatic that no one in a congregation has the option of being excused from being a steward, our only choice being the degree to which we give of ourselves for the keeping and enhancement of what we share in holding from God in trust. In the Book of Revelation, such perpetual stewardship of the things of God is seen as the work of heaven: "Therefore they serve God day and night" (Rv 7:15).

The term "stewardship" as a specific program category in congregational life should present few problems, as long as we take sufficient care to define our terms. As a general rule today, when we speak of Christian stewardship as a specific program area, we refer to *financial stewardship* and/or to what has come to be called *environmental stewardship*. The use of the term "stewardship" as related to one's financial support of the church's work has become increasingly widespread in this late twentieth century, although in my own continued readings and re-readings of the works of Phillips Brooks, I have discovered his use of the term as reflecting a new development in church life in the late 1800s.

Financial Stewardship

The continually growing importance of financial stewardship for Christian congregations stems from needs associated with dramatic changes in the political and economic life of Europe and the Americas over a period of at least several centuries. For a thousand years and more until roughly three centuries ago, churches in or near Europe were largely paid for or financed by a prevailing feudal structure.

It was the famous European Emperor, Charles the Great or Charlemagne (742-814) who is said to have been responsible for doing the most to institutionalize the system of rulers and the rich paying for most charities, including the church's bills. Vestiges of such a feudally-oriented system linger in much of the church, in Europe and the Americas especially, even to this day.

> From Charles the Great's 8th century
> There comes the lasting legacy
> Of patrons in their piety
> Controlling Christian charity.
>
> To make a Christian state, Charles aimed,
> And in this noble purpose maimed
> The sense that each must give, and be
> As Christ, ourselves God's charity.
>
> Each age has its own truths to teach;
> Today, as Christians, we must reach
> Not for some state community
> But everywhere Christ's Body be.
>
> As Bread and Wine surrendering,
> Redemption's goal, God's life we bring.
> So in the sense King Charles once blessed,
> Each age must give anew its best.

This meant in King Charles' day that the rich, who were the political and economic overseers, paid the church's bills. This seemingly handy system inevitably kept the vast majority of Christians from both the growth-enhancing opportunity of giving and the privilege of having a major voice in deciding on church affairs. Minority group members in largely white denominations in the United States and the Caribbean today may still remember the days earlier in this century when their congregations were "blessed" with the debilitating largesse of white persons or congregations who in their giving reinforced the notion of minority group dependence upon the majority and, importantly at the same time, kept them in non-voting or limited influence categories as "missionary congregations."

Unfortunately, this same basic or general practice is widespread in an unconsciously debilitating way among some religious groups today, where denominational subsidy support to some congregations has often continued for a matter of decades. A revealing statistic should be brought to mind here. On average, it is said to take only some fifty to sixty individuals living at the poverty line, and who tithe, to support a full-time ministry. In this light, perhaps the weight of denominational support for any local congregation—including overseas missions—might most appropriately be designated for help with financial stewardship development, rather than for the continued paying of maintenance bills. This would represent substantial improvement, enabling a sense of dominion to flourish in the place of building in dependency. Indeed, it may be said that the essential purpose of present-day financial stewardship parallels our commonly held democratic political purpose, which is to enable every citizen to become economically and intellectually (or skills-wise) self-sufficient so as to be in a position to contribute to and enhance the common good. In this light, current financial stewardship efforts may be seen as designed ideally to build sufficient financial stewardship habits and outlooks that individuals, along with congregations and larger church bodies, (1) may handily attend to their own maintenance needs, and then (2) may answer the gospel call of the church to "go into all the world," i.e., to be redeeming and restoring or re-creating agents, so that all of life may become what God has proposed in creation. The word "gospel," we must remember, begins with the letters "g - o," i.e., to Go!—suggesting that our principle work begins as Christians *after* our internal maintenance needs (which are largely matters for our own convenience) have been met. It has been said, and possibly well, that when a congregation or other church body meets its own internal maintenance needs, it has largely created a "chapel of ease" for its own convenience. It is only when we go beyond such local or internal needs that we may begin to answer in earnest the "gospel call."

Implicit here is the suggestion or principle that Christian financial stewardship efforts should not be geared primarily for meeting maintenance needs, since the accomplishment of such a goal does not much more than position a church body to "get up to bat" and begin to fulfill its fundamental reason for being. That reason is to redeem or to re-claim and re-create our world—including all of life's elements—as God would have them be. "And I, if I be lifted up, will draw all things unto me" (Jn 12:33). Also implicit here is the principle that church bodies should always seek to spend more for redemptive and enabling purposes beyond their own communities than they spend for local maintenance needs. This is often called "50/50" giving.

In such an understanding of Christian financial stewardship it should be evident that a thoroughly redemptive purpose or spirit must pervade the entire life experience and commitment of every Christian. Indeed, this goal must go beyond the church to include every person, so that we may serve along with all of nature and all other created things, as—in many instances—the human elements play "catch up" with much of life's non-human stewards in a faithful working out of creation's apparently intuitive or implanted purpose.

Environmental Stewardship

The current need for an interest in environmental stewardship stems essentially from a history of three hundred years or more of excessive exploitation and wanton waste by what are seen as the major developed nations of the world.

Primary and alarming signs of this exploitation and waste have become evident in the earth's ozone layer depletion, which threatens to drastically maim or modify all of the life on the planet. Rivers have been polluted to the point where their accustomed provision of drinking water and of a place for recreation is no longer possible. The disposal of garbage presents problems of staggering numbers, in large measure from the continued use—even unthinkingly by countless numbers of church organizations—of non-biodegradable plastic cups and plates, along with grocery bags, wrapping and other conveying materials of a similar nature. In the United States there are alarmingly high toxic emissions from automobiles, airplanes, and other motors using gasoline and oil, which altogether disproportionately and unconscionably, pollute the earth's air around the planet. These are only a few of the superficial signs that in our nation's and world's air, water, open lands, and households, factories, and mines, and through our failure to plant (air cleaning) trees, through overfishing and strip mining and the failure of population controls, the global place of our habitation has become endangered. Hence a thoroughly reasonable concern and justifiable alarm leading to the present urgency of what has come to be called environmental stewardship.

The problems just noted go far deeper than they may appear, investing environmental stewardship with a mantle of the most grave proportions. The pattern of European exploration, begun some five centuries and more ago, established and infused in our modern day world a tradition of brute exploitation of peoples and places as an almost unquestionably accepted way of life, even for Christians, In fact, Christian leaders most often enticed themselves into initiating these developments; and other leaders and nations followed throughout the world. Included in this pernicious process has been a seemingly ever-increasing sense of the denial of basic involvement or responsibility in the rape or the sack of Africa's people and produce, along with the plunder of the peoples and resources of the Americas, parts of Asia and the open seas. The resultant mind set still rests at the roots of sustained poverty and a growing economics-related racism in this country and throughout the world, along with the cruel and obscene invention of recent homelessness worldwide.

Recurrent calls for a perhaps structurally impossible redistribution of wealth hold little promise of relief, since at the base of most of world and national poverty is an inequitable enhancement of opportunity. Those who practice economic and educational discrimination build in social and economic problems in a criminal way, for which the public must pay an enormously unending price. Fair play and the deliberately equitable inclusion of all should not be seen as acts of charity but rather of necessity for order and the secure well-being of our communities, nations, and our world. Again, when in-groups become increasingly further ingrown, they also tend to increase alienation both in small communities and in the global community at large. It was St. Augustine who most eloquently reminded the church in its early years that a deliberate and self-conscious effort to make all Christians become one family through purposed intermarriage, as, across all national and racial lines, was the Christian community's ethical duty in an increasingly alienated world (see his *City of God*, Book XV, Chapter 16 in *The Fathers of the Church*, vol. 14; notice here the theme or the impetus toward inclusiveness). The pollution of thought processes—by the forgetfulness of the inclusive nature of creation and the Christian life—is thus added to the already staggering problem of deadly chemical pollution. In the recent period prior to the development of reasonably safe contraceptive devices (up until the last fifty years) many poor whites, along with perhaps the vast majority of the black and original American communities in this nation, were exploited sexually with the result of producing a new breed of peoples who, as of today, have been assumed (possibly by sheer oversight) to be barren or bereft of the pursuit of what otherwise would be normal out of wedlock inheritance rights. Implicit here is the reality of a nation where, according to a 1970s Tulane University study, an estimated eighty percent of its black population would, by blood composition, be considered "white" (or of "European" extraction) elsewhere in the world, and where an estimated at least one person in three of its white population meets the American criteria of being seen as black.

Add to this the infamous Davis-Bacon Act from the Great Depression era of the 1930s. This union-sponsored act put "grandfather clauses" into all federal construction trade contracts which have effectively barred, even to this present day, blacks in every state of the Union, north and south from participating equitably in federal construction projects which are paid for at taxpayers' expense. The political air of the nation is thus thickened and poisoned by what have become grave environmental hazards to this nation's legal and moral health. Such, as we have seen in this brief sampling, is only an introduction to the challenges faced by the trend toward environmental stewardship. Superficial or surface problems abound. But their resolution calls for a major surgical change of both outlooks and habits within our nation's—and the church's—life. It is against such a socio-political, ethical, and spiritual background as this that we may see most clearly the potential relevance of our test criteria involving the life-reordering purposes of (1) dominion, (2) growth, and (3) an inclusive-consciousness in the area of environmental stewardship.

The Relevance of What We Do

If it is to be assumed that the basic Christian purpose in everything that we do is to restore or reorder life as God would have it be, then in both our individual life outside the church and our shared or corporate life within the church, barring the emergence of something better, our three test criteria for the presence of the redemptive spirit should help us to assess just where we are or where we should be going.

Financial Stewardship Questions

We always need to raise the question as to how our activities in this area encourage dominion, growth, and an inclusive-consciousness. In response, we may see first that congregational financial steward-ship should be structured so as to foster congregational *dominion* in the sense of independence/integrity and self-sufficiency. On the personal level, such financial stewardship, especially through the mechanism of proportionate giving (i.e., the tithe of ten percent of what we have through God's church as "the beginning of Christian giving"), should foster the building of order and reasoned priorities in our overall budget-making. Such a mechanism should also in-crease the sense or fact of dominion in aligning our lives with God's purposes and God's presence, which is God's power whereby we may say, "I can do all things through Christ who [dwells] in me" (Phil 4:13).

We may say secondly here, in regard to *growth*, that as God is put first in our financial stewardship, we come closer to meeting Jesus' standard requirement (as in Mt 19:2-3 and Mk 10:22) for entrance into his kingdom—as a means of spiritual growth. Jesus did not say "Where your heart is, your treasure will follow." Rather, our hearts follow our treasure for "Where your treasure [already] is, there will your heart be" (Mt 6:21). Further, the tithe-oriented life style enables its adherents to see new opportunities and richly positive experi-ences which had remained unseen before. Typical among those who tithe is the recognition that most of their fellowship is not from among the rich but from among the economically poor who come to see themselves, with St. Paul, as "possessing all things" (2 Cor 6:10).

We may say, in regard to the third criterion of an inclusive-consciousness, that from a practical point of view financial steward-ship should be seen as inclusive of all in terms of fulfilling the giver's need to grow in the giving spirit and likewise in terms of the giver's need to participate in all of what might be seen as a covenant of sharing in the work of all creation. From a strictly "people of God" point of view, it may be said that in giving we are to share in God's redemptive purpose, and not simply "doing our part" to contribute for the payment of the church's maintenance.

> We give "the tenth" to God, and then
> We give and give and give again;
> For God has made our lives to be
> Like God who gives eternally.

> As Malachi has said, no less,
> For those who tithe the Lord will bless,
> From heaven's store—through windows wide—
> With endless gifts God's host provide.
>
> God gave in sending us God's Son,
> Who on the cross of glory won
> The right for us to walk the way
> Which leads by grace to endless day.
>
> God gives the Holy Spirit, too,
> Enabling us our whole life through
> To grow in givingness, that we
> May share God's gift of Victory.

"Bring the full tithes into the storehouse ... put me to the test, says the Lord of hosts, if I will not open the windows of heaven for you and pour down for you an overflowing blessing" (Mal 3:10).

It may be said that the whole of the created order of life and things tends implicitly toward the fulfillment of God the Creator's will, and that we humans (who are uniquely endowed with free will) are freed either to obey that life-fulfilling instinct or to disobey it.

In my own work at doubling and tripling church budgets, I share with those with whom I work a book of *Guidelines* which has the following preface directed to our three tests of relevance criteria:

> A congregation's annual stewardship endeavor is normally seen as successful when a 10% to 20% increase has been achieved. These guidelines—which should be used ideally with some professional assistance—are designed to achieve an increase of from 50 to 150% in the week-by-week pledge offerings of a congregation!
>
> Two further stewardship assumptions are implicit in the following material. One is that just the reverse of a 10 to 15 percent of customary involvement of church members as "insiders" (or as leader/managers) must be brought about. In the average Protestant congregation, the 10 to 15 percent of the membership who "run things" generally account for 80 percent or more of the congregation's income. For all to consider responsibly proportionate giving, every member must be optimally aided in participating fully in the program governance and/or other leadership ranks in the congregation.
>
> The final basic assumption is the increasingly normal expectation that every Christian is to see the tithe (or the provision of at

least 5% to 10% of one's income for the church's work) as "the beginning of Christian giving." Jesus encouraged good financial stewardship as a means of conversion and spiritual growth. This same premise is implicit in these guidelines.

Environmental Stewardship Questions

Here we need to ask ourselves on a far deeper level (and in a much wider range) the same three questions regarding the relevance of our plans and actions. Does what we do foster the establishment or extension of *dominion*? Our key question here regarding dominion enables us to establish an unmistakably clear pattern of action and of purpose in all our human relationships and with much of the world of creatures and of things. We are to see or envisage every life, in all God's varied order of things, in terms of its optimal (or ideal or divine) potential, and then we are to work to bring the beauty of that potential to its fullest flower.

I have often shared with others a model by which I might assess at the end of a day all that I have done in regard to others (1) in my family relationships, (2) in my church, teaching, or other professional work, and (3) in my community or in other public concerns. In this exercise I draw a line from the top to the bottom of a blank page, thereby making two columns—one column is entitled "Enablement/Redemption," the other is labelled "Relief." Then I list under each heading the things that I have done (or the relationship with which I have had encounters). If I have simply or primarily done things which "oil the wheels" and keep life moving happily along its way, I list that relationship or activity under the heading of "Relief." If, however, there have been activities where I had sought genuinely to help so that a life or a relationship or an activity may come to its fullest flower and thus possibly in some sense gain dominion, I would list that item under the heading of "Enablement/Redemption." You may guess regarding what proportion of my activities might normally have fitted under each category. I can tell you that "Relief" has counted each day for nine-tenths or more of what I have given my time at best for doing. The almost rote dynamics of our moving through each day must be willfully confronted on our part, if life's negatively-oriented inertia is to even begin to be overcome.

In regard to my own *growth*, here too I all too often find myself rusty. Whatever prevails around me, it is that to which I tend willy-nilly to adjust. Only when some dire or dramatic circumstance prompts me, do I tend—pretty naturally—to seek for new insights or new and non-defeating approaches to otherwise routine concerns. But fortunately there is much of the aberrant or the out-of-the-ordinary, sufficient to propel me into thoughtfully creative action or growing. At one point in my life, before a long series of illnesses (from which I have now recovered) took my life for a serious turn, I was asked what I felt it was that enabled me to receive a number of first place awards. I replied (in some profound sense honestly) that I was essentially lazy, so that I never wanted to do anything *twice*. Hence I worked for the most successful accomplishment on the very first try. That seems to be at least one scenario of how "God moves in a mysterious way (God's) wonders to perform." Would that all of life could be filled with some of such miracles of grace, regardless of how strange—or how disconcerting—they may seem to be.

With regard to an *inclusive-consciousness,* this has seemed for me to be the most difficult of all. I have worked and worked practically all of the seven decades of my life for life to become as beautiful as possible for humanity, for others among God's creatures, and for things. But I am at heart an introvert, and so I enter most frequently and most naturally into my own private world, castle, and even corner of my room. My felt need is to leave others out. I have had close friends says to me, "Nathan, what a blessing it has been that you were born black, which you have made into an infinitely great privilege and has enabled you to grow richly in your sensitivities in many ways." If such a statement is true, it is chiefly that way because I have been thrust into a position of the utmost felt sense of an urgent, clear necessity. For this I am deeply grateful, even as I am aware that my deep-seated infirmities of long-standing have all been associated in some way with my halting and stumbling attempts to probe life's problems, to help others to grow, and to set things right. Like so many others, and perhaps like you who read these lines, I have found that what I would do, I cannot, and that which I would not, I tend to do. Yet such an awareness keeps me alert to the need (however difficult) to relate to others and to probe the mind and the heart of God to include all creation in my inmost circles of awareness, relationships, and concern. So it may be with you. Maltbie Babcock (1858-1901), who became successor to Henry van Dyke as pastor of the Brick Presbyterian Church in New York City, in a hymn called "This is my Father's world," expressed something of the inclusive-conscious spirit which must motivate us toward the utmost reverence (and preference) toward all life, "in honor preferring over another," saying:

> This is my Father's world,
> Dreaming, I see (God's) face.
> I open my eyes, and in glad surprise
> Cry, "The Lord is in this place."

We must dream and will work relentlessly for a world and a universe of time and of spacelessness where always God's goodness, presence, and fulfillment reign.

Other sweeps Model Areas

Here we make the following brief relevance-related comments.

In our *Worship* life, in every service, there ideally should be some elements that specifically encourage and highlight a sense of our dominion through our identification and reunion with, in, and as Christ.

In our *Evangelism*, the basic area for this might be in the guest list of those who visit a church congregation. And among others who use the church in all of the "matching," "hatching," "patching," and "dispatching" activities which the church does both well and, in some sense, uniquely, there are fertile occasions to hold up the church's capacities for the encouragement of the three characteristics which comprise our test.

In our *Education* activity, the rich meaning of the liturgy-stewardship-creation relationship can be plumbed and set forth repeatedly, and this should emphasize the place of dominion, growth, and an inclusive-consciousness throughout the Christian life.

In *Pastoral Care*, those whom we serve—ideally through congregation-wide mutual ministry—should be encouraged most substantially in their altogether therapeutic sense of dominion, growth, and relationship with all of life's divine (and all-inclusive) processes and purposes.

In our *Service* to God's world, wherein lies our major challenge, throughout the length of every day and night, we are (in all things) to redeem and restore God's entire universe to God's eternal will and purpose. Liturgy tells us to "Go" and to "Serve." Our sense and grasp of stewardship impels us to accept God's work most fully and to do it well. Creation (or re-creation) is both the process and the product, the "eternal why" of all of our life's work.

Recapitulation - II

In reference to *liturgy*, we must see that all we do as Christians in terms of our gift of worship (i.e., "service" in its fullest, widest sense) to God. This includes overwhelmingly all our weekly activities and our interpersonal, intergroup, and family relationships. Formal worship collects, or brings together, these offerings of all that we each do in a public or corporate celebration; in this sense our public worship is always and implicitly a corporate act. The presentation of the bread and wine—which should always be a highly conspicuous act—is (or should be) designed to dramatize all our life's activities and labors since our last corporate weekly celebration. These gifts we collectively present to God under the forms of bread (symbolic of our manufacture) and wine (symbolic of our cooperative activity with nature).

Our *stewardship* represents how thoughtfully and well we perform our day to day and moment by moment liturgies by deliberately seeing *everything we do in life* as an act of worship. With this kind of recognition in mind, we may sense our oneness with all the rest of animate and ostensibly inanimate nature, as all together we hymn through our varied but shared liturgies in praise of the creator. In such a context both our financial and our environmental stewardship take on infinitely deeper, richer, and fuller meaning; for in all that we do we are stewards of the infinite and ineffable graces of a Creator God of unending aspects of glory and light. How exalted in this way we are! How one with creation and glory thus we become! How filled with "the music of the spheres" is every moment of life, as time begins to merge for us—and for all things—with that which is eternal!

Our *creative or re-creative work* (i.e., *creation*) is measured by the extent to which all that we do fosters (1) dominion, (2) growth into and as the very life of God, and (3) an inclusive-consciousness. All that we do or plan to do, individually or collectively, each day should be measured in this way. Then all that we have described or alluded to in our discussion above of the varied aspects of stewardship and church program life might be thought through sentence by sentence (or phrase by phrase) in regard to the three test criteria as to the fulfillment of Christian purpose. In this way, we may faithfully adhere to creation's theme or song, and so be prepared to mark or summarize and celebrate—as in each next Sunday's formal liturgy or worship—our oneness with creation, and in and as extensions and expressions of the Holy One "in [whom] we [all] live and move and have our being" (Acts 17:28).

Praise be to God, to whom be praise
In concert throughout all our days,
In heaven, earth, and in all things—
So all of life forever sings.

Our liturgies—the work we do,
Our stewardship—which leads us to
Creation's purpose, test the "why?"
Of everything we raise on high.

Dominion, growth, inclusiveness—
Promoting these, we make life best;
So may God smile, and heaven ring
With joy, while choirs of angels sing.

Such is the everlasting thrust
In doing all the things we must
To make life holy, right and meet
For offering at God's Mercy Seat.

So praised be God, all joyous praise,
In concert throughout all our days;
All nature sings! We lift our songs
To God to whom all life belongs!

14

Taking Down Our Harps: Deacons as Creative Artists

Ormonde Plater

As for our harps, we hung them up
on the trees in the midst of that land.
(Psalm 137:2)

HANGING UP THEIR HARPS, HEBREW PEOPLE IN BABYLON SIT DOWN AND WEEP. Too oppressed to praise the Lord, they cannot even sing alleluia. The darkest sign of their captivity is the inability of the people of God to make song.

Making song is an act of creation, making images of poetry and music. It is what people do when they expect to escape slavery and death, when they remember good times, when they celebrate freedom. Song is godly. Singing the Lord's song is praising God for making all images, for performing the divine act of creation in perfect harmony, and for giving life in the midst of death. Even when times are bad, we yearn to sing the Lord's song of creation and salvation. As we seek a just and peaceful world, in which God openly reigns over the music of the universe, we take down our harps and sing the songs of Zion. Joining God, we create.

Making song, as a metaphor for all creative art, is also one of the functions of deacons. This may not be clear to all who are acquainted with the deacons of the Episcopal Church and their work. The ordination prayer speaks of deacons as sharing in the humble service

205

of Christ who was "servant of all." Being a servant means care of "the poor, the weak, the sick, and the lonely."

The third-century ordination prayer of Hippolytus, by contrast, portrays the *diakonia* of Christ as a cosmic act of creation. The prayer draws a parallel between the service of Christ to God, "who created all things and set them in order by the Word," and the service of deacons to the church.[1] The creative activity of deacons thus reproduces and images the creative activity of Christ. By this definition, deacons are creative agents of the church who carry out Christlike missions in the world.

There is an old tradition of creative art among deacons, which includes the poetry of several prominent deacons in the early and medieval church. In the Episcopal Church deacons are creative artists in areas including art, music, and writing. They use their art in ministry with the needy, and they reflect on its theological meaning. They lead Christian people in making song. When they sing the Exsultet at the Easter Vigil, especially, they lead people in praising God for the supreme creative art of the Word made flesh, Jesus Christ risen victorious from the grave.

Early and Medieval Deacons

Two Syrian deacons of the early church used poetry to praise God and teach the orthodox faith. These are Ephrem of Edessa in the fourth century and Romanos the Melodist in the sixth century.

The poems of Ephrem originate in theological controversy. In 363 the Romans handed over Nisibis to the Persians, and Ephrem, at age fifty-seven, left the city of his birth and moved west to Edessa, an intellectual center. There he met followers of the popular heresies of the day, some of whom had written their doctrines in poetic form. To counter these heresies, Ephrem wrote hymns and organized choirs of women to sing them. He died in 373.[2]

As a poet who praises God in song, Ephrem became known among the Syrians as "the Harp of the Spirit." His extensive writing in Syriac includes two kinds of poetry: hymns (*madrashe*) in stanzas, sung by choirs, and verse homilies (*memre*) in couplets, probably recited. The subject matter covers heresies, faith, virginity, the church, resurrection, paradise, and the like. Ephrem drew upon Scripture for vivid imagery, and like many writers of his age he was fond of antithesis and paradox. Stanzas from a hymn on faith illustrate both the theological content and the style of his poems. The hymn, apparently sung at the eucharist, begins with a comparison of this feast with that wedding at Cana:

> I invited you, Lord, to a wedding feast of song,
> but the wine has failed, the speech of praise.
> You the guest filled the jars with good wine,
> fill my mouth with your praise.

In the fourth stanza the wedding at Cana becomes Christ's wedding with his bride the church:

> Others invited you, Jesus, to their wedding feast,
> here is your own pure and fair wedding.
> Cheer your new-born people, Lord,
> for your guests need your songs: let your harp speak!

Refuting the Arian heresy, which denied that Jesus was of the same substance as God, the hymn ends with praise of the divine and human natures of Christ:

> It is right for human beings to praise your divinity,
>   it is right for heavenly beings to worship your humanity.
> Heavenly ones were amazed to see how humble you became,
>   and earthly ones to see how grand.[3]

Ephrem's verse homilies display the same love of paradox as his hymns. A homily on the Nativity compares the birth of Christ with the birth of John the Baptist:

> A virgin is pregnant with God,
> and a barren woman is pregnant with a virgin,
> the son of sterility leaps
> at the pregnancy of a virgin.[4]

Romanos also was born in Syria and influenced by Syriac poetry, but he made his religious and literary career in the Byzantine culture of Constantinople in the early sixth century. There he became linked with the rise of the *kontakion*, a brief topical hymn used in the liturgy of the Orthodox Church, and earned the title "Melodist." Alexander Schmemann says that the *kontakia* of Romanos show a "striking combination of plastic literary form and genuine poetry with a profoundly theological, penetrating content."[5] Two famous examples are the *kontakia* of Christmas and Easter:

> Today the Virgin gives birth to one beyond all being,
>   and to one we cannot approach the earth offers a cave.

> Angels and shepherds sing his glory,
> the wise men follow the star,
> for to us is born a child,
> God in all eternity.

> You descended to the grave, O Immortal One,
> and overthrew the power of hell.
> In victory you rose, O Christ our God,
> to the myrrh-bearing women proclaimed: Rejoice!
> to your apostles granted peace,
> and to the fallen resurrection.[6]

The religious poetry of the Middle Ages, usually in Latin, seldom possesses the beauty or theological depth of earlier works. Two deacons of the eighth century, Alcuin of York and Paul the Deacon, lived in an age when poets began to listen more to courtly harps than to sacred ones. Both studied classical poets. Both served in the court of Charlemagne. Both wrote the typical court verse of the day—occasional poems, epitaphs, epigrams, poetical epistles, and a few religious poems.

Among Alcuin's early poems are two long hexameter pieces: a history of the church in York, where he had studied in the cathedral school as a child, and a life of his kinsman St. Willibrord. One of his later religious poems is an evening hymn in sapphic meter, *Luminis fons, lux et origo lucis.*[7] Paul the Deacon, a Lombard from a noble family in northern Italy, may have written a famous hymn in honor of John the Baptist, *Ut queant laxis resonare fibris.*[8]

In the thirteenth century Francis of Assisi used poetry to inspire and teach common people. Turning to Scripture and his natural surroundings for inspiration, Francis recovers the spiritual depth of earlier deacon poets. His best known work is "The Canticle of Brother Sun." This poem in Italian draws ideas and images from two liturgical texts in Latin, Psalm 148 and *Benedicite, omnia opera Domini.* Francis praises God for sun, moon, stars, wind and all weather, water, fire, earth, and finally, in strophes added just before his death in 1226, Sister Death. Through simple and pleasing personifications, Francis teaches people to respect creation and thank God for it.[9]

Francis (a nickname meaning "Frenchie") belongs to the southern European genre of the troubadour with its wandering minstrels, exuberant spirits, and chivalrous ideals. Like other minstrels Francis pursues romantic love, but instead of an idealized courtly lady he converts romance to faith and seeks Lady Poverty. "The Praises of the Virtues" stresses dying to self, beginning:

Hail Queen Wisdom! The Lord save you,
    with your sister, pure, holy Simplicity.
Lady Holy Poverty, God keep you,
    with your sister, holy Humility.
Lady Holy Love, God keep you,
    with your sister, holy Obedience.[10]

Deacons of the Episcopal Church

Deacons in the Episcopal Church who are creative artists range
from novice to expert. Their practice of art extends from part-time
hobby to full-time profession. They create art through means such as
needlework and crocheting, handbells, puppets and masks, garden-
ing, photography, praying in foreign languages, composing music,
journalism, watercolors and oils, making quilts, iconography, mu-
rals, singing, musical instruments, preaching in verse, writing short
stories and novels, clowning, and composing bawdy limericks. This
only begins the list.

Many deacons take their art seriously, regarding it as a gift from
God. They use it to praise God, heal the sick, bring order out of chaos,
enable others to minister, touch other people and get their attention,
spread the good news, and deliver the message of the poor. Here are
the stories of deacon artists, musicians, and writers.[11]

Artists

In 1990 Betty Noice of Grand Junction, Colorado, decided to paint
icons. She attended a workshop at Western State College of Colorado
taught by an Episcopal priest, Les Bundy. Along with applying gesso
and paints, she learned that iconography is "a spiritual exercise, an
act of worship, and a means of entering into the Christian vision as it
developed in the Byzantine world." Before starting an icon, she says
a prayer.

Even her naive first try came alive, and she began to share her art
with people in her parish church. She completed twelve traditional
icons and put them in various places, two under the hymn board, one
in the nursery prayer corner, and one (of a saint or season of the
church year) in front of the lectern. After she introduced icons to
Sunday school, for weeks children came to church after school to
learn to paint them.

She took two icons to the local youth detention center and passed
them around. "The boys were fascinated and wanted to know the
meaning of the Greek inscriptions. I told them if they could paint

model cars, they could paint icons. What a great project for incarcerated youth!"

Another deacon who has learned to paint icons is Brother Placid, a Benedictine monk at St. Gregory's Abbey in Three Rivers, Michigan. In 1990 Placid spent two weeks of his annual leave at the Antiochian Village in Ligonier, Pennsylvania, studying with Philip Zimmerman, a professional iconographer. The first week all the students worked on an icon of Our Lady of Korsun. The second week they were free to paint what they wanted at their own pace. Placid senses that God has led him to the practice of iconography. By rising a little early and using free time on Sundays and holy days, he manages to fit his painting into the monastic schedule and finish an icon almost every month. Making icons with the hands is "akin to a sacramental participation with God in the mystery of the Creation itself."[12]

The same understanding is present in the work of Nan Collins, a professional artist in El Paso, Texas. She describes her oil paintings, ranging from impressionistic landscapes and floral designs to abstractions, as "examples of God's creation in large uses of space and color symbolic of the southwestern part of the country." Although she does not use her painting for any specific work in the church, she feels that every canvas proclaims the love of God "for his people and the world he has made."

Marie Shirer of Arvada, Colorado, is known at "the quilt lady" in church circles and "the church lady" in quilting circles. An editor of magazines and author of books about quilting, she has taught a class at St. John's Cathedral in Denver on "Scripture and Stitching: A Theology of Creativity." In artistic terms, the persons of the Trinity are the creator, the created, and the act of creation. Shirer also works at a shelter for battered women and children, leading a quilting class. Making a quilt encourages abused women to share their stories and helps to heal them.

Shirer finds that quilting symbolizes God creating. Both activities are orderly, take time, and involve skills. Both carry an element of risk—rejection, damage, abuse, death, but also success. The work of deacons among the needy expresses the social and healing aspects of God creating.

Bill Rimkus of Summit, Illinois, runs a cottage industry. The part-time business started as sign painting and evolved into other forms of art—album covers, banners, book illustrations, icons, church booths. Most of his art he creates for the church. Art is a gift from God he is giving back.

In 1990 Rimkus painted a mural on pieces of paper and hung it in windows of the diocesan center in Chicago, facing the street. Lower windows depicted the holy family as *campesinos* surrounded by tropical foliage. Upper windows portrayed animals—donkeys, chickens, rabbits, pigs, sheep, goats, and beehives. This was part of Heifer Project International, a program that gives animals to people in the Third World. As children of the diocese brought pledges, the mural grew. Eventually it covered half the windows.

Musicians

Jerry Meachen of Stamford, Connecticut, has spent forty years as a church musician teaching the people of God to sing the liturgy. Rectors in three dioceses have hired him because of his record for leading congregations in song and attracting newcomers. Years ago a young college student, hearing the sound of a plainsong *Te Deum*, walked into a church where Meachen was leading music and stayed. Music is evangelistic.

Now retired, Meachen works as a volunteer at St. Paul's in Darien, Connecticut. At 8:00 A.M., an hour without music at most parishes, "a church full of folk sing anything we put before them from Pulkingham to plainsong." Meachen juggles being an organist with being a deacon in the liturgy. By 10:00 he is at St. John's in Stamford as deacon. At noon he rings the bells and leads prayers and intercessions.

Meachen's fame includes a simple chant he wrote as a young man trying to introduce the 1941 Hymnal in a Connecticut parish. The chant is printed as number S 415 in the 1982 Hymnal service music edition (a book seldom found in the pews). Wherever congregations sing the psalms and other liturgical texts, this is likely to be one of the chants they use. Many know it by heart, and Meachen suspects it may be as memorable to Episcopalians as the plainchant *Sursum corda*.

For Barbara Novak of Spokane, Washington, music is both a healing power and an expression of mystery. After seeing a man die in a motorcycle accident, she suffered post-traumatic stress syndrome for a year. "The only places I felt safe were at home and listening to music." Novak is a professional bassoon player with the Spokane symphony orchestra. "Music expresses things that we can't express any other way."

Writers

Robert Gard was a deacon at Grace Church in Madison, Wisconsin, from 1961 until his death in 1992. For even longer he was a regional writer, playwright, director, and encourager of the arts. For many years at Grace, he organized art exhibits in the undercroft and dramatic productions in the nave. He wanted to make Grace a leader in drama. When he tried to begin a national movement of the dramatic arts in the Episcopal Church, he met with indifference at church headquarters.

Gard's passion for uniting drama and religion derived from his concept of human beings as creative artists:

> Man's best side is his creativity, and this is manifest always in the arts. Because man in the arts is always striving to create the best product of which he is able, this side is close to God, in that God is perfection, and man in this striving is also striving for perfection. Thus creative man brings the best of himself, his talents, to offer to God when he kneels at communion. The eucharist, to me, is a celebration of man offering his best, creative self to God.

Gard was the author of a novel about Grace Church and the ghost of its founder, Bishop Jackson Kemper, entitled *The Deacon*.[13] In the story he speaks of the deacon as "a bridge figure," mediating between clergy and laity, and as a symbol of continuity in the parish, always there while rectors come and go.

Gard believes that every candidate for the diaconate—and for the other orders—should have a background in a creative art. Deacons especially "can do more than priests in ordinary church affairs to promote a deep spiritual relationship" between the arts and the church.

Berkley Forsythe of Waterloo, Nebraska, decided to write a short story for a Lenten discipline in 1978. He repeated the project in 1979, and in 1980 he began to write as a constant practice. About the same time, he and his wife Mary entered the "Education for Ministry" program of theological learning. "My writing and religious studies not only developed side by side, but became inextricably entangled. No matter what I write, religion and the church manage to find their way into the story." These include one humorous novel, *Expo '98: Sherlock Holmes in Omaha*,[14] an unpublished novel based on his courtship and early marriage, an unpublished collection of short stories, and many bawdy limericks. He was at work on a serious novel based on the life of James the brother of Jesus when he died in 1992.

Forsythe was ordained deacon in 1988. Although he had trouble seeing how his mainly humorous writing related to the diaconate, he considered writing as part of his ministry. He suspected that his writing served to "help to carry the church out into the world in a non-preachy manner."

Ted Malone of Chapel Hill is editor of *The Communicant* in the Diocese of North Carolina. When the standing committee interviewed him before his ordination in 1991, several members asked whether religious journalism is a legitimate ministry for a deacon. Malone replied that a deacon editor "can intentionally promote servant ministry."

> Having spent two years in the Army Signal Corps, six years as a newspaperman, seven years as a college English and journalism teacher, and seven more years as a government publications editor, it makes sense to take the skills that I have gained from those past experiences and put them to use—just as a deacon with medical, social work, legal, or other training would put his or her training to work.

Bishop Robert Estill agreed and named the editorship as Malone's primary ministry.

Malone is also a poet. One of his recent works is the hymn "Diakonia," inspired by the judgment scene in Matthew 25:

> The moss grows on the castle wall,
> the Lady's footsteps softly fall,
> the torches flicker in the hall,
> Lord Jesus come today to call.

> But where is Jesus? said the youth.
> I cannot see him. What is truth?
> Castles and towers are all swept away,
> where can I find Jesus Christ today?

> Oh, see him in the beggar's face,
> that homeless roams from place to place.
> The world's eyes see a ragged gown:
> in the eyes of love, a golden crown.

> Oh, see him in the hungry child,
> with tangled hair and features wild.
> The world's eyes see a castaway,
> in the eyes of love, our Prince today.

> Oh, see him old and poor and bent,
> forgotten, sick, his fortune spent.
> The world's eyes see the wreck of age,
> in the eyes of love, our worthy sage.
>
> Oh, see him in the stranger's face,
> with different language different race.
> The world's eyes see a mask to fear:
> in the eyes of love, our sister dear.
>
> Oh, see him in the seven seas,
> in forests tall and clean, sweet breeze.
> The world's eyes see to exploit their worth:
> in the eyes of love, our home the Earth.[15]

The words recall the folk ballads of England and Scotland. The waltz tune, which Malone composed, suggests the melodies of the southern highlands. At the biennial conference of the North American Association for the Diaconate, in June 1991 in Spokane, Washington, several deacons and others formed a choir to sing Malone's hymn and other texts by deacons.

The poetry of Bob Dewey of Lakeland, Florida, is strikingly different. Dewey suspects that he is "the only minister in Christendom who preaches all his sermons in verse, or holy doggerel as I call it." Not quite—if we include the *memre* of Ephrem, a large body of poetic homilies in the early church, and the free-verse sermons of black preachers in our own day. But Dewey makes us laugh.

The opening of "The Devil You Say," on Mark 1:21-28 (fourth Sunday of Epiphany in year B), illustrates the point:

> Whenever I'm asked,
> "Do you believe in the Devil?"
> I'm tempted to say,
> "Hey, are you on the level?"
>
> Not that in my own life
> I've got any doubt.
> But let's make sure that I know
> what you're talking about.
>
> If by Devil you mean
> some co-equal with God,
> some eternal bad spirit
> who ranges abroad,
>
> spawning devils and demons
> above and below,

if that's what you mean,
then my answer is "No."[16]

The sermon lasts forty-eight verses. Although his style owes more to Dr. Seuss than to Ephrem, like his ancient predecessor Dewey teaches orthodox theology. His sermon on Satan goes on to refute a dualism of good and evil and to promote catholic doctrines of the Trinity, creation, and resurrection.

Dewey regards his doggerel "simply as a device to get people's attention." Parishioners of All Saints Church in Lakeland, where Dewey has been deacon since 1969, undoubtedly stay wide awake during his preaching. In 1984 he collected twenty-two poetic sermons in a private edition called *Straight in the Desert*, which he also illustrated. He has more than enough new sermons for another volume.

Singing the Lord's Song

Deacons who are artists, musicians, and writers understand that their gift is a sacrament of God's creation. With their art, they do God's work of love and service in several ways. They find that art heals themselves and others. They use art to proclaim the Gospel of the Lord. They use art "to interpret to the church the needs, concerns, and hopes of the world." They use art to offer praise and thanksgiving, to reveal what is hidden, and to proclaim the mystery. They use art to send God's people into the world for *agape* and *diakonia*.

When deacons take down their harps, the primary song they sing is "Rejoice." Rejoice, cosmos and earth and church. My own version of the *Exsultet*, inspired by square dance, goes:

Dance now, angels, leap and fling,
grab a partner, circle round,
spirit hands who scrape the bow,
fiddle a tune for Christ our king.

Enter, earth, and orbit right,
swing your corner, now your own,
astral lanterns dazzle dark,
round all fly in cosmic light.

Push back pew, complete the ring,
mother church in shimmy gown,
bring your loud and rowdy crowd,
fling this night for Christ our king.[17]

The opening stanzas of the *Exsultet* are not the deacon's individual song of praise. They give directions for all creation to join as artists, singers, and actors in an lively dance. Singing "Rejoice," the deacon addresses the multitude whose creative gifts may be ordinary or exceptional but are nonetheless sacred. When Christians feed the hungry, they serve good food to human beings—and meet the divine image. When they care for the sick and visit those in prison, they listen with love to human beings—and meet the divine image. Every ordinary act performed in an encounter with Christ becomes sacred art.

The rare artistry of some deacons reflects the common artistry of all who serve. All of us, deacons and all the baptized, are to take down our harps and sing the Lord's song.

Notes

1. See the Latin text in H. B[oone] Porter, Jr., *The Ordination Prayers of the Ancient Western Churches*, Alcuin Club Collections, vol. 49 (London: SPCK, 1967) 10.

2. There is an introduction to Ephrem's life and work in Sebastian Brock, *The Harp of the Spirit: Eighteen Poems of Saint Ephrem* ([London:] Fellowship of St. Alban and St. Sergius, 1983) 5-17.

3. My version of the text in ibid. 18-20.

4. Ibid. 63.

5. Alexander Schmemann, *The Historical Road of Eastern Orthodoxy* (Crestwood, NY: St. Vladimir's Seminary Press, 1977) 195.

6. My version of the text in Isabel Florence Hapgood, *Service Book of the Holy Orthodox-Catholic Apostolic Church*, 4th ed. (Brooklyn, N.Y.: Syrian Antiochian Orthodox Archdiocese, 1965) 178, 230.

7. F.J.E. Raby, *A History of Christian-Latin Poetry from the Beginnings to the Close of the Middle Ages*, 2d ed. (Oxford: Clarendon Press, 1953) 159-162.

8. Ibid. 162-167.

9. For the text, see Marion A. Habig, ed., *St. Francis of Assisi: Writings and Early Biographies: English Omnibus of Sources for the Life of St. Francis*, 4th ed., rev. (Chicago: Franciscan Herald Press, 1983) 130-131. See also Roger D. Sorrell, *St. Francis of Assisi and Nature: Tradition and Innovation in Western Attitudes toward the Environment* (New York and Oxford: Oxford University Press, 1988) 98-124.

10. Habig, *St. Francis of Assisi* 132.

11. Unless otherwise noted, my information about deacons of the Episcopal Church comes from correspondence and conversations.

12. Br. Placid, OSB, "Light from Light," *Abbey Letter* 165 (Eastertide 1991) [5].

13. Robert E. Gard, *The Deacon* (Madison, WI: R. Bruce Alison Wisconsin Books, 1979).

14. Berkley I. Forsythe, *Expo '98: Sherlock Holmes in Omaha* (Omaha, NE.: Simmons-Boardman Books, 1987).

15. E.T. Malone Jr., "Diakonia" (Chapel Hill, NC, 1991). Reprinted by permission of E.T. Malone Jr. Copyright 1991 by E.T. Malone Jr. All rights reserved.

16. Robert O. Dewey, *Straight in the Desert* (Lakeland, FL: n.p., 1984) 12. I have taken the liberty of changing Dewey's style of capitalization (all his letters are upper case) and punctuation (two or three dots at every pause). Reprinted by permission of Robert O. Dewey. Copyright 1984 by Robert O. Dewey. All rights reserved.

17. Ormonde Plater, "Exsultet," *The Living Church* (15 April 1990) 13. Reprinted by permission of *The Living Church*. Copyright 1990 by The Living Church Foundation, Inc. All rights reserved.

15

On Creation, Creativity, and the Creator

Barbara Carey

As it is the created world which surrounds us, and it is through our created senses and faculties that we have knowledge of God, so the ability to perceive manifestations is a basic competence needed by the Christian pilgrim.[1]

HOW TRAVELERS PERCEIVE THE WORLD UPON WHICH THEY VENTURE DEPENDS both upon the character of their surroundings and the nature of the talents given them to deal with their journeys. Some are favored with penetrating intellect, keen eyes, superior hearing, or fine physical skills. Others may be challenged by their limitations but are given will, determination, or stubbornness enabling them to experience what we might otherwise expect to elude them. Some may live amidst beautiful surroundings, easily observing the fecundity of nature day by day. Other visions of natural life may be obscured by the products of civilization. The latter may require greater exercise of abstraction and imagination to understand nature's spontaneous generative power. To see stars through city skies is rare, not so in unpopulated land. To observe human dependence upon nature is easy in a rural setting, difficult in an urban one. Thrilling to the sound of a symphony orchestra is possible in cultivated society but not in primitive isolation. Avenues to understanding are always defined by circumstance.

219

The urge to search for meaning in life is universal. Some claim that children are born with a biological urge to make sense of it.[2] Indeed, philosophy has an emotional, sensual base rooted in the experience of the physical world. This experience is fundamentally perceptual. It engages us in intensely active examination of and interaction with our physical and intellectual surroundings. Creative minds never cease exploring, admiring, and wondering about the objects of their attention, their fascination even becoming obsessive at times.

These minds dissect the objects of their attention, reveling in detail, dismantling either actually or abstractly the objects of their admiration. In order to make something, one must know of what it is made. Discovering ingredients requires participating in a process that is the reverse of "making," and for this reason creative minds are essentially both iconoclastic and formative.

In the philosophical realm, iconoclastic thinkers decry blind adherence to orthodoxies and formalisms which restrict fresh visions of life and impede the pursuit of the cosmological urge, the urge to explain creation. Heretical defiance of tradition characterizes all worthy mystics, philosophers, artists, scientists, explorers, inventors, and the like. They seek intense personal experience based on their own examinations and understandings. Repeatedly they tell us that this fascination with the "is-ness" of an entity is what fascinates and activates them.[3]

For many, this dynamic perception of reality is spiritual in character. It constitutes personal contact with God with all of the intangible, emotional, sensual qualities that characterize an intimate relationship. The glimpse beneath the cloak of mystery which surrounds the creator is experienced as a profoundly personal privilege with spiritual dimensions.[4]

The search for meaning in creation occupies every creative intellect. To root out the is-ness of a musical idea, of a mathematical concept, of a design, of a sub-atomic particle, of the atmosphere of Saturn, of the confirmation of Pangaea, of the Marianas Trench or any other aspect of creation can totally absorb a person. Profoundly curious people disregard theories or observations that contradict their intuitions and perceptions, a quality Hans Christian Anderson's famous fairy tale, *The Emperor's New Clothes*, cleverly illustrates.

The creative mind concentrates on a particular notion, exploring its features, its functions, its behaviors—all of its distinguishing characteristics. Scrutiny may be applied as easily to a process as to an object. This mind has innocence, freshness, and simplicity that allow it to see life without prejudice and to resist applying conventional labels or explanations. It often makes unique comparisons and generalizations and is able to see the subject of interest in unusual contexts. The capacity to abstract, to imagine, to reshape, to consider alternatives and possibilities is endemic to this spirit. Its temperament is original, generating ideas which exist on their own merits. The greatest artists are those who give autonomy and integrity to their creations. We associate this same complexity, freedom, and autonomy with God's creation insofar as we are able to understand the creator's acts and motives at all.

The urge to create is so universally experienced that we need not attempt to enumerate the many forms it may take. An obvious common urge, one well-known to overwhelm reason and logic, is the sexual one. Similarity between its characteristics and other expressions should not be lightly dismissed. Its qualities of stimulation, its need to communicate, its obsession, activity, and total absorption, if considered in the context of activities such as painting, musical composition, ministry, philosophy, architecture, theology, and so forth, can give insight into these pursuits.

Intimate understanding of an is-ness relies heavily on what the adeptly creative identify as intuition. They simply "know" when something is "right." This knowing is the intellectual counterpart of physical satisfaction of an appetite. We all know when thirst is slaked, hunger quelled, pain relieved, stress disbursed, fatigue obliterated. Innate satisfaction with the rightness of an artistic or intellectual concept assumes the same relationship, and is an essential component of the creative process.[5]

Another essential component is imagination. When he examined his methods of thought, Albert Einstein came to the conclusion that the gift of fantasy meant more to him than his talent for absorbing positive knowledge.[6] Nobel laureate Hideki Yukawa described his work in meson physics in a similar way by saying that abstraction cannot work by itself, but must be accompanied by intuition or imagination.[7] It is no accident that Einstein also played the violin, that Winston Churchill painted, that Leonardo Da Vinci invented machines, that Bach was fascinated with mathematics. The inventive mind finds connections between art, literature, and science, not antagonisms.[8] In recognition of this phenomenon, one observer called Einstein's General Theory of Relativity a great work of art to be enjoyed and admired.[9]

Enjoyment in this sense is whole-hearted, not passive.[10] It is often described in sensual rather than intellectual terms even when referring to abstract mental activity.[11] Popular opinion would have us believe that deep thinkers and those involved in complicated and esoteric disciplines are detached and unemotional in their work, that their pleasures are qualitatively different from those of "ordinary" people. On the contrary, enthusiasm, excitement, and energy characterize their work; emotional vitality, curiosity, and zest fill it.

Curiosity, the driving force in the metaphorical fantasy, *Alice in Wonderland*, drives creative endeavor and is so potent as to be regarded as holy.[12] It motivates us to pursue and persevere for no reason except to satisfy its urgings. As such, it presses us to examine life's mysteries and to inspect the structure of reality. Curiosity stimulates our initial foray, whether bold or timid, and propels us along a particular path.

Each person's journey, both physical and intellectual, will stir emotion, emotion powerful enough to motivate further adventure or discourage it. The love of the adventure will excite further imagination, drawing mind and heart into the complexity of the task at hand. Finally, adventurers care deeply about their pursuits, defining the rest of their lives according to the involvement they have with the object of their passion and desire.[13]

Out of love and knowledge come creation. Out of passion and abundance. Out of an overflow of energy and vitality. Out of the innate fecundity of nature.

Appreciating the innate fecundity of nature is often difficult from the perspective of urban life. Animal companions and cultivated gardens sample nature. But they fail to provide the scale and magnitude of original creation or the concomitant understanding that living outdoors and depending entirely on one's wits and surroundings provide.

Through anthropological studies we can partially understand the culture of nomadic people. Closer to home, the contemporary culture of Native Americans reflects an appreciation of the natural world unique in modern times. Current popular interest in the culture of these people has stimulated an enlarged public to examine and respect values previously termed "primitive" or "occult."

Early in the twentieth century, Bert Greer Phillips, a southwestern artist whose paintings of Native Americans were commissioned by the Santa Fe Railway, observed that these people worshiped all things beautiful. He commented that the Native American attitude toward beauty is not the passive appreciation characteristic of other cultures. Their response to beauty is integral to their being, and their daily lives revolve around the rhythm and life of nature.[14]

Understanding the rhythm and life of nature implies realizing that living things exist by virtue of dependence upon and sympathy with their surroundings. These creations rely upon each other and cannot exist in isolation. None controls the other absolutely. In the Native American tradition, power is in nature, not self. To ally oneself with this power, one must realize that power resides not in a single person but in the entire created world. When individuals assume power, disorder ensues and suffering follows.[15]

Considerations of the meaning of power, its manifestations and uses color any discussion of creation and particularly of the creator. To say that any creative mind actually equates itself somehow with God is to unfairly assume hubris. Before 1500 C.E., *creating*, as distinct from *making*, was the prerogative of God alone.[16] Biblical authors evaded this issue by use of myth, poetry, and analogy. Phrases such as "God so loved the world that...," "And God saw that it was good," are anthropomorphisms which enable understanding. Thus in discussing the power of creativity and the experience which creative people enjoy during creative acts, we draw upon this imagery in reverse, inferring from it the presence of a tangible contact between human beings and a numinous creative force.

Many creative individuals echo playwright Arthur Miller's observation that he was exhilarated at his power to make life in the same way God had. He had unleashed creative power in himself by giving substance to an idea. He likened the process to prayer in its mystical dimensions. It was also a form of participatory worship since others involved in bringing the playwright's creation to life made decisions about the play, just as people participate in the decisions of creation in their everyday life. This freedom to "use" creation defines original sin and free will. We are separate from God and able to act according to any standard we choose. Making life and making choices are qualities humans share with the Numinous. Liberating ideas by giving them form and giving these ideas freedom is another. Thus, in God we participate in the endless process of creation. We are independent and autonomous creations ourselves.[17]

Autonomy and independence of the created should be respected, appreciated, and enjoyed. This is no less true of a play, a symphony, a pot, or a poem than of a cat, a cactus, a spotted-owl, an ocean, the atmosphere, an albino, a Kurd, a Gentile. Superficial appraisal and thoughtless "use" of anything outside of oneself is an offense to both the creation itself and its creator. The more obvious a creation's uniqueness, the more obvious the affront. The response one makes to any creation is esthetic, moral, emotional, and physical. It is not possible to fully isolate these responses, for one experiences them all whether acknowledging them or not. Further, one *acts* upon these responses without realizing it. Ignoring, rejecting, accepting, destroying, admiring, exploiting, or nurturing are optional responses to each creation we encounter. How we choose is the measure of our lives. Thus the flip saying, "Not to choose is to choose," is more profound than it at first seems, and highlights the fact that, in the face of knowledge, indecision is immoral. How we deal with the converse—decision in the face of incomplete knowledge—is the eternal dilemma.

Options for response vary according to the form of a particular creation. A piano rag is loosed upon the world by a composer. A pianist will re-create it on other than the composer's piano, at different tempi and dynamics and with different emphases. The performer's attempt to understand the work, to give it life in hands other than the composer's, to make it speak to whatever hearts are present constitute a participation in the reality of that creation. This re-creator has a responsibility to the work of another that extends well into the moral and metaphysical. That a work stands alone ready to be regarded, evaluated, used, manipulated, abandoned, enjoyed, discarded, abused, misunderstood, destroyed, or changed tells us as much about all creation as it does about that particular work.

Viewed in this way, every creation has value, and distinctions between sacred and profane blur. Creation is seen as an ongoing process. In this context, the creation of the world becomes a mythic prototypical event, a sacred time to which we repeatedly seek to return. We seek to recapture its freshness, innocence, vitality, and originality.[18]

Religions tend to organize and systematize this experience by creating cycles of observance which liturgize and commemorate both God's creative power and human experience of it. These systems are closed, circular organizations, commonly defined by the calendar year and related to observable natural phenomena such as phases of the moon or agricultural cycles. The belief in the reincarnation also reflects the impulse to cyclical organization and is another example of why cyclical time is considered sacred time.

Philosophical abstractions devised by religious mystics have counterparts in other disciplines. The concept of the curvature of space elucidated by Albert Einstein provides an elegant physical model of the philosophical concept of sacred time, as does Andrei Sakharov's integration of his observations of the indefinitely repeated cycles of existence into his cosmological theories.[19]

Other conceptual similarities between philosophy and science can be found. Quantum physics finds quarks so elusive that the very attempts to describe their locations make those locations impossible to determine. The process seems akin to defining the Trinity. Dionysius understood these paradoxes, suggesting that we intuit God's nature by embracing combinations of what we know and don't know.[20] Shifting images, kaleidoscopic in nature, form by using the same lens focused on the same colored shards. Countless varied and original patterns are created. The slightest shift of lens or shard or observer produces different visions from exactly the same substance.

Entropy, chaos, and indeterminacy are other slippery physical concepts the examination of which resembles efforts to systematize thinking processes dependent upon choices, sifting alternatives, recombining elements in numerous forms, or considering components from different perspectives. Cosmogony, scientific exploration, theology, and creative art, therefore, share common outlooks and methodologies.

They also require similar qualities in the effective observer. Happy, innovative, productive people share the same personal qualities. Though no one person can exhibit all of them, the properties include wholeness, perfection, completion, justice, aliveness, richness, simplicity, beauty, goodness, uniqueness, effortlessness, playfulness, truth, and self-sufficiency.[21] The similarity of this catalog to others and to attributes of the creator is obvious. Meditating on these qualities, we might, for example, observe beauty in nature and examine how God may be beautiful, may make beautiful things, may think beautiful thoughts. Our own experience supplies the examples and therefore *is* the sacramental contact. Though we acknowledge that the Incommensurate can never be fully comprehended, our nature compels us to *attempt* to understand our contact with the Undefinable.

Contact with the Numinous may occur in our act of creating something. It may occur in our experience of the art of others or in our direct experience of the art of the creator. Symbolic creation, like God's creation, excites new sensibilities in the observer. Appreciation, then, is also a creative act. In it, transcendence of time and self is demonstrated.[22]

Going beyond self, or more importantly, overcoming self-centeredness, amplifies our capacity for sharing life. Artists, philosophers, and scientists congregate as much for mutual stimulation as for appreciation of their efforts. Few of the most productive work in constant isolation. Certainly much of the effort to produce something unique or explain some phenomenon is directed at communicating with others. It is not enough to *conceive* of a thing; the thing must somehow take on a form others can fathom. Christian understanding of the Incarnation depends upon this very logic: that God required human form to be understood by humans. Our belief that God "needs" human understanding infers that without it he would feel alone, a condition many of us try to avoid.

But we know that loneliness can contribute to the generation of great works, for many studies show a correlation between the capacity for isolation and the incidence of creative thought. Sustaining imaginative effort, concentrating one's mental powers, and focusing on a single area of intellectual design require some degree of privacy and freedom from distraction. This situation resembles the image we have of God working in majestic isolation, particularly as the creator of all from nothing. Biblical myth and George Burns in our contemporary myth, *O God*, add the anthropomorphic notion that God did *indeed* feel lonely and unappreciated until human life was formed.

Transcending self has another important dimension, that of seeking immortality. Expressions of self can endure beyond the self. The flow of Life, the timeless stream in which all swim, contains singular monuments to productive people. The desire to leave an artifact is of itself a rebellious act, for no mere mortal is omnipresent. It is an act of insurgence to seek to enlarge authority beyond one's immediate surrounds and to prolong influence beyond one's lifetime.[23]

Many creative efforts are demonstrably rebellious. The science of Galileo Galilei, the writings of Ayn Rand, the ministry of Mother

Theresa, the music of Arnold Schoenberg, the theology of Martin Luther, the art of Pablo Picasso, and the movies of Oliver Stone are examples. That against which these "saints" rebel is not authority *per se*, but against narrow, unexamined formalisms imbued with authority by virtue of convenience, tradition, or social circumstances. *These* rebellious search for more "authentic" sources of order and explanation than the ones immediately at hand. These rebellious and their followers may become as loyal to their new authorities as the world was to its formerly traditional ones.[24]

Here we confront the realization that our understanding of the true nature of the creator's power is severely limited. Human beings know God by the evidence at hand, by what they are able to perceive. God's latent talents cannot be humanly understood nor can manifestations beyond human ken. A 1960s author pointed out to us that *our* God is too small, that as a Christian culture we are institutionally guilty of solipsism.[25]

Indeed, institutions as corporate entities dependent upon historical context for their effectiveness, are constitutionally subject to change. Required change follows inspired observation, a phenomenon attributed to individuals, not groups.

The capacity to see clearly and speak openly about what one sees— the Emperor's-New-Clothes Syndrome—is a capacity ascribed to prophets and one widely referenced in Scripture. The courage and daring required to give utterance to holy observation resemble the exuberance required to liberate a creative notion.

Supernatural courage and insight abound in biblical writers.[26] The Yahwist author of Old Testament Scripture is like Abram and Jacob themselves in being filled with spiritual vitality. The creative genius of the Yahwist is so immense that the image of God projected in the so-called "J" texts, written about 925 B.C.E., dominates Judeo-Christian understanding of God's nature to this day. J describes God as capricious, lively, active, and exuberant, and shows the essence of God to be surprise and originality, Romantic ideas which we often find applied to artists, inventors, philosophers, and the like.[27]

The biblical creation myth indicates that humans are made in God's likeness. They are most God-like when most vital, when filled with courage, vigor, accurate perception, action, movement, and exercise of will. When people are creative, they overflow with urgent power; they are lively, possessed of a super-abundance of essential energy, energy which floods out of all boundaries of time and space and cannot be contained. This activity and its results are a blessing, a form of The Blessing: more life, abundant life, eternal life.[28]

"*L'chaim!*" - "To life!" This exuberant Jewish toast exemplifies an appreciation for the immeasurable gift that life is, both individually and collectively. In the Jewish observance of Rosh Hashanah, personal repentance and reconciliation are sought as a means of assuring a place in the Book of Life.[29] The strength, power, and awesomeness of God's creation are observed in prayer; the incredible sound of the shofar represents "the power God gives us to make fresh every living moment."[30] A similar prayer from Lamentations, "Make our days full of newness, as You did long ago," is read during Tisha B'Av.[31] These prayers for more life, more Blessing, reflect an outlook on mortal existence which has sustained the Jewish people through centuries of unimaginable persecution.

More life. Into a time without boundaries. More Blessing. Days full of newness. Every moment fresh. How evocative of the lives of creative people these phrases are.

Freshness and newness are obvious attributes of the First Creation. No matter in what venue humans may act, the creation of the world becomes the archtype for every subsequent creative exercise.[32] And for many observers, artists constitute human metaphors for God's creativity.[33] Not only does an artist's activity echo the Original, it *interprets* the Original. Pop artists tap exactly the same vein as the traditional in this regard. Andy Warhol, Madonna, Garry Trudeau, and Spike Lee are all adept interpreters using contemporary metaphor.[34] The metaphoric mind either sees or invents unusual relationships and creates forms for depicting them. When such a mind comes upon the requisite metaphor, it knows in a perfect realization what is required. There is no hesitation; rather a sort of instantaneous recognition.[35] Even those who do not consider themselves particularly creative occasionally experience sudden realizations, ones which surprise and delight them. If the content of a realization is the solution to a dilemma or an idea for a painting, we term the experience "inspiration."[36]

Reflecting on the assertion echoed by others[37] that inspiration fires the creative process leads us to speculate on what might have "inspired" the creator to act. We have already touched on "loneliness" and found it wanting. Further thought yields the likelihood that God's motives are different from human ones, and that it is neither possible nor necessary for us to achieve full understanding of these motives in order to appreciate God's power. Given that no human understanding *can* be perfect and complete, we conclude that everyone's task is simply to seek, earnestly. The quality of such effort is improved by making the journey in faith and sustaining the search for fresh understanding and new appreciation day by day. Realizing that we see only between blinks,[38] we must strive for the best vision possible.

Creative people are missionaries for truth. They regard their occupations as callings, vocations as profoundly mystical as those to the priesthood. Like saints, they spend themselves in their revelations, bringing themselves entire to epiphanies in various forms. Even the misguided proceed with fervor and dedication, using up themselves and their worldly assets according to their desire. Sustained by their skills, they persevere, sometimes rewarded and encouraged, sometimes vilified and impeded. The physical nakedness of Joan of Arc is mirrored in the intellectual and artistic exposure of those in other expressive areas. Ultimately, all one can do is act; the judgment of time takes care of itself.[39]

Our sampled examination of creation, creativity, and the creator leads us to conclude, then, that this yearning for glimpses of absolute truth, ultimately undefinable but knowable in an intuitive sense, propels all humans. What makes the creative individual different is the overwhelming compulsion to give form to understanding, however limited that understanding may be. In considering what shape to give an idea, choices are made, alternatives weighed, discarded or accepted, details considered, variations measured, an audience addressed. As we apply such criteria to the creator, we find ourselves humbled to consider that humans may not be the sole audience for all of creation; that creating continues and alternatives are still being weighed; that at every moment there is purpose and motive power engaged in the action of the universe; that overflow of desire and inspiration propel creative acts; that ways of giving form to inspiration are found through love; that no created thing is ever complete; that beauty is not static and changes as it is examined; that all things stand alone and are affected by what surrounds them; that power exists everywhere and in everything and is available to experience in some way.

Can we know what that way will be? Art may show us; nature may show us, or poetry, or music, or architecture, or literature.

All artistic endeavor is mythic.[40] It is of itself, but connotes more. It describes a small reality, but embodies larger truths. It is of certain circumstances, but implies others. It exists in a particular moment, but transcends it. It is particular and concrete, but stimulates generalities and abstractions. For the creative, the power to create myth is paramount.

Zechariah suggests to us in his powerful eschatological myth, one partaking freely of images of nature and natural phenomena, that when the day of Yahweh comes—when our understanding of creation and the creator is complete—

> His feet will rest on the Mount of Olives, which faces Jerusalem on the east, and the Mount of Olives will be split in half from east to west, forming a huge valley; half the Mount will recede northwards, the other half southwards. The valley between the hills will be filled in, yes, it will be blocked as far as Jasol, it will be filled in as it was by the earthquake in the days of Uzziah king of Judah. And Yahweh my God will come, and all the holy ones with him. That Day, there will be no light, but only cold and frost. And it will be one continuous day—Yahweh knows—there will be no more day and night, and it will remain light right into the time of evening. When that Day comes, living waters will issue from Jerusalem, half towards the eastern sea, half towards the western sea; they will flow summer and winter. Then Yahweh will become king of the whole world. When that Day comes, Yahweh will be the one and only and his name the one name.

Notes

1. Harry Boone Porter, *A Song of Creation* (Cambridge, MA: Cowley, 1986) 130.

2. Morris Bergman calls this the cosmological urge, adding that "cosmology explains the order of things . . . We are creatures genetically programmed for meaning. "Interview," *Omni: The Search for God* 13:1 (August 1991) 87.

3. See also Ronald W. Clark, *Einstein: The Life and Times* (New York: Avon Books, 1971) 118, among others.

4. "Is-ness" is my word. Henry Miller, "Reflections on Writing," says that "understanding is not a piercing of the mystery, but an acceptance of it, a living with it, in it, through it and by it." See Brewster Ghiselin, *The Creative Process* (Berkeley: University of California Press, 1952) 187.

5. Ibid.

7. Hideki Yukawa, *Creativity and Intuition* (Tokyo: Kodanshu International Ltd., 1973) 10-11.

8. "Creative imagination is the vital factor in all of them." Clark, *Einstein* 208.

9. Hedwig Born said that the theory was "the greatest feat of human thinking about nature, the most amazing combination of philosophical

penetration, physical intuition, and mathematical skill. But its connections with experience were slender. It appealed to me like a great work of art to be enjoyed and admired." Ibid. 252.

10. One friend said of Einstein: "I have never known anybody who enjoyed science so sensuously as Einstein. Physics melted in his mouth." Ibid. 395.

11. Andrei Sakharov uses similar language to describe his work in theoretical cosmological physics: "Such models have attracted cosmologists' attention for quite awhile: Some authors have called them 'oscillating' models, but I prefer the term 'many sheeted,' which seemed *more expressive* and more in tune with the *emotional and philosophical implications* [italics mine] of indefinitely repeated cycles of existence." Andrei Sakharov, *Memoirs* (New York: Knopf, 1990) 542.

12. Einstein observed that "Curiosity has its own reason for existence. One cannot help but be in awe when [one] contemplates the mysteries of eternity, of life, of the marvelous structure of reality. It is enough if one tries merely to comprehend a little of his mystery each day. Never lose a holy curiosity." Clark, *Einstein* 755.

13. Pulitzer prize-winning author Annie Dillard characterizes this quest by observing that artists have always possessed "powerful hearts, not powerful wills. They loved the range of materials they used, the work's possibilities excited them, the field's complexities fixed their imaginations. The caring suggested the tasks; the tasks suggested the schedules. They learned their fields and then loved them. They worked respectfully out of love and knowledge, and they produced complex bodies of work that endure." Annie Dillard, *The Writing Life* (New York: Harper and Row, 1989) 70-71. Christian Zervos echoes Dillard with the observation that "art is not the application of a canon of beauty, but what instinct and intellect can conceive independently of the canon. When one loves a woman one doesn't take instruments and measure her, one loves her with desire." Christian Zervos, *Conversations with Picasso*, in Ghiselin, *The Creative Process* 52.

14. Sandra D'Emilio and Susan Campbell, *Visions and Visionaries: The Art and Artists of the Santa Fe Railway* (Layton, UT: Gibbs Smith, 1991) 78.

15. "One of the deep teachings in the Native American tradition is always to try to rid yourself of the impulse to feel powerful: to remember that the power is out there, the power is not in you." Interview with Robert Nelson in Robert Baker and Ellen Draper, "Exploring the Near at Hand," *Parabola* 16:2 (May 1991) 39.

16. Georgia Todd Temple, "Creating Works of Art," *Midland Reporter-Telegram* (21 July 1991) G 1-2.

17. "I felt . . . exhilaration for I had made life, just like God." Arthur Miller, *Timebends* (New York: Grove Press, 1987) 396. "One has control of a new power, a power to make real everything one is capable of imagining . . . An artist blindly follows his nose with hands outstretched, and only after he has struck the rock and brought forth the form hidden within does he and

explain what is forever inexplicable [my note: we might advance the notion that God "explains" his art through such as Christ and prophets] .. . I did not know how to do what I had apparently done and . . . the whole thing might as well have been a form of prayer for all that I understand about it." Ibid. 193. ". . . an idol tells people exactly what to believe. God presents them with choices they have to make for themselves. The difference is far from insignificant; before the idol men remain dependent children, before God they are burdened and at the same time liberated to participate in the decisions of endless creation." Ibid. 259.

18. "Since the sacred and strong time is the *time of origins* [italics his], the stupendous instant in which reality was created, was for the first time fully manifested, man will seek periodically to return to that original time . . . Religious man reactualizes the cosmogony . . . each time he creates something." Mircea Eliade, *The Sacred and the Profane*, tr. Willard Trask (New York: Harcourt Brace, 1987) 81. "Thus creativity is a sort of nostalgia for the perfection of beginnings, a desire to live in the world as it came from the Creator's hands . . . Every creation is a divine work and hence an irruption of the sacred; it at the same time represents an irruption of creative energy into the world. Every creation springs from an abundance." Ibid. 91.

19. See note 11 above.

20. Boyd Wright, "A Patron Saint for Writers," *The Living Church* (13 October 1991) 13-14.

21. Abraham H. Maslow, *Toward a Psychology of Being* (New York: Van Nostrand Reinhold Co., 1962) 83.

22. "The symbols only dreamt about by most human beings are expressed in graphic form by the artists. But in our appreciation of the created work . . . we are also performing a creative act. When we engage a painting . . . we are experiencing some new moment of sensibility; something unique is born in us. This is why appreciation of the music or painting or other works of the creative person is also a creative act on our part." Rollo May, *The Courage to Create* (New York: W.W. Norton and Co., 1975) 22. "In the creative exercise one transcends one's mortal limitations." Ibid. 25.

23. "By the creative act . . . we *are* able to reach [even] beyond our own death." Ibid.

24. "Artists are generally . . . concerned with their inner visions and images. But that is precisely what makes them feared by any coercive society. For they are the bearers of the human being's age-old capacity to be insurgent. They love to immerse themselves in chaos in order to put it into form, just as God created form out of chaos in Genesis." Ibid. 32. May also paraphrases a famous observation by Paul Tillich: "In religion, it is not the sycophants or those who cling most faithfully to the status quo who are ultimately praised. It is the insurgents . . . Those we call saints rebelled against outmoded and inadequate forms of God on the basis of their new

insights into divinity . . . into the meaning of godliness. They rebelled . . . against God in the name of God beyond God. The continuous emergence of God beyond God is the mark of creative courage in the religious sphere." Ibid. 34-35.

25. "The seeing of God is not like the seeing of man. Man sees only *between* the blinks of his eyes. He does not know what the world is like *during* the blinks. He sees the world in pieces, in fragments. But the Master of the Universe sees the whole world unbroken. *That world is good. Our seeing is broken . . . An artist, too, must see the whole world. He must somehow learn to see during the blinks, he must see where no one else can see, he must see the connections, the* betweennesses in the world. Even if the connections are ugly and evil, the artists must learn to see and record them" [italics his]. Chaim Potok, *The Gift of Asher Lev* (New York: Knopf, 1990) 100.

26. David Rosenberg and Harold Bloom, *The Book of J* (New York: Grove Wedenfel, 1990) 205, 211.

27. "Those who have contempt for Yahweh lack the capacity for change; they are fixed and obsessive builders of Babel, the inhabitants of Sodom, Egyptian slavemasters, backsliding whiners in the Wilderness. Beyond surprise, despisers of wholeness, they have no desire to be useful to Yahweh. That desire is elitist, and one of its fullest embodiments is the gorgeous career of David, and of Joseph before him. Human caprice, however dammed or deprecated by normative tradition, remains the essence of elitism and helps account for what it is that attracts Yahweh to David, and less fully to Joseph." Ibid. 277.

28. "If God's leading attribute is vitality, then his creature, the human, is most Godlike when most vital." Ibid. 277. "Why does someone of immense literary power write [and by extension we might ask here what motivates such as mathematicians, physicists, musicians, actors?] whether now or three thousand years ago? Doubtless there are hosts of reasons. But I think essentially it comes down to the Blessing: more life into a time without boundaries." Ibid. 277. See also Eliade, *The Sacred and the Profane* 29, 65.

29. "And therefore, Lord our God, cause all that You created to remember fully all that You have done; cause all Your creatures to revere Your doings and to tremble in Your presence; cause them all to act as one to do Your will wholeheartedly. For we know, Lord our God, that the strength of Your hand, the power of Your right arm, and the awesomeness of Your Name rule over all creation." Arthur Waskow, *Seasons of Our Joy* (Boston: Beacon Press, 1982) 11.

30. Ibid. 15.

31. Ibid. 222.

32. Eliade, *The Sacred and the Profane* 45.

33. Diane Apostolos-Cappadona, "God in Culture: Images of God in Christian Art" (manuscript) 13.

34. "The metaphoric mind is the natural mind. Its functions are enriched but never dominated by the natural order. It wanders through awarenesses, experiences, images, and all our tacit knowings like a gentle predator as it searches for being. If there are gaps in experience of knowledge, it hardly pauses but seeks an alternative route. If there is no valid alternative route, the metaphoric mind invents one. For that is what it does best . . . it invents." Bob Samples, *The Metamorphic Mind* (Reading, MA: Addison-Wesley Publishing Co., 1976) 62.

35. "The thing has already taken form in my mind before I start on it." Vincent Van Gogh, "Letter to Anton Ridder van Reppart," in Ghiselin, *The Creative Process* 47.

36. "Inspiration, then, is the impulse which sets creation in movement, it is also the energy which keeps it going. The [creator's] principal problem is that of recapturing it in every phase of his work; of bringing . . . the requisite amount of energy to bear on every detail, as well as . . . on his vision of the whole." Roger Sessions, "The Composer and His Message," in Ghiselin, *The Creative Process* 38.

37. See Harold Shapero, "The Musical Mind," in Ghiselin, *The Creative Process* 45.

38. See note 25.

39. "It is evident that faith in their vocation, mystical in intensity, sustains poets . . . [A] poet's [is] a sacred vocation like a saint's . . . Their ambition is of the purest kind attainable in the world . . . They are ambitious to be accepted for what they ultimately are as revealed by their inmost experiences, their finest perceptions, their deepest feelings, their uttermost sense of truth . . . Since there can be no cheating, the poet, like the saint, stands in all his works before the bar of a perpetual day of judgment . . . At the same time this faith is coupled with a deep humility because one knows that, ultimately, judgment does not rest with oneself. All one can do is to achieve nakedness, to be what one is with all one's faculties and perceptions, strengthened by all the skills which one can acquire, and then to stand before the judgment of time." Stephen Spender, "The Making of a Poem," in Ghiselin, *The Creative Process* 122-123.

40. ". . . what flows into you from the myths is not truth but reality (truth is always about something but reality is about which truth is) and therefore every myth becomes the father of innumerable truths on the abstract level." A.N. Wilson, *C.S. Lewis: A Biography* (New York: W.W. Norton, 1990) 219.

16

"The Care of the Earth" as a Paradigm for the Treatment of the Eucharistic Elements

Frank C. Senn

The Emergence of a Theme

THE ECOLOGICAL CRISIS IN THE NATURAL ENVIRONMENT HAS BEEN AN AREA OF major ethical reflection during the second half of the twentieth century. It has had a liturgical correlary in the development of creation themes in prayer texts and calendar observances. There has been less attention focused on the most creaturely elements used in Christian liturgical celebration: the bread and wine of the eucharist. Yet the ways in which we treat these earthly elements provide a model for our care of the earth.

The eucharistic controversies of the ninth century marked a change in the treatment of the eucharistic elements. In the debate between Paschasius Radbertus and Ratramnus, two monks of Corbie, the tension between the realism of Ambrose of Milan and the sacramentalism of Augustine of Hippo snapped. It became impossible to regard the eucharistic elements as "figures" of the body and blood of Christ.[1]

It would be another three centuries before the notion, emphatically stressed by Radbertus, that the eucharistic bread and wine "change" into the body and blood of Christ, would be philosophically defined by the doctrine of "transubstantiation."[2] What could not be analyzed by the great theologians who devoted themselves to this task was the impact of cultural change on the understanding of "reality" and its impact on notions of sacramental realism. In fact, Western European peoples were culturally incapable of sustaining the worldview of classical antiquity which pervaded the mind sets of the Greek and Latin theologians of the fourth and fifth centuries. For these Church Fathers, "figure" and "symbol" pointed to and participated in reality. For the empirically-minded peoples of Western Europe, what is "real" is what can be apprehended by the senses. Certainly changes in sacramental practice influenced eucharistic piety, and piety influenced doctrinal development.[3] But the fact is that the discussions which informed practice, piety, and theology were rooted in the empirical desire to experience reality through the senses.

Examples of this are found in *The Dialogue on Miracles*, c. 1223, by Caesarius of Heisterbach (c. 1180-1240). In Book IX, which treats "Of the Sacrament of the Body and Blood of Christ," the whole interest centers in providing proofs that what one receives in the sacrament is "the true body of Christ born from the virgin" under the species of the bread and "that the actual blood is present under the species of wine."[4] The proofs are provided from miraculous incidents which the master monk relates to the novice. Among the numerous miracles associated with the "change" and the "status" of the eucharistic elements, the ones that hold interest for the theme of this essay are: "Of the body and blood of the Lord which was stolen from a church and its place of concealment revealed by oxen in a field"[5] and "Of bees who built a shrine for the body of the Lord."[6] In the case of the oxen, as they were plowing a field they came to a discarded pyx and would not move forward over the consecrated elements. In the case of the bees, a women pretended to receive communion in order to sneak home a consecrated host, which she then put in her beehive to keep her bees from dying off. But the bees, Caesarius related, "recognized their creator, and built a most beautiful chapel with wonderful skill from their sweetest honeycomb for the most gracious guest, and placed it in an altar of the same material, and laid upon it the most sacred body."

The naiveté of this popular piety is charming; and we note that Caesarius of Heisterbach was a contemporary of Francis of Assisi, whose reputed delight in God's creation was only less sophisticated than the interest in the natural world that led to the rise of the natural sciences and the recovery of Aristotelian philosophy during this period. Indeed, Lynn White argues that "the emergence of Gothic art reflects a fundamental change in the European attitude towards the natural environment. Things ceased to be mere symbols, rebuses, *Dei vestigia*, and became objects interesting and important in themselves, quite apart from man's spiritual needs."[7] But this development of interest in the natural world led to technological mastery of the natural environment by western people. In the process humankind became alienated from the world of nature and could use it only as a pool of resources to be exploited. By the twentieth century, the very atoms were so abused as to become agents of the ultimate hurt rather than the glue which held the creation together.

In this context of potential ecological catastrophe, the late Joseph Sittler sounded a warning and issued a constructive challenge to develop a theology large enough to embrace and challenge humankind's vast, penetrating, and revolutionary domination and manipulation of the natural world. In his epochal address to the 1963 Assembly of the World Council of Churches at New Delhi, India, Sittler proposed a doctrine of creation large enough to view the world of nature redeemed from human abuse and freed for its God-given purpose. He said:

> The way forward is from Christology expanded to its cosmic dimensions, made passionate by the pathos of this threatened earth, and made ethical by the love and the wrath of God. For as it was said in the beginning that God beheld all things and declared them good, so it was uttered by the angel of the Apocalpyse of St. John, ". . . ascending from the east, having the seal of the living God; . . . he cried with aloud voice to whom it was given to hurt the earth and the sea, saying, hurt not the earth, neither the sea, nor the trees . . ." The care of the earth, the realm of nature as a theatre of grace, the ordering of the thick, material procedures that make available to or deprive men of bread and peace—these are Christological obediences before they are practical necessities.[8]

Two issues are raised here: the need to develop a wider sense of the scope of grace through an expanded Christology; and the need to see creation in terms of its redemption in Christ. In his *Essays on Nature and Grace*, Sittler probed the resources of an expanded Christology: the testimony to a cosmic Christology in the Epistles to the Colossians and Ephesians and the prologue to the Gospel of John; the image of Christ the Pantocrator in the Eastern Church; and the multi-faceted aspects of the doctrine of grace in western theology since the time of Augustine.[9] In his celebrated sermon on "The Care of the Earth," Sittler evoked a neo-Franciscan sense for the world as a place of wonder and delight. He set forth the proposition that "delight is the basis of right use."[10] Wine, for example, is to be enjoyed, not used. Or, rather, enjoyment of wine is the right use of it. Rightly used it may be a means of grace; abused it stores up wrath. Here is a sacramental principle not unlike that which St. Paul applied to the celebration of the Lord's Supper in 1 Corinthians 11. "Right use" has both sacramental and ethical implications.

The restriction of grace to the believer's personal relationship with God, especially in Reformation theology, left Christian theology resourceless in dealing with the ecological structure of reality and human interaction with it. And the attitude of utilitarianism, especially manifested in the ethos of practical usefulness, has imperiled Brother Earth.[11] This essay on the treatment of the eucharistic elements takes Sittler's teaching on "the care of the earth" as a paradigm for the treatment of the eucharistic elements, and the treatment of the eucharistic elements as a paradigm for the care of the earth. The offering, consecration, consumption, and disposal of the eucharistic elements must fit into an ecological structure. That structure must be informed by an understanding of God's saving love for the cosmos (Jn 3:16) and a Christological obedience which outweighs practical necessities.

Because this essay is written to honor an eminent liturgiologist who has been in the forefront of recovering the understanding of worship as "primary theology," and because I have expressed myself a number of times on the methodological question of the relationship between the *lex orandi* and the *lex credendi*, let me indicate at the outset that harnessing liturgical praxis to a particular theological vision in no way implies a subjection of liturgy to doctrine. Quite the contrary, the very building blocks of Sittler's Christology of nature are hymnological and liturgical materials in the New Testament and the early church. Indeed, the historic liturgy itself provides a witness to "the ecology of faith" and evoked a cosmic Christology in its acclamations and canticles even during those periods of rationalism when theology restricted grace to the realm of privacy.

Finally, it should be noted that data can be interpreted in various ways according to one's agenda. Caesarius of Heisterbach was concerned to shore up the sense of sacramental realism and belief in the "change" in the eucharistic elements at the moment of consecration. Stories about oxen kneeling before a consecrated host dropped in the field and bees building a Gothic honeycomb over a consecrated host fall into the category of "bleeding host" stories used to argue for the "real presence" of Christ in the elements. Apart from whatever veracity might might be ascribed to these stories, they do testify to the mute creation's recognition of the gracious visitation of the One who subjected it to futility in the hope of redemption (Rom 8:18ff.).[12] This proposed analysis of the "true use" of the eucharistic elements within the paradigm of "the care of the earth" should suggest redemptive possibilities for the natural world. It will do so by arguing for a practice of disposal of the eucharistic elements which demonstrates reverence for the earthly species that have served as means of grace; for an understanding of consecration that involves less an idea of "change" in the elements (thus denying their creaturely status) and more a "recognition" of a "true use" according to the word of Christ; and finally for an offering of the bread and wine which recognizes the complex matrix of nature and human endeavor from which these earthly elements are produced.

A Starting Point: Ecological Implications in Leftovers

When we prepare a dinner party or a special banquet, our concern is primarily to feed those who are present and to do so either as inexpensively or as impressively as possible. When our ancestors prepared a feast, their concern was to feed the whole community and to have leftovers for additional days of celebration when work would be kept to a minimum. This approach to feasting still survives in some family festivities, such as Christmas, reunions, or anniversaries, when, among other considerations, the economical homemaker asks: what can we serve that will provide food for latecomers as well as for ourselves in the days following the feast when we don't want to spend so much time in the kitchen?

As early as the full description of Christian eucharistic worship in the *Apology* of Justin Martyr c. 150, a part of the eucharistic celebration was the inclusion of the absent to whom the deacons took the consecrated bread and wine.[13] This means that the celebration was planned with leftovers in mind to accomodate a larger number of communicants than those gathered in the public assembly.

Archdale A. King, in *Eucharistic Reservation in the Western Church*, demonstrates that the primary purpose of reservation before the twelfth century was to commune those who were not present at the community's celebration: the sick, the imprisoned, and the dying (viaticum).[14] There was also the practice of the faithful taking home the consecrated elements in order to commune themselves at the end of a period of fasting, a practice discouraged after the fifth century.[15] The ancient *Ordines Romani* also indicate practices which connected liturgies of the Roman Church separated in space and time: the *fermentum*, or elements consecrated at the papal liturgy carried by acolytes to other liturgies in the city at which presbyters or suffragan bishops presided, in order to demonstrate the unity of all the faithful in the pope's echarist; and the *sancta*, or reserved particles from the previous eucharist which were added to the supply of elements at the present eucharistic celebration.[16] Reservation of the consecrated elements for the liturgy of the Pre-Sanctified developed in the Eastern Churches during the sixth century. This practice, which facilitated the communion of the faithful on the fast-days of Lent when the eucharist was not celebrated, was restricted in the Roman Church to Good Friday because the eucharist was celebrated daily and a distinction between feasts and fast days was not maintained.[17]

Nathan Mitchell, in *Cult and Controversy*, has discussed the process by which the consecrated elements were reserved, not for communion in special circumstances, but for the worship of the eucharist outside the Mass.[18] These practices included: visits to the blessed sacrament, processions (e.g., on Palm Sunday and Corpus Christi), solemn exposition of the sacrament to the people at communion, and Solemn Benediction of the Blessed Sacrament at the conclusion of Sunday Vespers and in Corpus Christi processions. By the fifteenth century, the worship of the sacrament outside of the Mass was replacing participation in the liturgy itself in popular devotion.[19] And people were more inclined to gaze at the elements than to eat and drink them. Indeed, by this time the people did not ordinarily receive the cup of wine in communion. And the quantity of bread had been reduced to a minimum by the use of wafers.

Here is the source of the Reformation's polemic against the adoration of the sacrament. The "true use," according to the Reformers, is to eat and drink the bread and wine in thankful remembrance of Christ's sacrifice for the forgiveness of sins.[20] There was no "true use" if the sacrament was not consumed by the communicants. But inclusion in the feast was handled differently by different reforming parties.

In the Lutheran churches, the sacrament was offered every Sunday and festival to those who desired it after they had been examined and absolved.[21] Announcing for communion became an important practice since that determined whether there would be any communicants (Mass would not be celebrated without communicants), as well as providing an opportunity to catechize and absolve those who intended to receive communion. The sick and homebound were included within pastoral care and there is some indication, in the *Manuel* of Olavus Petri (1529) and the Mark Brandenburg Church Order (1540), of communion from the reserved sacrament.[22] We are aware of some instances of Martin Luther's strong objection to mixing the consecrated with the unconsecrated elements, so intense was his belief in the sacramental union of the body and blood of Christ with the bread and wine.[23] While this might have led to the retention of the old practice of eucharistic reservation, and to the communion of the sick and dying from the reserved elements, the tradition that developed in Lutheranism was to consecrate the elements in the presence of the communicants (in effect, a kind of "private Mass," although the presence of others was often encouraged). There has not been much discussion about the reasons for this practice. But we would suggest that a major concern centered less on the status of the elements than on the importance of the proclamation of the words of institution as a "summary of the gospel"[24] in the hearing of the communicants.

In contrast, the Reformed Churches emphasized the fellowship aspect of the Lord's Supper, and conscientious effort was made to include the whole congregation in the celebration and reception of the sacrament four times a year. Within this tradition provision for the communion of the sick and dying was not firmly established. Among the Reformed there was absolute resistance to the adoration of the elements. By contrast, the elevation of the host was retained in many Lutheran Mass-orders. For the Reformed there was certainly no sense that the consecration involved any kind of "change" in the elements. Nor was there a concern to keep the consecrated and unconsecrated elements separated after the celebration of the Lord's Supper.

The Anglican tradition was a *media via* between the Lutheran and Reformed traditions in its sacramental practices. The Book of Common Prayer has always provided a form for the communion of the sick. The 1549 Prayer Book followed the Mark Brandenburg Church

Order in providing for communion from the reserved sacrament, but also provided for an abbreviated eucharistic rite in the home of the sick. As in Lutheranism, this latter practice came to prevail in Anglicanism. But the 1979 Book of Common Prayer of The Episcopal Church and *Occasional Services: Lutheran Book of Worship* (1982) have each provided an order for the ministration of communion to those in special circumstances, like the Roman Catholic rite of Administration of Communion and Viaticum to the Sick.[25] An ecological principle is involved here: the whole community should be included in the celebration. The celebration should accomodate those who are absent from the assembly.

But even if elements from the congregation's celebration are sent out with ministers for the communion of the sick and homebound, there are bound to be additional supplies of consecrated bread and wine that are not so used. Invoking the practice of *Ordo Romanus I*, these elements could be set aside for inclusion in the next eucharist. This becomes less practical when "real bread" is used for communion rather than individual wafers, since the bread will probably not keep for a week. In situations where a reverent consuming of the elements is not possible, excess bread and wine can be scattered onto and poured into the ground. There could be even a solemn procession to the place where the elements are to be disposed and a prayer of thanksgiving for the use of the elements as they are returned to the earth from which they came.

A theory of consecration as "change" in the elements might make some squeamish about treating the bearers of the body and blood of Christ in this way. I believe it could be argued that the body of Christ broken on the cross and the blood of Christ spilled for our redemption cannot be desecrated by being broken and poured onto the ground which also provided a final resting place for the human body of Jesus before his resurrection. It may be a part of our religious sensibility that sacred things should be protected from defilement, but we note the statement of Mircea Eliade that the ". . . ambivalence of the sacred is not only in the psychological order (in that it attracts or repels), but also in the order of values; the sacred is at once `sacred' and `defiled'."[26] Mary Douglas also notes many examples where corruption is enshrined in sacred places and times, especially symbols of suffering and death such as the crucifix in Christian devotion.[27] A reverent disposal of the elements which have been the bearers of Christ's sacramental body and blood can be a model for the reverential treatment of any of earth's creatures which have been the gracious bearers of life through a "true use."

At the same time we need to consider whether the theory of a "moment of consecration" which produces a "change" in the elements at the words of institution or the epiclesis even squares with the biblical and patristic view of consecration.

Thanksgiving as Consecration

What does Christological obedience require when it comes to the central act of the eucharist? What is the referent of the dominical command related by St. Paul in 1 Corinthians 11:24 and 25, "Do this in remembrance of me." Much discussion on this text has focused on the biblical concept and content of "remembrance" (anamnesis). But to what does the command "do this" refer? The plain sense of the text is that "Do this" points to the action of giving thanks and eating and drinking the bread and the wine.[28] If there is no thanksgiving, or if the bread and wine are not received and consumed, the dominical command has not been obeyed, no matter what other pious practices are observed.

So important is the idea of "thanksgiving" in Holy Communion that it has given its name to the entire service—the eucharist. But *eucharistia* comes to focus especially in the Great Prayer of Thanksgiving proclaimed over the bread and wine. Thanksgiving is essentially an acknowledgment of a gift received.[29] This is the fundamental insight of the Jewish *berakoth*, from which models the Christian eucharistic prayers evolved.[30] When, in the Jewish meal prayers, the Lord is blessed for the fruit of the vine or the bread from the earth, this is an acknowledgment of the true Giver of every good and perfect gift, which requires a "right use" on the part of the recipient. It might be noted that the blessing of God at the breaking of the bread is tied in with Semitic practices of hospitality, which says something about the connection between prayer and human behavior.

The eucharistic prayer acknowledges our indebtedness to God for all his gifts, including all the gifts of creation, redemption, and sanctification, but takes the bread and wine as the focus of the praise of God for his grace in Christ. This is why the eucharistic institution narrative found a place in the eucharistic prayer. Its purpose was neither to provide a warrant for the celebration nor a consecration formula, but rather a way of focusing the jubilant acknowledgment that all is grace. The institution narrative is noticeably lacking in the eucharistic prayers of the *Didache*, chs. 9-10, and in the earliest known text of the East Syrian Anaphora of Addai and Mari.[31] But a consecration formula was not needed; thanksgiving itself is consecratory. It acknowledges the source of the gift and implores a right use of it. By focusing on the bread and wine, these elements become typical of all created things. But a special grace is attached to them because of the command and promise of Christ. This is recollected in the words of institution, and it was a logical development to include an institution narrative in the prayer. In the Anaphora of Hippolytus the institution narrative was connected with the anamnesis because the words of Christ (in Hippolytus' text), "When you do this, you make my remembrance," were followed by "Remembering, therefore, his death and resurrection."[32] In the *Euchologion* of Sarapion of Thmuis, however, the words of institution are directly connected with the offering of the bread and the cup and there is no formal anamnesis.[33]

Thanksgiving is not the reason for gathering. The reason for gathering is to celebrate a fellowship meal, and consuming the elements is essential to the meal. The cause of the celebration is that participation in "holy things" makes us one with Christ Jesus himself. But the Great Thanksgiving articulates the meanings and dynamics of this celebration. It does so by employing a "rhetoric of celebration" which existed prior to the exegetical language of analysis and the theological language of proposition. Thanksgiving is occasioned by remembrance of the gracious gifts of God. But there is, as Joseph Sittler observed, a "way of testifying-forward by recollecting-backward."[34] The promises and mighty acts of God in the past (e.g., the promise to Abraham, the event of Exodus) become stimuli to reflection on fresh instances of hope and acts of redemption—in Israel and in Christ. Recollection leads to participation and reenactment. A classic example of this is Romans 6:1-11, in which recollection of Christ's death and resurrection becomes the occasion for reflection on our participation in Christ's death and resurrection through baptism. In eucharistic prayers the recollection of the Christ's redemptive acts in the anamnesis becomes the impetus for imploring a Spirit-engendered participation (*koinonia*) in the fruits of Christ's redemptive acts. This *koinonia* includes sharing in the bread and the cup and the fellowship of the ecclesial body. The epiclesis in the eucharistic prayers has tried to include both of these dimensions of *koinonia*.[35]

Joseph Keenan has rightly lamented the lack of cosmological themes in Christian eucharistic prayers, especially as contrasted with Jewish prayers such as the *berakoth* preceeding the *Shema*.[36] But we note that the usual progression of sections in a eucharistic prayer from the epiclesis to the intercessions, commemorations, and concluding doxology employ what Sittler called a "rhetoric of cosmic extension."[37] Especially in the more developed prayers, intercessions include all sorts andconditions of humanity, the commemorations of the saints inject a sense of eschatological fulfillment, and the concluding doxology praises Jesus Christ who is worthy and capable of bearing the glory and honor of God. The prayers acclaim, finally, a cosmic Christ who rules all things.[38] It is here, in eschatology and doxology, that cosmological ideas are found—properly—in Christian eucharistic prayers. For, as Sittler proposed, "the realm of redemption cannot be conceived as having a lesser magnitude than the realm of creation."[39] Creation themes cannot be limited to the preface-section of the eucharistic prayer as if the creation itself is unaffected by that reality which Christian theology calls "the fall." The destiny of the whole creation must be included within the great eschatological salvation.

Creatures of bread and wine have been taken from the creation and presented for use and acknowledged by thanksgiving and the word of Christ as the bearers of Christ's sacramental body and blood. We now look at these elements as typical of the creation when they are presented in that part of the liturgy known as the offertory.

The World as Sacrament

Alexander Schmemann, like Joseph Sittler also of blessed memory (and equally a mentor), wrote that "The world was created as the `matter,' the material of an all-embracing eucharist, and man was created as the priest of this cosmic sacrament."[40] The Christian eucharistic meal declares the eucharistic nature of the whole world. Even if "fallen man" does not acknowledge this reality, humanity redeemed by Christ does acknowledge it.

We have resisted a notion of consecration which regards it as an act of sacralization. Sacralization is an act of separating persons and things from the profane realm to place them in a "religious" compartment. Consecration as acknowledgment enables human beings to understand that all matter can be a sacrament of communion with

God, and by the inclusion of the words of institution it is declared that, by Christ's specific command and promise, these elements of bread and wine shall be a sacrament of communion with God. Schmemann asserted that the eucharist is "the end of cult, of the `sacred' religious acts, isolated from, and opposed to, the `profane' life of the community."[41] At every point the eucharist is connected with "the life of the world." This is so even with the consecration of the elements. It is not a matter of making something sacred out of something profane, for the world is not profane. It is the creation and gift of God, and bears the imprint of its creator no matter how marred. Consecration is the acknowledgment or recognition of that which has been sacred or holy from the beginning. As Louis Bouyer put it, consecration is "simple acceptance on the part of man of the divine having its own way, a `liturgy', that is, a `service', through which he hands himself over and submits himself to the will on high."[42] Consequently, the eucharistic consecration, far from expressing a separation, indicates the unity of all things in Christ (see Col 1:15-20). By making *eucharistia*, we acknowledge the true nature, the right use, and the promised destiny of God's creation.

Life in this "fallen" world is not whole. If we are not interested in sacralization, neither does secularization present an alternative because a characteristic of secularization is individualism and the differentiation of persons and roles: i.e., the division of labor and the multiplication of specialized tasks. But the offertory enacts the divine mission by reconciling that which is alienated and separated. In the presentation of the bread and the wine we see the unification of all industry, whether of farm or factory, in an act of dedication to God. As J.G. Davies once wrote, "We do not present just grain and grapes, but bread and wine which are a microcosm of our present industrial system."[43] The bread and wine we use at the eucharist are not just products of nature; they are products of farming and harvesting with tools and equipment made from iron mined and forged and propelled by fuel that has been extracted from the earth and refined; then transported by a vast system of commerce and shipping; sometimes imported under a complicated system of international exchange involving governmental regulation and scrutiny; then processed by another network of trade and finally distributed by another network of transportation and retailing. Well does the offertory prayer in the Roman Catholic Mass refer to elements that "earth has given and human hands have made." Moreover, the bread and wine are presented in containers and then placed in other vessels which have gone through similar processes from natural material to manufactured products. In most churches, the offering includes a monetary collection, which represents the value of our exchange of goods and services, and at least a part of this is usually used to purchase the bread and the wine.

It is this bread and wine, presented at the offertory, which serves as a means of grace by Christ's choice and specified use. We must understand that grace is not nature and nature is not grace. But, as Sittler was at pains to point out, nature and grace are related. For as a sheer phenomenon grace is, as Sittler proposed, ". . . the sheer *givenness-character* of life, the world, and the self—the plain *presentedness* of all that is."[44] This appeal to the phenomenological core of grace as "sheer givenness" cannot be dismissed as pantheism. It proceeds rather from the Trinitarian assumption embedded in Thomas Aquinas' statement that "God is above all things by the excellence of his nature; nevertheless he is in all things as causing the being of all things." "It does not follow," wrote Sittler, "that man can move from nature to grace. It does follow with immutable force that he must move from the focal point of the incarnated embodiment and disclosure of grace to the creation as a theatre of grace."[45] Communicants cannot have received the life-giving gift of grace through the sacramental bread and wine without returning to the world to celebrate the world's sacramental potential as the means of communion with God. This potential may be only partially and fitfully realized, but it is precisely the task of Christian mission to proclaim by word and deed the world's eschatological destiny in Christ.

It is right and salutary that poets should express their delight and astonishment in the world by using the genre of *eucharistia*, from Gerard Manley Hopkins's "Pied Beauty":

> Glory be to God for dappled things -
>> For skies of couple-colour as a brinded cow;
>>> For rose-moles all in stipple upon trout that swim;
> Fresh-firecoal chestnut-falls; finches' wings;
> Landscape plotted and pierced - fold, fallow, and
> plough;
>> And all trades, their gear and tackle and trim.
>
> All things counter, original, spare, strange;
>> Whatever is fickle, freckled (who knows how?)
>>> With swift, slow; sweet, sour; adazzle, dim;
> He fathers-forth whose beauty is past change;
>> Praise him.[46]

to e.e. cumings's ecstatic ascription:

> i thank You God most for this amazing
> day: for the leaping greenly spirits of trees
> and a blue true dream of sky; and for everything
> which is natural which is infinite which is yes.[47]

If all of nature would be offered and acknowledged and used and disposed of like the eucharistic bread and wine, if "the care of the earth" was as eucharistic as the eucharist is a paradigm of "the care of the earth," then the ancient image of "the morning stars sang together, and all the children of God shouted for joy" would return with something more than mere poetic force. But in the meantime Joseph Sittler was right to employ poetic force to give us a deeper sense for the world in order to enlarge our perception of the scope of grace. And H. Boone Porter was right to advocate the inclusion of Eucharistic Prayer C in the current Book of Common Prayer of the Episcopal Church, with its extended references to creation,—"At your command all things came to be: the vast expanse of interstellar space, galaxies, suns, the planets in their courses, and this fragile earth, our island home"—as reflective not only of the scientific interest of our century but of "the desire to see God's purposes carried out in man's stewardship of the natural world."[48]

Stewardship is what "the care of the earth" is all about. To demote human beings back into the animal kingdom because of humankind's ecological folly, as some environmentalists would do, negates any hope of redemption from futility for human beings and nature alike. But a vision of the world as sacrament and of human beings as priests of the world, offering it to God in a eucharistic sacrifice of love and praise, embraces redemptive possibilities. The eucharistic celebration itself is a paradigm of the "right use" of the creation, and the treatment of the eucharistic elements provides a model for the treatment of all of God's creatures by those creatures created in God's image and given a mandate to tend the garden of the Lord.

Notes

1. See Gustave Martelet, *The Risen Christ and the Eucharistic World* (London: Collins, 1976) 127ff.

2. See Hermann Sasse, *This Is My Body*, Eng. trans. (Minneapolis: Augsburg Publishing House, 1959) 13ff.

3. See Nathan Mitchell, *Cult and Controversy: The Worship of the Eucharist outside Mass* (New York: Pueblo Publishing Co., 1982) 86ff.

4. Caesarius of Heisterbach, *The Dialogue on Miracles*, vol. 2, trans. H. van E. Scott and C.C. Swinton Bland (London: G. Routledge, 1929) 105ff.

5. Ibid. 113f.

6. Ibid. 114f.

7. Lynn White, Jr., "Natural Science and Naturalistic Art in the Middle Ages," in *Medieval Religion and Technology. Collected Essays* (Berkeley: University of California Press, 1978) 33.

8. Joseph Sittler, "Called to Unity," *Ecumenical Review* 14 (1962) 175-187.

9. Joseph Sittler, *Essays on Nature and Grace* (Philadelphia: Fortress Press, 1972).

10. Joseph Sittler, *The Care of the Earth and Other University Sermons* (Philadelphia: Fortress Press, 1964) 91.

11. See Paul Santmire, *Brother Earth* (New York: Thomas Nelson, 1970).

12. It simply will not do to spiritualize the verses of Romans 8:19-25. While Paul develops no theology of nature as such, he assumes that the act of God in Christ has consequences also for the redemption of the natural world which has already experienced the consequences of human sin.

13. Justin Martyr, *First Apology* 67.

14. Archdale A. King, *Eucharistic Reservation in the Western Church* (New York: Sheed and Ward, 1965) 3ff.

15. Ibid. 19ff.

16. See Michel Andrieu, ed., *Les Ordines Romani du haut moyen âge*, vol. 2 (Louvain: Spicilegium Sacrum Lovaniense, 1948) 65-108.

17. See Robert Taft, *Beyond East and West. Problems in Liturgical Understanding* (Washington, D.C.: The Pastoral Press, 1984) 66ff.

18. See Mitchell, *Cult and Controversy* 163ff.

19. Lambert Beauduin, *Mélanges liturgiques* (Louvain: Abbaye du Mont César, Centre liturgique, 1954) 211.

20. Note the words of administration in the 1552 Prayer Book of King Edward VI: "Take and eate this, in remembraunce that Christ dyed for thee, and feede on him in thy hearte by fayth, with thanksgiving. Drinke this in remembraunce that Christ's bloude was shed for thee, and be thankefull." *The First and Second Prayer Books of King Edward VI*, Every Man's Library vol. 448 (London: Dent; New York: Dutton, 1910, 1968) 389.

21. See *Augsburg Confession*, art. XXIV.

22. See Frank C. Senn, "Holy Communion outside the Assembly: Two Models," *North American Academy of Liturgy Proceedings* (Valparaiso University, 1989) 190-210.

23. See Edward F. Peters, "Luther and the Principle: Outside of the Use There Is No Sacrament," *Concordia Theological Monthly* 52 (1971) 643-652.

24. See Carl F. Wisloff, *The Gift of Communion*, trans. Joseph Shaw (Minneapolis: Augsburg Publishing House, 1964) 32ff.

25. See Philip H. Pfatteicher, *Commentary on the Occasional Services* (Philadelphia: Fortress Press, 1983) 113ff.

26. Mircea Eliade, *Patterns in Comparative Religion*, trans. by Rosemary Sheed (Cleveland and New York: World Publishing Co., 1963) 14-15.

27. Mary Douglas, *Purity and Danger* (London, Boston and Henley: Routledge and Kegan Paul, 1966) 7ff.

28. See Robert W. Jenson, *Visible Words. The Interpretation and Practice of Christian Sacraments* (Philadelphia: Fortress Press, 1978) 67ff.

29. See Robert J. Ledogar, *Acknowledgment: Praise Verbs in the Early Greek Anaphoras* (Rome: Biblical Institute, 1968).

30. See Louis Bouyer, *Eucharist*, trans. Charles U. Quinn (Notre Dame: University of Notre Dame Press, 1968). But note the refinement of Bouyer's presentation in Thomas Talley, "From Berakah to Eucharistein: A Reopening Question," *Worship* 50 (1976) 138-158.

31. See *Prex Eucharistica*, ed. Anton H nggi and Irmgard Pahl (Universitaires Fribourg Suisse, 1968) 66f., 375ff.; *Prayers of the Eucharist, Early and Reformed*, ed. R.C.D. Jasper and G.J. Cuming, 2d ed. (New York: Oxford University Press, 1980) 14ff., 26ff.

32. *Prex Eucharistica* 80; *Prayers of the Eucharist* 22f.

33. *Prex Eucharistica* 131; *Prayers of the Eucharist*, 40.

34. Sittler, *Essays on Nature and Grace* 31.

35. See John H. McKenna, "The Epiclesis Revisited," in *New Eucharistic Prayers: An Ecumenical Study of their Development and Structure*, ed. Frank C. Senn (Mahwah, NJ: Paulist Press, 1987) 169-196.

36. Joseph Keenan, "The Importance of the Creation Motif in a Eucharistic Prayer," *Worship* 53 (1979) 341-356.

37. Sittler, *Essays* 36.

38. Sittler draws extensively and appreciatively on Allan Galloway, *The Cosmic Christ* (London: Nisbet and Co., 1951).

39. Sittler, *Essays* 37. Sittler's exposition of the Epistles to the Colossians and Ephesians (pp. 40ff.) is simply breathtaking!

40. Alexander Schmemann, *For the Life of the World* (Crestwood, NY: St. Vladimir's Seminary Press, 1974) 15.

41. Ibid. 25f.

42. Louis Bouyer, *Rite and Man. Natural Sacredness and Christian Sacraments*, trans. M. Joseph Costolloe (Notre Dame: University of Notre Dame Press, 1963) 80f.

43. J.G. Davies, Worship and Mission (London: SCM Press, 1966) 100.

44. Sittler, *Essays* 88.

45. Ibid. 89.

46. Gerard Manley Hopkins, *A Selection of His Poems and Prose*, ed. W.H. Gardner (Baltimore: Penguin Books, 1953) 30f.

47. e.e. cumings, *Poems:1923-1954* (New York: Harcourt, Brace and Co., 1954) 464.

48. H. Boone Porter, "Episcopal Anaphoral Prayers," in Senn, ed., *New Eucharistic Prayers* 69.

17

New Beginnings
and Church Dedications

John Wilkinson

WHEN I WAS INVITED TO WRITE AN ARTICLE TO HONOR BOONE PORTER, I HAD a question I wished to explore. "Was the doctrine of creation related to the dedication of churches?" Without further thought I sent in the title. But when I started to ask this question with regard to very early dedication services, I discovered that they hardly mention creation. Creation was certainly one of God's acts at the beginning: thus a Roman dedication prayer addressed the "Creator of the things to be consecrated to thee."[1] But I have changed my heart. This article now seeks to describe the aims of the dedication service. There will be a section about creation, but greater attention will be paid to imitation, in its negative and positive aspects.

In the fourth century there were two kinds of "dedications," according to Eusebius. In 329 the Empress Helena visited Palestine and "dedicated"[2] the church in Bethlehem. This was at a stage when the builders were only beginning their work, and the service is now known as "the blessing of the foundations." Ten years later the church was finished, and Eusebius again says it was "dedicated."[3] This was a "dedication" in the modern meaning of the word. It is the final preparation of a finished building for its first regular service. Both services were needed for a new church.

The early services will be represented by two examples of blessing the foundations and four dedications. At the beginning of the eighth century the Byzantine and Armenian Churches had both types of service. The Armenian text is missing, but in about 720 John of Odzun, Bishop in Etchmiadzin, wrote a detailed commentary which gives a good idea of the contents of the services.[4] The earliest text of the service is slightly different, possibly because it comes from a different area. The Armenians borrowed from the Byzantine rite,[5] but by the date when we first witness the service, it has developed its distinctness from the earliest remaining Byzantine dedication.[6]

Both Eastern Churches had both services. The other two are both dedications from the west. One is from the Roman Church and although it was written in about 750,[7] some of its prayers were over a century old.[8] If this service was ever performed as it was written, it did little to explain its meaning. The other, much richer in teaching and symbolism, was copied out at about 810 from some place near the Rhine.[9] It was perhaps influenced by "Scotti" from Ireland,[10] and by the Byzantine service. There is also a commentary on a service very much like the Rhenish one entitled *The Treatise on the Dedication of a Church*. Scholars formerly supposed that Rémy of Auxerre (c.841-908) was its author, but it must be by someone earlier, since it was first copied out when Rémy was a small boy.[11] Manuscripts often contained both the texts of the service and this Treatise, a useful guide to a service which in most periods must have been extremely rare.

The blessing of the foundations is outlined below, with common features of the Armenian and Byzantine services in bold type. Such features may go back to Byzantine roots.[12] There was no clear biblical precedent for ceremonies at the start of a building. Thus the biblical account of the start of building the Temple describes the date,[13] but not much else. The Christian service was therefore an original composition. The Byzantine service is short, and blesses the church before the sanctuary.

In the following service the bishop publicly takes spiritual responsibility for the plan. The architect was in fact responsible for the measurements,[14] laying out the building physically "according to Ezekiel's vision concerning the Temple,"[15] and proportioning it to represent the earth and heaven.[16]

Blessing the Foundation

Both	Armenian	Byzantine
	Bishop receives twelve stones; psalms are sung.	

Preparatory prayers

		-CHURCH- Censing the church foundations while the choir sings.
	-SANCTUARY-	-SANCTUARY- Bishop prays, signs the cross on a stone.

Bishop sets the stone in the middle of the sanctuary

-CHURCH-
Twelve stones for
  corners are
  washed with water
  and with wine.
Procession and prayers.
Bishop draws the measure
  of the size of the building.
Twelve stones are anointed
  with chrism.

Psalms and readings in
  the church.

Bishop prays

Bishop digs three times.

Builders begin their work

At the altar there are psalms,
  prayers, and readings.

The bishop blesses[17] the church and the sanctuary. He sets a stone in the center of the sanctuary which is later to be replaced by the altar.[18] The bishop then starts the task of the builders with a prayer.

When the church had been finished, the dedication took place; the outline of this dedication follows. Bold type indicates common points. There are several biblical precedents for the dedication, but the common points go beyond these, and suggest that the Armenian and Byzantine services sprang from a common liturgical root.

The more one studies the details of these different services, the harder it is to see their precise aim. Three of the traditions make use of relics, but relics are not essential. They are not in the Armenian dedication, and there were times when the western rite omitted them.[20] Indeed Pope Vigilius once held that a celebration of the

---

Dedicating Altar and Church

All Western	Eastern
(Rom. Rhi. and Byz.)	(Armenian)
Relics to a church nearby. They are brought in procession when needed.	Service with altar in the middle of the church. Altar taken outside. Approach door three times. "lift up the gates." Altar enters church and is raised to bema.
	Assembly of altar. (Byz., Arm.)
Prayer outside doors. (Rom.) 12 candles. Prayer. Writing Alphabet. (Rhi.)	Prayer outside doors. (Byz.)
1. Washing altar with water and wine.[19]	
And washing church. Rest of water poured at base of altar. (Rhi.) Relics laid in altar. (Rom.)	
2. Anointing altar with chrism (as in baptism)	
Bishop censes church. (Rhi.)	Bishop censes church. (Byz.)
3. Anointing church (except Rom.).	
Church sprinkled with water. (Rom.) Blessing linens, vessels. (Rhi.)	
4. Dressing the altar.	Lamps are lit. (Byz. Arm.) At the main door "Lift up the gates is sung three times. Entry prayer. (Byz.).
Relics laid in altar. (Rhi.)	Relics laid in altar. (Byz.)
5. The Eucharist.	
Eight days feast. (Rom.)	Eight days feast. (Byz.)

eucharist was enough to consecrate a church,[21] and the question has to be asked whether any other ceremonies were needed.

Although Vigilius may have been theologically correct, a full service, so the church believed, should correspond with dedications in Scripture. Christian dedications imitate the detailed biblical descriptions of Moses and Solomon consecrating the holy building and the altar. Thus the bishop anoints the building either with water or chrism, imitating Moses when he anointed the Tabernacle; and when the dedication ends, which is a service only once held in the Tabernacle and in a new church, the first regular liturgies begin. Such imitations are not merely a literary convenience but a serious search for biblical precedents.

This type of imitation consisted in human action which hoped for the action of God. Two things were commanded of Moses: first, to consecrate the altar[22] and the Tabernacle first by anointing the structure "and all its furniture,"[23] and consecrating, and secondly by holding the first service in it.[24] God's response to this was that "the glory of the Lord filled the Tabernacle."[25] Later on in Jerusalem, when Solomon dedicated the Temple and brought the Ark into its place, God responded in the same way: "The glory of the Lord filled the House of the Lord."[26] This was before the regular sacrifices began. When the altar had been placed, Christians too prayed that the glory of God should enter the new church. The Christian altar copied the heavenly altar as described in the Letter to the Hebrews and Revelation,[27] but it was also the final preparation for the first regular eucharist.

It had been true that God gave commands about the form of these dedications. It had been true that God made his response. So for the early dedications the directions in Scripture were taken literally: for instance, Scripture says that Solomon consecrated the place of the altar for eight days; so some communities made a rule that "the liturgy must be said in the church for a week before the altar is fully consecrated."[28] The Bible was followed, whether or not it meant much to the congregation, in the hope that God would renew his response.

And the use of the Bible went deep. The biblical source, some verses from the Pentateuch, is in the left column on the next page, and the instruction to the priest, derived also *verbatim*, on the right.[29] This quotation is from the Rhenish service.

	Phrases from the Bible	Instructions from the Rhenish Service[30]
	Then take some of the bull's blood	First then take some of the wine mixed with water,
Ex 29:12	place your finger on the horns of the altar . . . when you have	place your finger on the horn of the altar and
Lv 8:11	poured it on the altar seven times . . .	pour it on the altar seven times . . .
Ex 29:12	But the rest of the blood	But the rest
Ex 29:13	you shall pour onto the base.	you shall pour onto the base.
Ex 29:18	. . . and you shall offer incense on the altar . . . a very sweet savour to the Lord.	And you shall offer incense on the altar, a very sweet savour to the Lord.

A later commentator, William Durandus, said that the consecration of a church did two things. One of them is "to make the material church belong to God,"[31] and this, as we have seen, was done by carrying out a recognizable imitation of the biblical ceremonies. The authority for the Roman dedication service was certainly the Bible. But if the service followed the text we now have, it could well follow the Bible exactly without being intelligible to the congregation. One development in later services was that the biblical ceremonial was more and more affected by Christian symbolism. Thus while the Eastern Churches had separated washing the altar with water from washing with wine,[32] the Rhenish service mixed the liquids together as a symbol of the "water and the blood" which came from Jesus' side.[33]

To lay out the site of a new church, the measures of the Temple were used from Ezekiel's vision.[34] For a start, this is to emphasize that the church's forerunners were the holy buildings of the old covenant, the Tabernacle,[35] the Temple of Solomon,[36] and the restoration of Zerubbabel.[37] But, in addition, all these three earthly buildings of the old covenant were copies of God's heavenly dwelling. The dwelling was the pattern Moses saw for the Tabernacle on Mount Sinai, and was no doubt essentially copied in God's plan for the Temple which he gave to David.[38] And in that dwelling in heaven will be the church in its future age,[39] in Holy[40] Mount Zion and heavenly Jerusalem,[41] the place of the true Tabernacle.[42] There in due time its members will recline at the table of his kingdom.[43] Even though the church is still on earth, it is already linked with this dwelling, since its prayers rise to God's "holy and intelligible altar."[44]

When the Rhenish service describes a ceremony in the nave, it touches on the doctrine of creation. This description has to be seen in the light of the ancient Jewish symbolism of the long room in the Temple. In a passage often quoted by Christians, Josephus says:

> [The Tabernacle] was capable of serving as a representation of the nature of the universe. For one-third of it [the "Holy of Holies"]... which priests could not enter, resembled heaven and was for God. The space... which was assigned to the priests [the "Holy Place" or *naos*] ... was like earth and sea, which are accessible to man.[45]

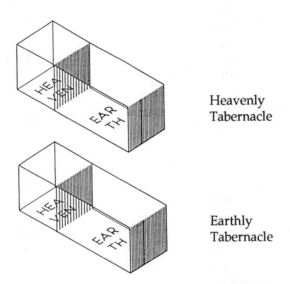

Heavenly Tabernacle

Earthly Tabernacle

Josephus' explanation of the Tabernacle

An obvious example that Christians accepted this Jewish symbolism is provided in the Revelation of John the Divine. Revelation opens in the long room of the heavenly Tabernacle, containing the lampstands, representing the lampstand in the Tabernacle,[46] and the Son of Man dressed as a priest. There is a door (possibly leading out of this long room) into the sanctuary of the temple containing the throne of God.[47]

In other words, the heavenly Tabernacle or Temple is like that in the First Book of Enoch.[48] The interpreter who assumes, as Josephus did, that these two rooms represent heaven and earth, can easily explain the angel who filled his censer from the sanctuary altar and then "threw it on the earth."[49] And in the context of the heavenly temple he can understand that when the veil (the sky) is removed, the wicked men of the earth can see God's throne in heaven.[50] The Temple and the universe are indistinguishable and the same.

This assumption about the church nave also explains a very odd sequence in the Armenian dedication. The altar is being carried to its place. But the description, if taken literally, means that it first approaches heaven, then crosses earth, then enters heaven:

> 1. The altar is taken to the door of the new church, representing the entry of the heavenly Tabernacle. This symbolizes Christ entering heaven, "restoring us that were exiled to the garden of life."[51]
>
> 2. Although the new church as a whole is like heaven, there is still a semblance of earth to cross: the altar in the church nave symbolizes Christ incarnate upon earth: "Our Lord walking in the house of our nature through the flesh he took from us."
>
> 3. The priests greet the altar, when it is lifted up into the sanctuary, with the angelic chant Alleluia, "because the sanctuary is the image of heaven."[52]

The Rhine service also treats of the nave when it says that alphabets should be written there. The four corners of the nave represent the corners of the earth, as they do in Revelation,[53] and the two alphabets were written diagonally between these corners. The *Treatise* made the following comment:

> What then is one meant to understand by the alphabet but the beginnings and roots of holy doctrine . . . For just as the recognition of individual letters fits with the education of small children, and gradually they come to syllables, then words, and then come to recognize sentences, so there are different grades of mental capacity in the family of the church . . . The corners of the church represent the four directions of the world, to which the church's teaching has come, symbolized by the letters written on the ground.[54]

There seems very little doubt that Plato's *Timaeus* was the source of the idea of differing mental grades. It contains a comparison of the elements to letters, and goes on to mention syllables.[55] But this explanation fails to account for the alphabet in the dedication. The letters are all over the nave, and not just at the outer edges. In fact, the *Treatise* failed to give the full explanation. The Latin word *elementa* (like *stoicheia* in Greek) has two meanings: both "letters" of the alphabet, and "elements" of the universe. So it is possible that in the dedication the letters of the alphabet were conceived as elements. A parallel notion is that of the Armenians, to whom the area between the four sides of the church symbolized the four elements of our material bodies,[56] and the world which we can perceive through our senses. To write them in the nave implied that it symbolized the solid and visible earth, as opposed to the insensible and intelligible things of heaven,[57] and again implies an idea of creation which is much influenced by Plato.[58]

A standard dedication reading[59] is from the Letter to the Ephesians, which is a valuable clue to what the dedication services mean. The author sometimes sees the church as a spiritual building and at other times as people:

> You are fellow-citizens with the saints, and members of the household of God, built upon the foundation of the apostles and prophets, Christ Jesus himself being the cornerstone, in whom the whole structure is joined together and grows into a holy temple in the Lord (1:19-22).

This line of thought was linked to the second effect of consecration according to Durandus: "To present a picture of our betrothal to God, not only as a church but as regards our Christian souls."[60] The early Roman dedication was poor in this regard, but the Armenians and the *Treatise* treated the dedication as an opportunity of teaching about the church's past, present, and future. The fact that the church symbolized the people underlay the fact that the church was hallowed like a person, with baptism and confirmation.[61] The altar was also taken to symbolize the people of God; the eastern rites had words about baptism,[62] and the Roman service "baptized" the altar with water and "confirmed" it with chrism.[63] A sermon, often copied out with the Latin services, enlarges on this symbolism.[64]

On the one hand, Christians in consecrating the altar imitated Moses. Moses had literally sprinkled bull's blood over the altar and anointed it with oil.[65] The Christian's aim became markedly different. The Christian was concerned with the literal following of the Bible only insofar as it could be symbolized into an acceptable meaning for Christians.

In fact, the *Treatise* almost turns the Rhine service from a dedication of a place into a dedication of people. So in the dedication services twelve stones or twelve candles represent the apostles.[66] Twelve candles are a symbol that in the future the church must be a place for "apostolic teaching."[67] The bishop knocks on the church door three times to show that the heavenly, earthly, and infernal powers are subject to his apostolic authority.[68] And when he enters he finds the new building still in darkness. At once he prays for those inside it,[69] those who are ready to be converted from ignorance and faithlessness.[70]

When the bishops reaches the altar he uses ash to purify it, recalling the red heifer's ashes on the day of atonement.[71] Then he cleanses it with wine and water representing Christ's blood and Christ's heavenly sacrifice in Hebrews 9:11-14.[72] He sprinkles the altar seven times to represent the Holy Spirit, and similarly the altar and church three times to cleanse them from sins of deed, thought, and speech.[73]

The relics of the saints form part of the Rhine service, and—to make it clear that the sanctuary is the heavenly Jerusalem[74]—the veil is drawn,[75] and their relics installed in the heavenly altar, for God's House can be seen as the company of saints.[76] The dedication ends with the first eucharist in the church, when the earthly altar is linked with the heavenly altar.

The *Treatise*'s interpretation is very Platonic, but, looking back at them, so are the texts of the services. The church dedication service is a copy of Moses with the Tabernacle and Solomon with the Temple. The church as a building is identified with at least six holy places from the old covenant. In the *Timaeus* Plato thought that copying of this kind, of God's thoughts or of ideas in the intelligible world, is extremely close to creation.[77] But in fact both the main models to which the church is compared, the heavenly Tabernacle or the Temple, are very like Platonic ideas. Jews believed that these ideas existed in themselves before the creation of the earth, like God's wisdom which also existed before creation.[78] The pattern which Moses saw for the Tabernacle was also independent of earthly time, for the Tabernacle was in the heavenly eternity of God's existence; and much the same could be said of the Temple.[79] The material Tabernacle was simply an example of following these heavenly ideas in the sensible world, and the material church was one of many such examples.

The late Middle Ages saw Greek prayers adopt Platonic vocabulary. An example is the prayer which begins "O Creator of the whole universe, both sensible and intelligible."[80] So if one accepts that imitation is part of creation, then to imitate heavenly ideas is in some Platonic sense to create, even though it has little to do with the act of creation in Genesis.

Creation is perhaps too strong a word. Christian dedication services aimed to hallow a new place where God's people could hear the apostolic preaching, could gain access to the one and heavenly sacrifice of Christ, and could turn their hopes to the heavenly Jerusalem. This was a place once created by God. It was new not by another creation, but newly dedicated by a minutely organized ceremony of blessing.

Notes

1. Second Mass Collect of the Gregorian Sacramentary, in L.A. Muratori, *Liturgia Romana Vetus*, vol. 2 (Venice, 1748) 241.

2. The Greek word in Eusebius, V. Const. 3.43.1 is aphierou.

3. 31 May 339. See G. Garitte, *Le Calendrier palestino-géorgien du Sinaiticus 34*, Subsidia Hagiographica, vol. 30 (Brussels, 1958) 430f.

4. F.C. Conybeare, *Rituale Armenorum* (Oxford: Clarendon Press, 1905) 11-18.

5. See Conybeare, *Rituale*, Note III, p.18.

6. From Vatican Ms. Barb. gr. III.55 (now Cod. Barber. graec. 336) in J. Goar, *Euchologium, sive Rituale Graecorum* (Venice, 1730) (Graz: Akademische Druck- und Verlagsanstalt, 1960) 485-490, and 655-671.

7. Ordo XLII, in M. Andrieu, *Les Ordines Romani du Haut Moyen Age*, vol. 4, Spicilegium Sacrum Lovaniense, vol. 28 (Louvain, 1956) 396-402. Abbreviated Rom.

8. Originally some were used for other purposes. In Ordo XLII, Sec. 1, the prayer is so general that it is used as a collect for the Sundays before Lent (see Andrieu, *Les Ordines* 397, last note).

9. Ordo XLI, ibid. 338-347. Abbreviated Rhi.

10. See for instance ibid. 319.

11. See PL 131:845-866 (abbreviation TDE), and P. Salmon, *Analecta Liturgica extraits des manuscrits liturgiques de la Bibliothèque du Vatican*, Studi e Testi, vol. 273 (Citta del Vaticano, 1974) 278. The *Treatise* quotes from a service whose text is very like the one we have named "Rhine".

12. The bishop was responsible for Laying the Foundations. There was an additional patriarchal service known as the Fixing of the Cross, which was resented by some bishops; see Goar, *Euchologium* 489f.

13. See 1 Kgs 6:1.

14. Professor R.W. Thomson translates the Armenian explanation to mean that the bishop "asks to be given the tool for digging" (not as

Conybeare, *Rituale* 12). The text of the service says that the bishop and the archgitect go round the church together when laying out the plan; see the last instructions on Conybeare, *Rituale* 1 and 2.

15. Conybeare, *Rituale* 12.

16. See ibid. 12 and 16.

17. At least as Simeon of Thessalonica later interpreted the bishop's actions they are blessings; see Goar, *Euchologium* 486f.

18. The Armenian rite likens this stone to the one in Nebuchadnezzar's dream (Dn 2:34f, 45). The Byzantine symbolism is different: see Goar, *Euchologium* 486f.

19. Rhi. adds "and ash" (Andrieu, *Les Ordines*, Sec. 7, 341). Rom. omits "and wine" (ibid., Sec. 4, 398).

20. See ibid. 329.

21. See PL 84:832 and comments in Andrieu, *Les Ordines* 369.

22. Moses gave instructions for building the altar in Ex 20:24.

23. Ex 40:9.

24. See Ex 40:29.

25. Ex 40:34.

26. 1 Kgs 8:11.

27. Heb 9:4, Rev 8:3, referring perhaps to Is 6:6.

28. See 1 Kgs 8:65-66, 2 Chr 7:10, and 1 Mc 4:56. Goar, *Euchologium* 664; see also Rom., Andrieu, *Les Ordines* 402.

29. As P. de Puniet was the first to notice; see F. Cabrol and H. Leclercq, eds., *Dictionnaire d'archéologie chrétienne et de liturgie*, vol. 4, p. 392.

30. L.C. Mohlberg, ed., *Missale Francorum*, Rerum Ecclesiasticarum Documenta, Series Major, Fontes, vol. 11 (Rome: Casa Editrice Herder, 1957) no. 57, p.18.

31. William Durandus, *Rationale Divinorum Officiorum* (Lyons, 1672) 1, 6, 8.

32. Conybeare, *Rituale*, bottom paragraph p. 16; Goar, *Euchologium* 659.

33. Jn 19:34, 1 Jn 5:6.

34. Conybeare, *Rituale* 12; Goar, *Euchologium* 659.

35. Ibid. 657.

36. Conybeare, *Rituale* 16f.; Goar, *Euchologium* 659; Andrieu, *Les Ordines* 340, 343, 348.

37. The three buildings in the sentence above are mentioned in Conybeare, *Rituale* 13.

38. Ex 25:9; 1 Chr 28:19.

39. Conybeare, *Rituale* 11.

40. Andrieu, *Les Ordines* 400.

41. Conybeare, *Rituale* 13.

42. Goar, *Euchologium* 657 (Heb 9.11) 658; Andrieu, *Les Ordines* 344, and with vessels 346.

43. Conybeare, *Rituale* 18.

44. Goar, *Euchologium* 658.

45. Josephus, *Ant.* 3.123.

46. Rv 1:12-13.

47. Rv 4:1-2.

48. 1 En 14:9-22.

49. Rv 8:3-5.

50. The veil is often equated with the firmament, and Josephus, *War* 5.214 said that the veil of Herod's Temple was decorated like the sky. See Rv 6:14-17. Compare also the *Treatise*, PL 131:863C.

51. Conybeare, *Rituale* 15.

52. Ibid. 16.

53. Rv 7:1; see also the Armenian service, Conybeare, *Rituale* 12, and the *Treatise*, TDE 851B.

54. TDE 851A-B.

55. Plato, *Timaeus*, 48C.

56. Conybeare, *Rituale* 17.

57. Some Jews believed that creation rested on only one letter of the alphabet; see the rendering of the *Second Alphabet of R. Aqiba* 50-55 in L. Ginzberg, *Legends of the Jews*, vol. 1 (Philadelphia: The Jewish Publication Society of America, 1947) 5-9, in which the letter is beth. This account is clearly distinct from the writing of the full alphabet in Christian dedications.

58. But see Wis 11:17, Justin, *1 Apol.* I.20 and 59, which are not yet free of the Platonic idea of creation.

59. Conybeare, *Rituale* 14 and Morin, *Sermones*, Part 2, p.859 (= CCL 104, p. 905).

60. Durandus, *Rationale* 1, 6, 8.

61. ArmD. 16-17; see Durandus, *Rationale* 1, 6, 9, and 1, 7, 18 who no doubt interprets it correctly.

62. Conybeare, *Rituale* 16f.; Goar, *Euchologium* 659.

63. Andrieu, *Les Ordines* sec. 6 and 18, pp. 399, 402.

64. Caesarius of Arles, *Sermo in Dedicatione Templi*, "Natalem Templi hujus Diem," ed. G. Morin, *Sancti Caesarii Arelatensis Sermones* (Maredsoux, 1937) 859 ff. (= CCL 104, p. 905 ff.).

65. Ex 29:12, Lv 8:11.

66. Stones, Conybeare, *Rituale* 11-12; or candles, Andrieu, *Les Ordines*, sec. II.1, p. 339 and *TDE* 846A.

67. PL 131:846A.

68. PL 131:848B.

69. PL 131:850A.

70. PL 131:848C.

71. Nm 19:9.

72. PL 131:853C.

73. PL 131:854D, 855B.

74. PL 131:862D.

75. PL 131:863B.

76. PL 131:863A.

77. See, for example, *Timaeus* 29B.

78. Prv 8:22-23.

79. Ex 25:9, Wis 9:8.

80. Dedication prayer by Nicephorus Callistus, Goar, *Euchologium* 654.

tions or it doesn't work; there is no magic. The most important ingredient of dance, a truly mysterious ingredient, one that must never be missing but often is, one lucid and cloudy at the same time—that one is nameless. Poets know this, as do the great religious leaders. It's the transforming alchemy that everyone seeks; it's inscrutable, cannot be taught, but when found it turns lead into gold.[1]

Paul Taylor makes a good point. But I am of two minds about the mystery. We all love mystery, but the fact is, we also need some clarification of thought. I will describe myself as an Episcopalian, not because I am so special, but because my story is so ordinary.

I am a birthright Episcopalian, reared by parents who attended the parish church, who worked on it inside and out, and who gave generous if not sacrificial financial support. My parents made their children attend. This was not democratic or permissive. In our household God was assumed in the way that God is assumed by the Hebrews in Genesis.

St. Augustine's, Santa Monica, CA, was certainly an ordinary church. We always had seventeen-year-old girls teaching Sunday School. One of our rectors wanted to build a garden that corresponded to the Holy Land, but the project failed since no one but he had seen the Holy Land, and no one remembered to water the plants. My grandparents had planted ferns around the church, and these plants had spread like wildfire, burning off other plants in the process. We had a real estate salesman in the parish who became a monk and a distinguished leader in the church. We had a boy who used the parish hall to teach the Bible but who discovered his vocation was not religion but philosophy and is teaching today at Stanford. All of our little ones took part in the choir, and most of the girls had at least one year playing the part of Mary in the Christmas pageant. I can still hear the rector intoning: "We will read the *Venite* on page 9 of the Prayer Book." Those were the days before our church centered its worship in the eucharist. Some of us children were obdurate and refused to call the new rector "Father." The old one had been called "Mister." My father now crossed himself with a gusty sigh. I hated the way we worshiped one way, and then another.

I began to chafe at the things that could have been changed but never were. Why did my uncle read the lesson as though he were reading from the telephone directory? Why did he read as though he hadn't the remotest notion of what the lesson was about? Why was it a mystery to him and to so many of us?

Now that I am grown, I think the real failure of religious education is simpler. There are just too many things that distract us from teaching or learning more about the faith that would enrich us.

Raïssa Maritain tells an amusing story in a children's book about Thomas Aquinas. It seems the great scholar came to town riding a donkey, his ample girth bulging over a red saddle. Addressing a villager about the difficulties of attending to God in prayer, he challenged the man. "I'll bet this donkey," Aquinas said, "that you can't say the Lord's Prayer through, without being distracted." The man thought eagerly of owning the donkey. "That's easy," he said. "Our Father—Who art in Heaven—Hallowed be thy Name—Do I get the saddle, too—?"

Distraction is one problem. Perhaps our distance from biblical culture is another.

Robertson Davies, the lively Canadian author, notes that a century and a half ago the number of people who read was much smaller than it is now.

> Classical culture was not the only culture; there was a wide-spread biblical culture also, and it was a powerful shaper of thought and expression. The Bible is a classical literature of history, poetry, legend, and prophecy, which used to be reasonably familiar to all educated people in the great King James Version. What if it were not understood completely, as modern scholarship reckons completeness? What if it were uncritically reverenced? . . . It is characteristic of the classics that their influence is not dependent so much on critical understanding as on love and familiarity.[2]

This is not the case today. Davies goes on to say:

> The classical culture has shrunk so that it has no appreciable influence: the biblical culture scarcely exists, and the writer or speaker who draws a parallel or quotation from the Bible today would not be understood by any more people than if he made this allusion to something in Homer.[3]

Nor is religious illiteracy confined only to the Bible. If most lay people were asked to take a simple quiz on the Christian faith, many would respond defensively, or not at all, to such questions as the following:

What is salvation?
What is grace?
How are we to understand the Resurrection?

What did Jesus mean by the Kingdom of Heaven?

What is the Covenant?

What does it mean to be made in God's image?

The Kingdom of Heaven is believed to be the heart of Jesus' message but it is never actually defined. It is mentioned twice in the Lord's Prayer. Thomas Groome, in his *Christian Religious Education*, quotes Hans Küng on the summary of Jesus' view of the Kingdom:

> It will be a Kingdom where, in accordance with Jesus's prayer, God's name is truly hallowed, his will be done on earth, men will have everything in abundance, all sin will be forgiven and all evil overcome.
>
> It will be a Kingdom where, in accordance with Jesus's promises, the poor, the hungry, those who weep and those who are downtrodden will finally come into their own; where pain, suffering and death will have an end.
>
> It will be a Kingdom that cannot be described but only made known in metaphors as the new covenant, the seed springing up, the ripe harvest, the great banquet, the royal feast.
>
> It will therefore be a Kingdom—wholly as the prophets foretold—of absolute righteousness, of unsurpassable freedom, of dauntless love, of universal reconciliation, of everlasting peace. In this sense, therefore, it will be a time of salvation, of fulfillment, of consummation, of God's presence: the Absolute future.[4]

Study and self-help groups are sometimes an opportunity for religious insights or practicing the faith.

A number of years ago some friends and I organized a Layman's School of Theology (at least that was the grand name we put on it), which was sponsored by several Episcopal parishes and held at Calvary Church in midtown Manhattan. Each church was solicited to put up fifty dollars, and when we had five hundred dollars working capital, we arranged for seminary professors to address us. They were good-hearted people and agreed to give a talk for a stipend.

What embarrasses me now is to think how enthusiastic, even evangelical, I was. I promoted and publicized and hustled and tugged as though my life depended on it. Strange to say, the clergy said that no one would be interested.

The scholars were interested because they were addressing lay persons, not clergy-in-training. At that time, there were some distinguished people available: John Macquarrie, John Knox, W.D. Davies, and Daniel Day Williams, among others. Lay persons attended, young people came, men and women took part, and clergy also came. We had two hundred people paying admission for one night a week—two hours each night—for a six-week session. We sold books the speakers had written. Boone Porter was one of the lecturers. He also suggested resources and strategies in setting up the series and thus helped to ensure its survival for several years.

In my naiveté I believed that if everyone had a short course in systematic theology, we lay people would learn the fundamentals. This would patch what we had failed to learn listening to a ten-minute sermon, and recalling what we had learned from a seventeen-year-old girl. General Seminary students were enlisted as discussion leaders. I remember that one seminary student wrote on his evaluation sheet afterwards: "I was surprised how much older women knew about their faith. It must be because of their life experience."

Despite the fact that there is a lot of uninformed faith in most congregations, religious education continues to concern us. Biblical illiteracy can be addressed. Nor should concern for change be confined to words and reading.

David Hurd, Professor of Church Music at General Theological Seminary, believes that reading music should be taught to children at the same time they are learning to read words. He remembers attending St. Philip's, Brooklyn, with his parents as a child. "It wasn't an intellectual thing with me. I was eight or nine. I remember the smell of incense, the scent of women's face powder with cigarette smoke, seeing the choir in their white cassocks, and the clergy wearing colors of the church seasons. And of course, the sound of the organ."

It helps to know that liturgy involves more than just the words. As Neil Alexander, Liturgics Professor at General Seminary, said at All Saints Church recently: "It's music, it's performance, it's architecture, it's the priest and the People of God."

Some of the laity may not think of themselves as participating members of the People of God.

"But isn't love enough?" a cleric asked, perplexed by this concern for religious education. Most people find that love without content lacks staying power. If love and understanding were coupled, love *would* be enough.

Robert Capon, the theology professor who writes readable cookbooks, once wrote a litany to baking soda, extolling its virtues as an ingredient for cooking, a balm for wounds and as a cleansing agent.

This small, witty example helped me to understand the idea behind performing the liturgy. How we worship should be self-explanatory, but there are always some people—like me—who have to be told as well as to be shown.

Scott Peck, author of several best-selling books on psychiatry and religion, said that the addiction group meetings which often meet on church premises provide a model of what the church should be because their members love and care for each other.

I was skeptical until I joined Weight Watchers, one of the most effective addiction groups around. It is not exactly like A.A. and no prayers are involved. Its founder, Jean Nidetch, explains what should motivate a person to join:

> Whatever the reason please don't start the W.W. program unless you are desperate. Deep down desperate. So desperate that you are miserable. So desperate that you are indeed earnest. And when and if you reach that point, we can help you . . .[5]

This provides the acknowledgement of transgression and the therapeutic power of confession which follows, something the church has understood since its founding. At the same time, W.W. is quite clear about the necessity of discipline and commitment: "This program will require your desperation, your sincerity, your cooperation and your patience."

Few people enter the church with that feeling of desperation. In fact, it is more likely that persons are apt to attend church with a little glow of self-congratulation. But most of us try to be sincere, cooperative, and patient. W.W. doesn't talk about diets and denials, but of a new kind of behavior.

When some friends heard that I was attending meetings, they asked if I could loan them the printed material. In this way, they could save money and skip the meetings. It crossed my mind that there was no salvation outside the group. The meetings keep you on track, remind you of your goals, and generally are a *locus* of encouragement. The early Christians insisted there was no salvation outside the church, but today a person would be unwise to insist on it, for fear of being thought too orthodox.

A year ago I attended a week-long bible study program under Roman Catholic auspices in another state. If Anglicans do not study the Bible much, Roman Catholics have only been encouraged to do so since Vatican II some twenty-five years ago. So it was interesting to meet lay persons from throughout the northeast who were attending courses, studying in small groups, and enjoying the Bible by exploring more of its books. I met several lay educators who were hired by diocesan leaders to be circuit riders, driving out to selected parishes to conduct adult education programs.

The average class consisted of twelve to twenty adults, mostly women in their 40s, who had raised their children and were now ready for reading, reflection, and increased church involvement. There was little money for this enterprise, and most thought it would not continue, at least in that form. Some lay persons attending said that many Roman Catholic clergy did not seem interested in serious adult education. One person summed it up by saying that he didn't blame the clergy for what they failed to do; he only wished that they would read a serious book once in a while.

A year ago some friends and I agreed to meet for bible study for an hour a week, rain or shine. Six of us from three Episcopal parishes meet at 8:00 A.M. Wednesdays in one of the member's law offices on East 42nd Street in Manhattan. This was reasonably near everyone's work. We serve freshly brewed coffee at each session. We start with each person reading alternately a paragraph from the Family Prayer section in the Prayer Book so that we can start with an attitude of prayerful attention. Two of us are recent graduates of New York Theological Seminary and are enthusiastic students of the Bible. We share the commentaries and spend a little time with the Bible Atlas. We have a leader, though all comment and respond to questions. We are getting more comfortable with reading the Bible because we are making a consistent effort.

During the time we have been meeting, the husband of one of our members died of a heart illness. One of our members lost her job, and one changed jobs. A man who had been fired from a Wall Street job joined us for morning prayer one day, then left. Our morning prayer, brief as it is, always includes prayers for those who are working, looking for work, the bereaved, those who are lonely, anxious, the old and the young. Sitting in an office with law books around you, and with the only view out the window being that of office buildings and a water tower, one feels a special gladness at being able to offer praise and thanksgiving early in the morning before the city starts to hum.

At the other end of 42nd Street I meet with a bible study group on Thursday evenings. The pastor of the Presbyterian church and I are board members of a small social welfare agency that helps older people live at home as long as it is reasonable. A life-long bible scholar, he shares his learning gladly, and this small group includes inquirers.

The *Didache* (the "Teaching of the Twelve Apostles") which the leader wanted us to read before we essay First Corinthians, is thought to be an authentic teaching of the first-century church on Christian behavior and on the elements of a church service. I am struck by its simplicity and its stress on behavior. The section called "A Way to Live" is about how the Christian community is to conduct itself. The liturgical service contains the Lord's Prayer and a litany.

In my ideal church there would be an instructed eucharist at least once a year.

Some say that the liturgy does not need to be explained. It is all very clear as to what is happening, and its lessons are absorbed in the doing. This is true sometimes, such as at St. Thomas's Church, Manhattan, in Holy Week. My own particular favorite is Maundy Thursday: the stripping of the altar, the choir singing Psalm 22, the scattering of the choirs mid-hymn, the silence. Of course it is theatrical: otherwise, it would not have so powerful an effect as this church provides with music, words, light, sound, and silence. I have never left the service without seeing people in the pews visibly moved, a number of them in tears. This is theater, and it is powerful teaching.

In Third World countries there are riches in liturgy that we know little about. I attend Roman Catholic churches as well as Episcopal churches in Mexico. The last time I was present for the rosary and Benediction at Soledad, Oaxaca, I saw a man standing in front of a crucifix, and simply meditating on it. Across from me a man stopped for two or three minutes to reflect before a large wooden image of Christ on the cross. When he finally kneeled, he made the sign of the cross on his lips; he then made the sign on his forehead, mouth, and chest, and finally his mouth again. Perhaps this means: God in my mind ... in my mouth (words) ... in my heart. He makes the gestures, but does he know what they mean? I don't know. No doubt, for him this devotion is by rote, yet he seemed engaged. I got the idea that the rosary is a prayer wheel, and a prayer wheel is part of the practice of several religious cultures.

There are other forms of education, such as education through service. I have spent quite a few hours as a volunteer chaplain at a nearby acute-care hospital. Although I go there under the guise of comforting, cheering, and consoling the patients, it is really where my inarticulate faith seems to gain strength. I particularly am grateful that it is an interfaith ministry since I have learned so much from patients of diverse backgrounds: their bravery and their honesty, often when they are most vulnerable. Doctors say they hear things from patients that no one else hears. Chaplains can say the same.

It was a thirty-year-old Anglican from Trinidad, dying of cancer, who asked me to sing a hymn with her. She wanted one that I did not know, so she sang it for me: "There is a balm in Gilead," which was haunting and lovely, given the circumstances.

> There is a balm in Gilead
> that makes the wounded whole.
> There is a balm in Gilead
> that cures the sin-sick soul.

Her father and brothers came, dumb giants, to stand by her side and say their prayers. Her husband and her girl friend came at other times. The cruel disease can kill slowly; I visited her for three months until her death. The patient knew many psalms by heart, and sang hymns dear to her in a sweet, true voice.

Many Jewish patients recite the great Shema and the prayer that asks God our healer to restore them to health and a useful life.

Another terminally ill cancer patient, an English teacher who is devoted to his Episcopal parish church, said, "I am not afraid because I am in God's hands."

A volunteer chaplaincy can be undertaken by lay people with training and continuing supervision. It is another kind of religious education.

It is fascinating to realize that the Gulf War and the collapse of Marxism in Eastern Europe have impacted not only our world view but even our ideas about religious education.

We in the west have the riches of resources for education. Eastern Europe has overthrown Communism but finds itself without the capacity to compete. A Romanian, who was released after fifteen years in prison, said: "I came out and I was ordained a bishop. I have no priests. I have no church. I have no people." He corrected himself to say: "No, I have the people. We had a ceremony in an open place because we had no church, and eighty thousand people came."

Rocco Buttiglione, an Italian seminary professor, notes:

> So there are people. But they are a people that has no religious
> education. They love the church but they don't know the cat-

echism. They love Christ but they don't know anything about Christianity. There is tremendous work to be done in order to create a concrete presence of the church that is near the life of the people.

The comments he makes are about the uses of faith in a free market economy.

Switching from communism to capitalism will mean a great deal of hard work. Before these countries can engage in consumerism to the same extent the West does, they will need a religion for hard-working people. Perhaps later they will lapse into the same kind of laxism we have in Europe . . . and in the U.S.[6]

Religious education in our day has to encompass new issues. The use of faith must also be linked to other causes even more important than consumerism in East Europe. And that is the environmental movement. To love God with all your heart and soul, and your neighbor as yourself, does not explicitly include saving the earth. But Thomas Berry, a Roman Catholic cultural historian, makes a powerful case in his book *The Dream of the Earth*[7] for the churches to preach, teach, and act on the subject of saving the only world we have, and without further delay. He gives a compelling theological rationale for conserving the earth as a priority for religious institutions.

The first Earth Day was celebrated in 1970, and there certainly have been efforts by various environmental groups to educate the public about the dangers we face if we neglect the earth. Unfortunately, they have not succeeded in getting the public to understand the issues.[8] The churches have hung back, and it was only in 1988 that the Episcopal Church put the issue of the environment on the agenda before the General Convention.

John Macquarrie, that most considerate of systematic theologians, responded once to a query as to why the church is so conservative, replying that it was because the church was based on tradition. Some complain now that the church is too absorbed in trends but on important issues like the environment is slow to change. Perhaps our task now is to see where doctrine rests on a theology of creation.

I am sure that what makes up a seminary curriculum is one of the arguable topics in religious higher education. In my ideal seminary, the Old Testament scholar would have to design a mandatory course on the doctrine of creation. God created the world and all living things. Men and women may kill or cure, may hinder or help. They have the freedom to choose, but they are responsible. In that sense, we are co-workers with God, which is awesome to contemplate.

Students would have to devise their own six-week series for teaching children. "What We Believe" would be a short course for interested adults who are too embarrassed to admit that they have forgotten what Christianity is. This series would be conducted three times a year. There would be a course called "Religion for the Third Age"—those of the congregation in the harvest of years from seventy to ninety.

Even if only a faithful remnant are in the churches, communicants represent an important minority in the world who are among the caring community.

Some see world issues so serious that they demand a response through Christianity combining with other world religions.

Hans Küng believes that the church uniting with the other inheritor from its Jewish source, Islam, may meet the challenge of secularism with a new ethic.

> . . . I do not believe a new unifying religion will emerge. Rather I see a new set of universal ethics, based on the humane conviction of the great world religions . . . the ethical goal for the third millennium is "planetary responsibility." That is the slogan for the future.
>
> Among the several general ethical rules: There must be no scientific or technological progress, that, when realized, creates greater problems than solutions; for example, the eradication of hereditary illness by genetic manipulation . . . The more urgent value of survival must have priority over the less equal value of self-fulfillment. The ecosystem must have priority over the social system.[9]

To these observations about religious education, I would add that there are some things that clergy ought to know. One is that lay persons have an unquenchable hunger for religious ideas and moral philosophy. We crave imaginative teaching. We are seeking community. The clergy should discuss theology, not so that people think it is the jargon of a clerical vocation but as an attempt to be reasonable.

The clergy shouldn't be lazy. "Our people wouldn't be interested" is really no excuse for lack of effort.

Some lay persons routinely criticize their church. As a sign of their disapproval, they cut their already modest support, or they drift away. But we should realize that when we criticize the church, we are criticizing ourselves. The church is us. If there is a choir practice for the congregation, a workshop, a retreat, lay persons should join in. Neither clergy nor laity should be slothful. Our criticism of others in the congregation, or the clergy, will diminish when we are participating in the church's teaching.

In a recent book on the sacraments, a German priest wrote:

> Liturgy really begins with the fact that we are totally present, with body and soul. But that is not the case when abstract intellect and purposive will smother everything else. If liturgy has something to do with feasting and joy, all the senses should be engaged: hearing, seeing, smelling, tasting and feeling.[10]

In this kind of theater, the congregation is not the audience. We are participants. The divine liturgy is—or can be—a very enlivening play.

Notes

1. Paul Taylor, *Private Domain: An Autobiography* (San Francisco: North Point Press, 1988) 213.

2. Robertson Davies, *A Voice from the Attic: Essays on the Art of Reading*, rev. ed. (New York: Penguin, 1988) 24-25.

3. Ibid. 25.

4. Thomas Groome, *Christian Religious Education: Sharing Our Story and Vision* (New York: Harper and Row, 1980) 53.

5. Jean Nidetch, *Weight Watchers Cook Book* (New York: Hearthwide Press, 1966) 14.

6. Rocco Buttiglione, "The Free Market of Faith," *New Perspectives Quarterly* (Spring 1991) 28-29.

7. Thomas Berry, *The Dream of the Earth* (San Francisco: Sierra Club Books, 1988).

8. Rose Gutfeld, "Americans Flunk Test on Environment," *Wall Street Journal*, 8 November 1991, B 6A.

9. Hans Küng, "The New Ethic: Global Responsibility," *New Perspectives Quarterly* (Spring 1991) 45, 47.

10. Klemens Richter, *The Meaning of the Sacramental Symbols: Answers to Today's Questions* (Collegeville: The Liturgical Press, 1990) 33.

The Legacy of
H. Boone Porter

19

Harry Boone Porter:
A Biographical Sketch

H. Boone Porter

I was born on 10 January, 1923 in Louisville, Kentucky, the son of H. Boone Porter, Sr. and Charlotte Wiseman. My mother died when I was an infant, and some years later my father married Edith Robinson Wood, a young widow with two children slightly older than myself. The three of us grew up happily in the beautiful rural area which at that time was on the east side of Louisville. Later going to boarding school, I graduated from St. Paul's School, Concord, New Hampshire, in 1941 and then proceeded to Yale College.

Pearl Harbor occurred during my freshman year. Continuing in college through the subsequent summer and fall, I was able to complete my sophomore year before going into military service early in 1943. As a soldier I received training in various locations, including Syracuse University, where I was fortunate to meet my future wife, Violet Monser of Oneonta, New York. I then served overseas in the Southwest Pacific. I was discharged early in 1946 and resumed college, from which I graduated in 1947, having been elected to the Phi Beta Kappa Society. On 28 June of that year Violet and I were married, and I entered Berkeley Divinity School in New Haven, Connecticut as a junior that fall. Our eldest child, Charlotte, was born in New Haven the next year, and our eldest son, H. Boone III, two years later. I was ordained a deacon in the Diocese of Kentucky shortly after Easter 1950 and subsequently graduated from seminary. I was pleased and surprised to be offered a position as "Fellow and Tutor" at the General Theological Seminary in New York.

We lived in New York City for two years while I performed the teaching responsibilities of a tutor in the seminary, and worked for my degree as a Master of Sacred Theology. My topic was the Liturgical Reforms of Charlemagne. I had some of my courses at St. Vladimir's Seminary and Columbia University. In the summer of 1951 we were able to go to England where we attended for the first time the summer conference of the Fellowship of St. Alban and St. Sergius in Abington. There we met many distinguished theologians, and also discovered that there was no obstacle to my pursuing future doctoral work at Oxford. In 1952, again shortly after Easter, I was ordained a priest in Kentucky. I completed my Master's Degree at General Seminary, and we then moved to England. We lived in rented premises near Abington, a short distance from Oxford, and I pursued my studies, carrying forward the topic of my previous Master's Degree. I was fortunate in being able to complete my dissertation within two years and was offered the position of teaching church history at the seminary of Nashotah House in Nashotah, Wisconsin, with the rank of assistant professor. I was later promoted to associate professor.

We lived in the pleasant rural setting of the Nashotah campus, about twenty miles west of Milwaukee (1954-1960). In this period our son Michael and our daughters Gabrielle and Clarissa were born. On Sundays I officiated in local churches and was often invited to preach at Grace Church in Madison, Wisconsin, then known as the "A.P. Cathedral" because it served as the center for the Associated Parishes, Inc. This was then a small and demanding group working effectively to disseminate the teaching of the liturgical movement. I was elected a member.

In these same years I pursued topics from my doctoral dissertation and had articles published in England in the *Journal of Theological Studies* explaining the origin of the Roman rite of extreme unction. I also wrote articles for *The Living Church* and *Holy Cross Magazine* introducing to the Episcopal Church the concept of priestly concelebration at the altar. I wrote my first book, *The Day of Light*, published in England in 1960 by SCM Press, and in the United States by Seabury Press. It was reissued in this country by The Pastoral Press in 1987.

Meanwhile my interests had shifted from church history to the field of liturgy. I was asked to come to the General Seminary of the Episcopal Church, at Chelsea Square in New York City, as a full professor, the first in the field of liturgics.

I was also invited in 1960 to travel around the world under the auspices of the Overseas Mission Department of the Episcopal Church to make a series of short stands as visiting professor or conference leader in overseas locations ranging from India, through southwest Asia, and around finally to Alaska. I then rejoined my family at Chelsea Square in New York and began my new teaching duties in January, 1961. Part of each summer we spent in Cuttyhunk Island in Massachusetts and part visiting Violet's mother in Oneonta, New York. At General Seminary I was privileged to direct the graduate work of several promising students, but became dissatisfied with living in New York City. These were turbulent years, and I accompanied a group of students from the seminary to the Montgomery March in Alabama and some other civil rights activities. During this period I was active in the Anglican Society and contributed to its publication *The Anglican*. I became a member of the executive committee of this small organization and have continued my involvement with it.

I found another position outside New York City, but was offered a new arrangement by the Dean of General Seminary. I would retain my professorship, but could live outside the city and commute in. I also had a sabbatical term. Meanwhile I had been appointed to the Standing Liturgical Commission in 1962, and the activities of this body began to increase. I was also appointed to the so-called Home Department of the executive council of the Episcopal Church, this department being concerned with domestic missionary activity under the creative leadership of Bishop Daniel Corrigan. While we were still in New York City, our youngest child Nicholas was born.

In 1965 we moved to 67 Westway Road, Southport, Connecticut and began half a decade of happy residence in that locality. During my sabbatical term I worked on my book *Ordination Prayers of the Ancient Western Churches* which was published in England by Alcuin Club. I also completed about this time my book *Growth and Life in the Local Church* published by Seabury Press in 1967, reissued by the William Carey Press in 1974; I also edited *A Prayer Book for the Armed Forces*. Meanwhile, I was engaged as a consultant by the Home Department and visited various missionary locations in the American Indian field. I also worked with the Church Army, a lay evangelistic organization, and was elected president of its board for several years. During the late 1960s I only taught half of each year. For the other semester the Home Department remunerated General Seminary for my time while I served on various assignments and projects. I was able to arrange for Fr. Alexander Schmemann of St. Vladimir's Orthodox Seminary to teach a course in my department the semesters I was not there.

I was still hoping to see my own ideas about theological education implemented, and in 1970 was pleased to be elected Director of the National Town and Country Church Institute (Roanridge) outside Kansas City, Missouri. At that moment I was among those who agitated successfully for General Convention to legitimate the position of priests serving in secular occupations. We moved west and had what were on the whole seven happy years living at Roanridge Farm. We held a variety of interesting conferences, including one which introduced and publicized theological education by extension, at that time a new Central American development. Our one-day Lenten conferences and our Easter Vigil to which people came from the greater Kansas City area, were great occasions.

During the years at Roanridge I was invited to various ecumenical meetings, being the person regarded as representing rural and small town work in the Episcopal Church. I was also invited to join the board of A Christian Ministry in the National Parks, which holds an interesting meeting in a different National Park each year. I continue to belong to this. In 1976 the meeting was held at Colonial Williamsburg, and Violet wrote an engaging account of it which was printed in the publication of the Rural Workers Fellowship, *Crossroads*. The latter organization had been for many years closely linked with Roanridge, and I was of course active in it. I also worked closely with the Commission on the Church in Small Communities of the national Church. I was pleased to be invited to preach at the ordination of David Cochran as Bishop of Alaska in 1974.

In these years I contributed to several volumes of collected essays, and wrote articles for several publications. I was pleased from time to time to be a speaker at the Valparaiso Liturgical Institute, held in Indiana, and one year in the Twin Cities. While at Roanridge I became a member of the Corporation of the *Anglican Theological Review* and began attending its annual meetings, as I have done subsequently to the extent possible. One summer I taught a course in liturgy in the graduate summer school at Notre Dame University, where I also attended other meetings. I devoted much time to the Standing Liturgical Commission, especially as Chairman of the Sub-Committee on Ordination Rites. I also became president of the Associated Parishes for two years which involved further writing and publishing. Having had some contact with *The Living Church* since student days, I now began writing for it on a regular basis, with the monthly column "Feasts, Fasts and Ferias." During 1970-1982 I was a member of the General Board of Examining Chaplains which provides national pre-ordination examinations for Episcopal clergy. On Sundays I commonly officiated at the Episcopal service in the Old Post Chapel at Fort Leavenworth. In the secular sphere I served for some time on the Mid-American Regional Council, a local body which screened federal grant requests. A more important body was the Missouri Governor's Advisory Council for Comprehensive Health Care on which Violet served, and within which she was a member of the very active committee for the counties of the greater Kansas City area.

Unfortunately Roanridge had no adequate base of financial support, and to the distress of rural churchpeople the directors disbanded in 1977. Shortly after, I was chosen to be the new editor of *The Living Church*, and we moved back to Wisconsin, renting a house in Nashotah not far from where we had lived twenty years before, and resuming contact with friends and the community of which we had been a part. I commuted daily to my office in Milwaukee. I also soon became priest in charge of St. Peter's Church, North Lake, a small semi-rural church which we had been attending.

With the closing of Roanridge, it was possible to salvage and continue the program known as Leadership Academy for New Directions. This was an advanced training course for archdeacons, canons missioner, and others involved in planning, coordinating, etc. work in small churches, mostly in rural areas. The residential sections of "LAND" were now held in different conference centers in different parts of the country, most frequently at the DeKoven Institute in Racine, Wisconsin. I participated in this every year for about half a dozen more years. It continues under an incorporated board. I attended many other conferences and meetings each year in this period, including the quarterly executive council meetings of the Episcopal Church, the General Conventions every three years, the Associated Parishes, and the annual conferences of Diocesan Liturgical and Music Commissions which A.P. initiated. There were also the conferences each other year on the revival of the diaconate which I and others in A.P. started. I was elected a member of the North American Academy of Liturgy, which meets every year in early January. I was also invited to join the board of the Canterbury Cathedral Trust in America.

A high point in my editorship was involvement in the Pacific Basin Roland Allen Conference held in Hawaii in the spring of 1983. Since visiting the Philippines in 1960, I had pursued an interest in the British missionary theologian Roland Allen (1868-1947) and spoke and wrote about him many times. From this conference three of us produced the small book *Setting Free the Ministry of the People of God*, published by Forward Movement in 1984. Smaller Roland Allen conferences have subsequently been held in this country.

When I came to *The Living Church*, selections from my column in that magazine during the previous years formed a book *Keeping the Church Year*, published by Seabury. I was also able to complete a book on which I had been working for many years, on Bishop Taylor, the famous seventeenth-century Anglican writer. *Jeremy Taylor, Liturgist* was published by the Alcuin Club in 1979. Selections from my column "The First Article," which appeared each week in *The Living Church*, formed a book *Song of Creation*, published by Cowley Press in 1986. That same year *The Living Church* moved its offices to a location proximate to All Saints' Cathedral.

In 1985 our family moved somewhat farther from Milwaukee to River Bridge Farm. Meanwhile I served a term on the Standing Committee of the Diocese of Milwaukee and was made an Honorary Canon of the Cathedral of Our Merciful Savior in Faribault, Minnesota, also in 1986.

In 1990 I retired as Editor of *The Living Church*, but retain the title Senior Editor, and continue to write from time to time. I was pleased to leave the magazine free of any debt or deficit.

Violet and I chose to move back to Southport, Connecticut, next door to where we had lived twenty years earlier. In the spring of 1991 I was honored to receive Doctor of Divinity degrees from Nashotah House and the General Theological Seminary. We have become much interested in the Episcopal Diocese in Jerusalem and in St. George's College, the Anglican study center there. And we are currently making arrangements for several American seminary students to have a short period of study in the Holy City.

20

The Porter Impact
on Church Reform

Joe Morris Doss

THE EPISCOPAL CHURCH DOES NOT YET UNDERSTAND THE IMPACT WHICH THE Rev. Harry Boone Porter, Jr., D.Ph. has made on its life. Some have a sense of it, but a rather grand breadth of perspective and a most penetrating eye would be required to comprehend fully what this person has done for the church. This is an attempt to begin focusing on Dr. Porter's influence.

On most Wednesday nights during 1969-1970 at General Theological Seminary, a man with a broad grin, usually carrying a bottle of Spanish wine in a basket, would cross the hall from the dorm room where he spent that single night of each week, and sit on the floor of my room to regale students with his wit, knowledge, and insight. On nice evenings we would sit outside the dorm on the grass and talk on into the morning. Boone Porter's combination of common sense, scholarly knowledge and zany imagination shaped a compelling vision for what the church should be in our time. Our personal relationship has continued throughout the years since. I am writing about a close friend and a lasting mentor.

A Man of Worship

Dr. Porter's life has been a consistent whole; his beliefs and his actions are remarkably harmonious. One can sense that his faith has become internalized as a part of his very identity. Boone Porter authentically believes, and his belief is palpable. The depth of Boone's faith and belief is grounded in worship. Perhaps he is best known to the public as a liturgist, a scholar who knows his discipline. People who know him personally know him as a man of worship. This is the first thing his friends would say about Boone.

His understanding of the correspondence of action and worship derives from his theology of the church, and informs all facets of his liturgical scholarship. Nothing has been more influential than his grand conceptualization of the interconnectedness of liturgy and mission, his comprehension of the integration of liturgical renewal with the Christian imperative for service and justice. No one who has been exposed to Boone Porter's vision can reduce prayer and liturgy to anything less than the mission of the church: the building of the Body of Christ and the offering of service.

His life of prayer is highly disciplined. Boone genuinely enjoys his life of prayer, both private and corporate. This liturgical scholar's eucharistic piety is central, but the daily offices are of great importance to him. The Rev. Samuel E. West remembers an interesting scene just off the floor of the House of Deputies during one General Convention. In the moments before the House was called to order Boone was absorbed in the morning office. Beside him another person was just as engrossed in *The Wall Street Journal*. Neither person was remotely aware of the other. Samuel observed how each man seemed to have selected his choice of daily office.[1]

One may be certain that any meeting which Boone attends will have morning and evening prayer at regular times. If it isn't on the schedule he will see that it is included, or, if necessary, he will invite others to join him at an appointed time and place. One person who attended such a conference came away with a new appreciation of the value of listening to the words of Holy Scripture, simply from observing Boone during the reading of the lessons. This was about the time when printing lectionary leaflets for congregational use was coming into vogue. People were encouraged to read the lessons silently along with the lector, thus using two senses rather than merely one. During the readings this person watched Boone listen to the word: quietly seated, intensely attentive, sometimes with his eyes closed, sometimes gazing off into space, but never reading. His whole being seemed to be focused on listening to the word. Since then, this man has been unable simultaneously to read and listen to Holy Scripture during the liturgy.[2]

Another long time friend, Jean Smelker, recalls a long bus ride from a Mexican airport to a meeting site. There was a great deal of talking and noise. At one point, she looked back to see Boone slumped down into his seat like the headless horseman, his white rimmed Mozarabic-styled collar pulled up over the top of his head. When his head reappeared she confirmed her suspicion that he had ducked his head for better concentration on evening prayer, which he had recited from memory.[3]

But Boone's worship is also evident in his work and his play. Readers of *The Living Church* are familiar with his deep and abiding love of God's creation. He is a naturalist and an anthropologist with the theologian's eye. No one can fail to be struck by his affinity with the things of this earth. One standing joke enjoyed by the Standing Liturgical Commission during the days of Prayer Book revision was the assumption that if a prayer referred to the Heavenly City it was probably written by the New Yorker, Howard Galley; if it referred to the Heavenly Country, it was written by the naturalist Boone Porter. Boone was, in fact, responsible for most of the rogation prayers.

Samuel West tells two stories on Boone to which he was an eyewitness. The first occurred at an Associated Parishes seminar for members of the liturgics commissions of the three dioceses in Michigan. Boone was the seminar leader and president of the closing eucharist, situated around an outdoor altar on the shore of Lake Michigan. Samuel noticed the celebrant's bare feet sticking out from under the chasuble, the toes gently caressing the soil, as he bid the *Sursum corda*: "Lift up your hearts".

The second took place at an Associated Parishes for Liturgy and Mission (A.P.) conference for lay people, during the most controversial period of Prayer Book revision. Someone asked what Boone would take with him if he were stranded on a proverbial desert island and he could only have two books. Without a pause Boone responded, "The Holy Bible, *National Geographic*, and if I could sneak one along, the Book of Common Prayer."[4]

Personally, it isn't just the instruction I received about eucalyptus trees as we walked across the campus of the University of California at Berkeley, or the discussion of the mountain range wildlife overlooking the Diocese of Olympia church camp outside of Seattle, or the way his famous class lecture described a primitive hunt in the ice-age snow of today's Long Island and how it necessitated a community of interdependence on which each person staked his or her life, or any of the other ways Boone has shared with me his knowledge and special appreciation of nature. It is also the way I see him having fun, enjoying food, drink and good company, that I know something of the joy in his worship of the God of creation. A man of straightlaced morality, someone to whom the word "frivolous" would never apply, he knows how to enjoy himself and people and "stuff". This man is able to appreciate fully the delights of one of the best neighborhood restaurants in New Orleans, the venerable Mandina's of Canal Street. (Many visitors would see only a loud little hole-in-the-wall bar with some tables—albeit, always full.) One day I looked up from my office desk to see Boone walking in. He had booked an extra leg on a cross country flight in order to gain a four hour lay-over in New Orleans—just enough time for a proper lunch at Mandina's.

The Discovery and Championing of Roland Allen

As renowned as Boone may be as a liturgist and, as one of the main editors of the 1979 Book of Common Prayer, with all his historical scholarship, for all his personal creativity, and even after his contribution in interpreting a very difficult time for the church during his years as editor of *The Living Church*, Boone may be remembered most for his influence on the church's approach to mission and ministry. His championing of Roland Allen's insights and his understanding of the ministry of the early church have planted seeds which have made more difference than most realize. The reforms they demand could radically alter basic assumptions about the church. Certainly, that is Boone's intention.

When Boone was Professor in the General Theological Seminary, and one of the most popular, a special arrangement was made by the Seminary and the Executive Council that allowed him to serve in a capacity they called Seminary Field Extension worker. This allowed him to devote half his time to a variety of field activities directed toward development and training for indigenous leadership, lay leadership, and church growth. He especially worked with clergy and lay people in rural areas, Indian reservations, and other special missionary fields.

In 1960 Dr. Porter was sent to Southeast Asia where he conducted liturgical conferences and lectured in mission seminaries. He was not entirely sanguine about what he saw. Nor was he terribly popular with the missionaries to whom he lectured, for he was quite free with his criticisms. Two young missionaries with whom he was more *sympatico* were stationed in the Philippines: George Harris, who became Bishop of Alaska, 1981-1991, and Richard Rising, later to serve as Dean of the Episcopal Theological Seminary of the Caribbean, 1963-1968 and Associate Director of the Board for Theological Education, 1970-1976. They were part of the highly structured "missionary compound," "clergy-in-charge" missionary style of the era, but they were questioning it. Having discovered Allen, they could see that what they were involved in was the exact antithesis of what he would have advocated.

George Harris had attended an Outgoing Missionary Conference sponsored by the National Council of Churches in Meadville, Pennsylvania. The lecturer was the Rev. Kenneth Cragg, a veteran Anglican missionary, author of several excellent theological works, including *Sandals at the Mosque*, and recognized as one of the Anglican communion's foremost expert on Islam. His lectures were largely on indigenous ministry, during which he introduced several of Allen's ideas. When George Harris arrived in the Philippines, Roland Allen's books were sitting on his shelf. With hindsight, he now says that Allen's works were a time bomb waiting to go off in the right hands.

Allen himself had recognized this. Accepting the fact that his life's work was going unheeded in his own lifetime, he anticipated a future in which they would be discovered. Late in life, his grandson Hubert asked him whether he could read his books, Allen responded: "You can read them by all means; but you won't understand them. I don't think anyone'll understand them until I've been dead 10 years."[5] Roland Allen died in 1947.

Then, along came Boone Porter in 1960, observing the problems of traditional missionary work and alert to new ideas. His lectures on liturgics were almost finished in the islands when a typhoon struck. The narrow mountain highway was blocked by a landslide and the bus he would have taken could not pass. Boone was stuck in the missionary compound. Boone turned to the library of his friend, George Harris. Harris remembers sitting in his living room as Boone came bursting in from the library with a copy of Allen's *Missionary Methods* in hand and talking excitedly about having found exactly what the church needs. Boone Porter understood Roland Allen. He saw far more than a simple methodology for effective missionary work abroad; here was a vision of a more complete fulfillment of the implications of baptism for all Christians and congregational communities. The prophet's ideas were in the right hands for the seeding.

From that moment on Boone has been industriously planting these ideas, which quickly became adapted to his own.

Perhaps a few words will be helpful in understanding the scope of Boone's influence in applying Allen's ideas to the church's mission and ministry. Allen contended that St. Paul's missionary success, especially as opposed to modern missionary and growth efforts, was the fact that he founded churches, not missions. He meant that Paul founded purely indigenous churches, fully endowed with all necessary spiritual authority, self-supporting, self-determining, and self-expanding. Paul did not hesitate to call on his personal authority when he needed to or to admonish the congregation when it was in error. But the churches he founded did not depend on him or any other outside person for the full sacramental, preaching, and teaching ministry. He ordained and appointed leaders as needed to administer discipline, teach orthodox doctrine, and manage financial affairs. Once the church was established, he and his missionary colleagues moved on, leaving an independent congregation to make its own mistakes and to determine its own selfhood. That local congregation was given the task, entirely, of evangelizing the surrounding populace. They assumed they should be growing internally in the Christian life and externally by gathering pagans. This system worked like none since.

"In sharp contrast is the way in which most missionary activity has been conducted in modern times, resulting in the establishment of `missions': congregations remaining almost wholly dependent upon the outside `sending' body for financial support, leadership, administration, discipline, and further evangelization. This dependency is rarely broken, even after decades. Growth is generally at a very slow rate . . ."[6]

Few would argue that Boone was the single most responsible person for bringing Roland Allen's contribution into the consciousness of today's church. It was a Herculean effort. By 1983, Boone's work had yielded such fruit that some 150 Anglican and Episcopalian lay persons, archbishops, bishops, priests, and deacons of some twenty-four different nationalities and fifty different ethnic backgrounds gathered in Honolulu, Hawaii, for a conference with the stated theme: "The vision and legacy of Roland Allen." The outcast prophet had become recognized by the establishment, even if his ideas had not yet achieved much implementation. That, Boone recognizes, is not likely to come about until and in those places where economics forces reality upon the church. Only when the church is forced to recognize that more clergy and more money will not be the solution, will it recognize that this should not be the solution.

At this conference Canon David Paton, of England, summarized Allen's basic doctrine as follows:

> 1. A Christian community which has come into being as the result of the preaching of the Gospel should have handed over to it the Bible, creed, ministry and sacraments.
>
> 2. It is then responsible with the bishop for recognizing the spiritual gifts and needs in its membership and for calling into service priests or presbyters to preside at the eucharist and to be responsible for the word and for pastoral care.
>
> 3. It is also required to share the message and the life with its neighboring communities not yet evangelized.
>
> 4. The Holy Spirit working on the human endowment of the community's leaders is sufficient for its life. Don't 'train' them too much! Don't import from outside.
>
> 5. A Christian community that cannot do these things is not yet a CHURCH: it is a mission field.
>
> 6. The Bishop and his staff (cf. Timothy, Titus, etc.) are crucial.[7]

Lay Ministry, Native American and Ethnic Ministry

The implications of Roland Allen's vision are several and Boone has followed almost all of them into efforts for reform of different aspects of the church's life. Compared to the rest of his work, Boone may not be known as a leader in the movement for lay ministry, but he certainly convinced many of his students and colleagues of the need to develop it. He saw that this was the real revolution, and he saw it in his own inimitable terms.

Boone has a remarkably sensitive feel for the way people form communities, whether it is a neighborhood, or a hunt, or a nation, or a church, or a group of colleagues, or any of the other ways folks come together and identify with a sense of interdependence and purpose. Boone knows how to respond to the given community, whatever it is: a small rural area, a neighborhood pub, a reservation, a military camp, a parish. He appreciates the little things which make the community stay together and give it cohesion.

This sensitivity to the life which forms community leads Boone to appreciate the parish as the key to the life of the church. He understands how a priest or a deacon must be in a parish long enough to become fully integrated into the community and accepted as one of the people, as well as to become a leader in the broader civic community. Only in this way can a priest or deacon genuinely affect the parish's life and have some lasting influence.

Boone himself has always been related to an active congregation, usually as pastor. This has had the intended effect on his broader contributions to the church as scholar, teacher, interpreter, and reformer.

Consequently, he has a deep appreciation for the kind of natural leadership which emerges in a community, whatever its structures. This leads him to appreciate the importance of the lay leadership which is necessary to form the parish community and enrich it most fully. He knows how to look to the key lay leadership which keeps a parish going over the years and provides its unique character and identity. Thus he understands how important it is for lay people to be well trained and fully authorized.

However, he doesn't think of lay leadership as something opposed to ordained leadership. His concern is for the total ministry of the church, and that includes ordered ministry. Ministry does not exist as a means for each individual to satisfy the implications of her or his baptism. It exists for the service and salvation Christ offers to the world through those who are baptized into the life of Christ. Thus, people are to be trained and given the opportunity to fulfill the ministry implicit in their baptism. Ordained or ordered ministry exists for the ministry of the whole body, the *Laos*. Consequently, when Boone thinks of the value of having the leadership and ministry of a community emerge from within, he thinks about the need for both lay and ordained leadership.

Boone was one of the first Episcopalians to comprehend the potential which education by extension has for serious and in-depth lay educators. He also understands its possibilities for training ordained leadership without taking candidates from the community where they have been recognized as leaders. Boone is very much in favor of local, non-seminary training for indigenous clergy, especially for rural and ethnic ministry, best accomplished by education by extension. He was excited by what the Presbyterians were doing in Guatemala and Korea, under the leadership of Ross Kinsler. They were training people for ministry in their own environment—without removing them from their culture or from the specific community from within which they had emerged as the recognized and selected leaders. The program seemed to understand that sending them away to seminaries in metropolitan centers would forever distance them from the people they were selected to serve.

Boone foresaw how this concept can be applied to lay training for ministry. He had high hopes that someone would develop materials for the United States. I remember when he obtained a translation of the text Kinsler had developed in Guatemala for the study of the Gospel of Mark. He ask me to examine it, but he already understood that it would not be the appropriate instrument for use among relatively sophisticated American Episcopalians. I can testify that no one was more thrilled to hear that Charles Winters was working on materials for education by extension, and then more pleased to see the results.

An example of how supportive Boone was of the effort to develop EFM can be seen in the way Boone brought Frank Cohoon, formerly Archdeacon of the Diocese of Kansas, into the small network of those interested in education by extension: "When Boone learned that my wife and I were moving to Guadalajara to work for the Episcopal Bishop of Western Mexico, he invited me to Roanridge for lunch and a visit . . . He also told me of Charles Winters' sabbatical that he was planning to spend in San Miguel de Allende. He was to work on . . . theological education by extension . . . I had known Winters at General Seminary where he was a Fellow and Tutor while I was a student. We did visit about his project a couple of times while he was in San Miguel. The result of Winters' work is now known as the `Education for Ministry' (EFM) of the School of Theology at Sewanee, TN. Boone alerted me to this and gave me the documented reports of the work in Guatemala which we did find useful in Western Mexico. EFM has been of enormous value in the United States by helping lay persons discover their gifts and training them for ministry."[8]

It does not appear that Boone had any direct influence on Dr. Winters, either to develop EFM or in the actual materials, but I know that he helped create the community of interest in the development of education by extension. I would like to think that those of us who had recognized the need for someone to address the challenge Charles Winters finally took up with such creativity and success, had some indirect influence in the process. I know that both Boone and I talked to Dean U.T. Holmes of St. Luke's Seminary at length about the need and the opportunity for a seminary to develop materials for education by extension. My personal interest in it fell on sympathetic ears during several conversations Terry Holmes and I engaged in about education by extension. Whatever the actual influence they may have had on Terry's thinking, it is worth noting that he was the Dean of St. Luke's Seminary who approved the plan, granted Dr. Winters his sabbatical, provided the resources, and sponsored EFM.

Bishop William Gordon of Alaska, believes that Boone became "The interpreter of Total Ministry".[9] This is a movement which emphasizes the ministry of the baptized, and suppresses clericalism. The role of the ordained clergy as trainers and enablers of ministry is understood as primary. The clergy are never to be understood as the expert or the elite in terms of training, function or status. "Lay" is never used as a term to refer to the relatively ignorant or to those who appear as clients to a professional expert.

Boone has especially focused on ministry to ethnic peoples. I can testify to his support for ministry to Hispanics, to whom Boone is particularly sensitive and highly appreciative of their culture. If nothing else, their deep commitment to the family would be enough to endear them to Boone. He believes they have much to offer for the enrichment of American culture and, specifically, for the church.

I had the opportunity to become involved in Hispanic ministry, and it has enriched my ministry immeasurably. I am not certain that I would have recognized the first opportunity for Hispanic ministry which presented itself to me had Boone Porter not so impressed on me the need while I was still a student at General. I would not have made it through the first few lonely years of hard work, lacking the proper language and cultural skills, had it not been for Boone's support and encouragement.

It is interesting to note how many times Boone personally drew on the Mozarabic tradition in writing portions of the Book of Common Prayer. He published a most informative article tracing the Hispanic influence on the Book of Common Prayer, an influence no Hispanic I have talked to realized prior to his explanation.[10] Boone has also worked with me to have A.P. materials, including his article, published in Spanish.

Most of his work with ethnic peoples has been with Native Americans, including those of Alaska: the Eskimo or Inuit, and the Athabaskans. Boone's influence for work with Native Americans has been extensive: teaching and holding workshops, consultation on a range of subjects of ministry, facilitating the emergence of a "middle management" of church officers sensitive to new ways of ministering to Native Americans, helping develop programs of education—especially for those to be ordained. A most important contribution has been political. This is reflected in the changes in canon law for which he has been directly responsible and which have opened opportunities for indigenous ministry.

If anyone fails to appreciate the political savvy of Boone Porter, they simply are not paying attention. He has a way of being in the right place at the right time to initiate programs which result in lasting and important changes in the church. We will see that happening for non-stipendiary priests, deacons, the community of liturgists and musicians, diocesan executives, rural ministers and others. But he also has the capacity to write legislation and to move it skillfully through the necessary process for adoption at diocesan and General Conventions. He understands the system; he understands how the Episcopal Church works; he understands how to get things done.

For Native American ministry he opened up the canons at the General Convention at Seattle in 1967. In 1966, after consultation with several people involved in Indian ministry, Boone met with David Cochran (later Bishop of Alaska, 1974-1981) who was stationed on the Standing Rock reservation in North Dakota. Together, at the Cochran home at Fort Yates, they worked out the first draft of a revision of Canon 26 on the educational requirements for postulants whose "native language" is "other than English," or who are "of a distinctive culture." This was the first step towards making an indigenous ministry for Native Americans possible in the Episcopal Church. The old canons, as in 1964, Canon 26, section 5, virtually required that one be a college graduate, or the equivalent, in order to be a postulant within the United States. Persons who were not college or university graduates had been required to take examinations in a number of subjects. That requirement was eliminated for postulancy to the priesthood and to what the canons then referred to as the "perpetual diaconate". The canon which passed read:

> If the native language of the Postulant be other than English, and he is to exercise his Ministry among peoples of his own language, or if he be of a distinctive or foreign culture, the Bishop may, at his discretion, dispense him from all such examinations; *Provided only*, that he shall satisfy the Bishop and the Board of Examining Chaplains that he possesses good mental ability and sufficient competence to enable him to pursue a course of study preparatory to the work of the Ministry.

As Fr. Cochran was grinding out the proposed revision on the mimeograph machine, Mrs. Cochran and Boone joined a group of Indian children for a swim in the Missouri River. The earthiness, enthusiasm, and playfulness of that moment is vintage Boone Porter: work hard, play hard, and embrace the earth.

It was also typical of Boone's practical appreciation of the way things actually work, that he made sure, largely through the good offices of Bishop Daniel Corrigan, that a resolution was passed charging the Church Pension Fund to consider new provisions for clergy who earn a living in secular occupations and who make other arrangements for their insurance and retirement. Subsequently the changes were made. Quite possibly the most impressive work in bringing the whole matter off was the lobby effort, practically a one man operation. Friends have vivid memories of Boone: walking down hallways with an arm around the shoulders of a voter, face bent to face and mouth working to articulate the logic of his position, on the move going from room to room to speak at committee meetings and at the relevant hearings—tending to business with consummate success.

In 1967 Bishop Gordon of Alaska asked Boone and Fr. Cochran to present the ideas behind the canonical change to the diocese. They already had been wrestling with a vision of a self-supporting indigenous ministry. Here was a bishop ready to act. Boone and Fr. Cochran helped the diocese to put flesh and blood on their local vision. Boone challenged them to a five-year plan for having local ordained leadership in all of their mission communities. He did it so powerfully and positively that they almost made it. The influence of the Alaskan experience has been far and wide. Bishop Gordon said this: "That pioneering step was the forerunner of the 'local' clergy development that emerged in Nevada and Utah and a couple of dozen other U.S. dioceses, and significantly overseas in places like Ecuador and slowly in Africa."[11]

At the special General Convention in South Bend, 1969, a canon was introduced to facilitate the ideas Boone had suggested during that conference. The creation of what Bishop Gordon was to call "sacramentalists" had been initiated.

Boone and his colleagues moved forward for the convention in 1970 with lengthy proposals for changing the canons so that persons might be ordained who would continue in secular work and that persons already ordained might enter secular work without penalty.

This was a convention in which I had a slight hand in the canonical changes as the Consultant to the Board for Theological Education. The canons for ministry underwent pervasive changes, for example, creating the present systems of Commissions on Ministry and The Board of Examining Chaplains. I was assigned to assist Canon Charles Guilbert, who was Secretary of the convention at that time, for most of the drafting of these new canons and amendments. One thing we were able to contribute was technical advice to Boone for the redrafting of the sections 10 of Canon 10 and 11. The most important canon Boone wrote, in terms of our discussion, began:

> A man of Christian character, proven fitness, and leadership in his community, who is willing to serve in the capacity of Deacon without relinquishing his secular occupation, may be proposed and recommended to the Bishop, for enrollment as a Postulant, by the Minister and Vestry of the Parish in which his service is desired . . . [III.10.10(a)]

Bishop Gordon and others sympathetic to his needs in Alaska for local "sacramentalist" priests, made sure the canons applied to the ordination of priests as well as deacons. It is important to note the imaginative change in the use of the term "proposed." This introduces the concept of local selection by a congregation for the first time since the practice of the ancient church. Rather than waiting for someone to present herself or himself in response to a personal call from God, the local congregation is to propose someone. The distinction which may be made between the "Petrine call," wherein the individual responses to God's call which the church is to test, and the "Pauline call," wherein the church issues the call which the person is to test (an opportunity not always granted to those called by the early church), has vast implications if we ever gain the nerve to use it as intended.[12]

The Diaconate

Central to Boone's purpose in the creation and implementation of these canons on ministry was the restoration of the diaconate as a permanent order with local ties in accordance with the ancient church's practice. Originally, the canon [III.10.10(a)] establishing the opportunity to be ordained while continuing in secular work, or to enter secular work after ordination without penalty was intended to establish the opportunity for the development of this "vocational" or "permanent" diaconate. It provided for deacons only. As previously mentioned, it was Bishop Gordon who saw to its expansion by adding a clause about subsequent ordination to the priesthood. Boone's heart, personally, was with the diaconate more than anything.

In 1973, thanks to Boone's continuing leadership, the movement to introduce flexibility to a previously rigid system regarding preparation for ordination to the diaconate was completed by amendment. "It divided preparation into two equal parts, academic and practical, thus shifting the emphasis from solely academic study (often modeled after seminary preparation) to include practical training and recognition of the value of practical experience in *diakonia*. The canon also required `an evaluation of the Candidate's attainments' instead of the usual formal examinations. The sum of these changes implied a new kind of deacon, formed more in the hospitals, prisons, and soup kitchens than in the study hall."[13]

Frank Cohoon realized that Boone was called to promote the restoration of the diaconate in the way the young scholar exercised his own diaconate while at General. Boone was completing his Master's degree in Sacred Theology and serving as a Fellow and Tutor at the seminary when their paths crossed during 1951-1952. Cohoon remembers that in those days being a deacon was considered a necessary discipline on the way to priesthood, the "real" ministry of the church. The Ordinal referred to the Diaconate as "this inferior Order" (1928 BCP, p. 535). In the liturgy of the seminary Chapel of the Good Shepherd, priests always read the gospel and led the intercessions. There was no provision for the deacon to send the community out into the world. If a deacon was scheduled he (there were no female deacons) was permitted to read Morning Prayer and assist in the distribution of communion, but only by ministering the chalice.

Boone provided the only model for an authentic diaconate, and other students took notice. The Rev. Peter Moore remembers from the same time, "Boone was a clear and ardent spokesperson for the diaconate."[14] Archdeacon Cohoon admits that he began for the first time to become aware of the diaconate as something worthwhile by watching Boone function as a deacon at St. Peter's Church, Chelsea, half a block from the seminary. He performed all of the traditional (but largely lost) eucharistic functions of the diaconate, except for the rubrically impermissible dismissal. In retrospect, Boone was at least two decades ahead of almost everyone else. He was to have his moment in changing the Prayer Book's regard for what it had termed "the inferior order." As Chair of the Standing Liturgical Commission Draft Committee, Boone was in position to ensure the diaconate a more appropriate theological definition in the new ordinal of the 1979 Book of Common Prayer—and did.

Cohoon finished his remembrance of Boone's diaconate by saying, "It was rumored at General that Boone believed his vocation should be fulfilled as a deacon; that he never aspired to be ordained Priest. But in the church of that day, priesthood offered the only avenue of study, scholarship and influence that would make it possible for him to do what he was called to do. So in April, 1952, shortly before leaving for England and Oxford University, the consummate deacon became a priest."[15]

Boone provided the leadership for restoration of the diaconate until the order grew to the extent that it started producing its own leadership, usually people who had been greatly influenced by the master himself. With Boone's tutelage A.P. made its seminal 1977 declaration calling for the restoration of the diaconate: The Wewoka Statement. A.P. has enjoyed no success more than its ability to call the church's attention to the issues that the council believes it is time for the church to face. When A.P. issued the call for renewal of the diaconate, the church began to recognize that this was a major issue on the church's agenda for reform. The first national conference on the diaconate was called by Boone as President of A.P. and held at Roanridge. The first item on the agenda was an informative and moving speech by Boone. Soon, the national conferences at Notre Dame sponsored by A.P. were gathering a movement which was picking up such speed that no one could claim to be in charge of it. Then, in its typical style, A.P. backed away from its front and center public role after parenting the beginning of a new organization of deacons in the United States and Canada. In the same way, Boone stepped back to make room for leadership within the order itself.

While Boone served as A.P. President he also organized the first conference for chairpersons of diocesan liturgy commissions, held at Roanridge. The representatives of some fifty-three dioceses were present. Soon it developed into a stable and important organization, expanded to include the chairs of diocesan music commissions. This was another organization A.P. was to parent and then leave to its own leadership, but not before Boone put the revival of the diaconate on its agenda and made it one of their causes. No one had more to do

with the success to date of the restoration of the diaconate than Boone
Porter. Of course he would be the first to acknowledge how far there
yet is to go. Boone has given the church a legacy which continues to
beg for action.

Small Church and Rural Ministry

Many of the same ideas and reform through canonical change
which applied to ethnic ministry and the revival of the diaconate
were also dedicated to developing ministry in rural areas and for
small churches, especially for churches lacking in resources. This was
Porter's primary task as Director of the Roanridge Conference and
Training Center. Boone is convinced that ordained leadership in such
communities, as in those for ethnic ministry, must come from the
local congregation and be largely non-stipendiary. The first reason
comes from simple economic realities. Many dioceses have a large
part of their internal missionary budget tied up in static little congregations which after seventy-five or a hundred years are still no closer
to being able to support a resident priest or deacon. The time when
we simply will not have the money to continue in this way is upon us.
Yet few dioceses are taking significant action to solve the problem.
We keep looking for more money and more seminary trained ordained ministers.

However, Boone is convinced that continuing the present practice
is a bad idea even if the money is available for a few more years. He
believes that local "amateur" (remembering the root of the word
implies a labor of love) leadership which relies on local training is the
best form of ministry under any circumstances. It isn't only that we
can't afford to send people from these places to receive a seminary
education, it is also that such an education would ruin them for
purposes of that particular local ministry. It would change them
culturally, removing from them the perspective and the qualities
which raised them into positions of respect and leadership in the first
place, probably motivating them to want to live in more exciting
places and enter into the career ladder system of Episcopal clericalism, devoid of the amateur's love of the job.

People continue to worry about lowering the standards of the
ordained clergy. In answer Boone says that, "it is not a question of
lower standards, but of more relevant standards. A middle class
young man of college education usually has no difficulty in entering

a seminary or passing canonical exams, although he may have grave deficiencies of character and no power of leadership. On the other hand, a Kentucky mountaineer or a Mexican American who happens to be a mature man of proven Christian character will find so many obstacles to ordination that he will be forced to conclude that the church does not want him. Yet it is precisely this kind of man who could work most effectively with his own people."[16]

Very early in his career, Boone wrote one of a series of biographies, published in the immediate post-war years by the old National Council of the Episcopal Church, called *Builders for Christ. Truman Heminway: Priest Farmer* rather perfectly pictured his ideas for small church rural ministry. In the medieval church the priest might farm what was called "the parson's glebe," by which he would earn his income from the Lord of the Manor, while exercising his parish ministry. This style of rural ministry continued well into colonial Virginia, tobacco normally serving as the legal tender. It lasted into our era in at least one isolated instance in Vermont. Truman Heminway performed his priestly ministry for the Episcopal Church on a mission farm in Sheburne, Vermont. Jay Lowery remembers hearing Fr. Heminway speak and testifies that it affected his entire life and ministry. "He smelled of horse manure and spoke of holy things. It made wonderful sense."[17] Boone's biography wondered why such ministry should die out. He suggested instead that this was one good and lasting model for the non-stipendiary ministry which rural areas need today.

In another work, *Growth and Life in the Episcopal Church*, Boone portrayed a living example of a tent-making ministry which was proved worthy. During the depression a small church in Evansville, Indiana found it necessary to institute a priest without stipend. It turned out to be a benefit rather than a drawback. In this work, Boone discusses how much local ministry depends on the little meaningful details and local idiosyncracies which a non-stipendiary minister who is a part of the community as a peer can recognize and attend to, and which the "pros" who come and go are likely to overlook or neglect.

Sitting on his porch at Roanridge Boone conceived LAND, Leadership Academy for New Directions, a ministry training school to develop leadership and programs for churches in small communities. Boone became the Dean of LAND during its infancy. Still operating out of the cathedral in Faribault, Minnesota, the primary elements include increased lay responsibility, indigenous local clergy, a well trained clergyperson serving as regional supervisor, and a cluster of several small places which operate independently and together— especially for more sophisticated programs than any one of them could afford. One successful aspect of this project was Boone's search for people to become supervisors and consultants. He discovered and trained a significant number of people with very real talent.

Man of Middle Management

Boone recognized that if the church is to undergo reform and renewal it will be important that those who have positions of "middle management" should play a major part in the process. Archdeacons, Canons to the Ordinary, Diocesan Administrators, Chairpersons of Diocesan Committees are "key" people in the renewal of the church. They can make things happen and they can block things from happening. We have already observed how instrumental Boone was in developing key people for middle management positions in special areas of interest, such as LAND, schools for lay education, training for ethnic ministry and programs for the diaconate. While at Roanridge, Boone also put together the Conference of Diocesan Executives or CODE, to act as a training and support group.

Implementer of Liturgical Renewal

Since Boone's accomplishments and reputation as a liturgist are well established, and are elsewhere treated in this work. I think it is particularly important for the public to understand just how much of the Book of Common Prayer owes its authorship and translations to Boone Porter. He did more than anyone else to see to implementation of liturgical renewal. It is one thing to teach ideas; it is one thing to revise the Book of Common Prayer and have it placed in every pew. It is yet another to have parishes begin to make the proper use of the ideas and the Prayer Book. That struggle is far from over. More than any other single person, Boone has been responsible for progress in the acceptance and practical application of liturgical renewal in parishes.

Much of what Boone has accomplished as implementor has been through the offices of A.P. This is a role which that organ of liturgical renewal has recognized and accepted for itself largely because of

Boone's insight. At one time A.P. hired one of Boone's former students, The Rev. Michael Merriman (formerly Precentor and Associate Dean of Grace Cathedral, San Francisco) with the specific job description of consulting with parishes for the implementation of liturgical reform. Unfortunately, there were few takers and the job was soon abandoned, but the experience pointed to the drastic need for parochial reform—as well as to the fear of it.

Rather than attempt to cover the field, let us take one example: the Easter Vigil. Boone introduced this rite to the students and faculty at General Theological Seminary long before it became an official service in the Prayer Book, convincing an advance generation of students of its value. As a member of the Standing Liturgical Commission during Prayer Book revision and Chair of its Drafting Committee, Boone was the prime mover for seeing that it was placed in the Prayer Book itself. Because it was only designed for use once a year, other members, like Massey Shepherd, argued that it should be placed in the *Book of Occasional Services*. Boone insisted that it was the very heart of the revised Prayer Book and that it must be placed in its very heart. He argued that it would be prohibitively difficult to introduce, much less to be given prominence as the main Easter service, if it wasn't placed in the Prayer Book. Those opposed argued that it was too long, but Boone insisted that it be published in full.

While Boone was at Roanridge he did more to introduce the service to the ordinary parish than can be imagined, simply by modeling it for the relatively small groups of people he invited to participate. Here, in the middle of the country, with a people who are not known for strange or exotic liturgies, he proved the benefits of a long and complicated service which contained the vast sweep and full imagery of the whole story of the people of God and which used a wide variety of symbols and rituals, which offered baptisms and celebrated eucharist—followed by a substantial party.

The Rev. Walter Guettsche, on the diocesan staff of the Diocese of Los Angeles, testifies to the importance of being involved in the liturgical life at Roanridge as pivotal to his decision to enter the Episcopal Church and become a priest. Images of gathering around a huge bonfire as the New Fire, of lots of smoke, of lots of movement, of lots of singing, of children sitting in a tub on a great *bema* in the middle of a large room while water was poured over their heads in the baptismal rite—images which set free the power of symbols and ritual actions—captured his religious imagination in a way which was formative.

It is also worth noting that Walter was another of many students who saw in the liturgical life which Boone demonstrated the all important unity between liturgy and mission, particularly the mission of justice. He says, "This was very powerful for me, you understand. There may be those who see liturgy as something merely supportive of spirituality and of the ministry of the church, something aesthetical which, when successful, enhances the inner spiritual life of the individual and the community. But through Boone's eyes I was able to see that liturgy is not successful, doesn't do what is intended until the church is servant, until it struggles for justice. I suddenly understood why A.P.'s full name is Associated Parishes for Liturgy AND MISSION."[18] His was the story of a significant number of people who attended the Easter Vigils and participated in the liturgies at Roanridge, all of whom have spread the message.

Boone has an ability to bring liturgy to the ordinary day to day human round. He can take the most complex matters and make them understood in simple, practical, and terribly concrete, application to our lives and to the day. On the other hand he can take something which seems rather esoteric, or trivial, or irrelevant, and use it to shed light on the most important of matters, develop it into the most important of generalizations. One student who arrived at General in 1950 discovered that Boone was his tutor. The topic assigned to the students for the first tutorial paper and discussion was: What is Christianity? When the time for the crucial first session arrived, the student was in a fit of anxiety, hopeful that his paper would be acceptable—or perhaps even to be judged as a work of quality, showing potential. When he returned to his dorm room his roommate found him puzzled. How did it go? The paper had been read, followed by one response from the young tutor: "Very interesting." Then Boone began to talk to him about the influence of the dromedary camel on near eastern religion. They never did go back to the awfully general topic which had been assigned.[19]

The Armed Forces

Boone served in the Army in World War II, and saw action as a staff sergeant in the Southwest Pacific. He has remained sensitive to the special stresses and needs of the communities formed by Armed Services. One special mission was to serve the church's liturgical, educational, and pastoral ministry to the Armed Forces. He has done this in a variety of ways which reflect his talents and personality.

In 1967 Boone served as editor for updating the *Armed Forces Prayer Book*. It reflected the thinking of that time of the liturgical movement and anticipated the Book of Common Prayer revision which was soon to follow. He has visited armed forces installations at home and oversees, such as in Germany, to consult with the troops and their families, as well as with duty chaplains. On occasion he has accompanied the suffragan bishops to the Armed Forces. Bishop Burgreen says that he fondly remembers their trips together.[20]

I hope that this very personal and relatively limited survey helps the church to begin to grasp something of the impact Harry Boone Porter, Jr. has made on its life, especially as a reformer. He hasn't supported every move for reform which has been addressed by the church. He is particularly wary of issues which are defined by society and, in his view, seem to be adopted by the church as it seeks to be responsible to society. For Boone, the issues which are truly going to reform the church arise from the clear mandate of Scripture and from our relatively new knowledge of the practices of the ancient church. This is, in fact, the source of most issues for reform, and no one has been more in the forefront, more important, and more influential in bringing these issues to life in the Episcopal Church during the latter half of the twentieth century than Boone Porter.

Notes

1. Samuel E. West, to Joe Morris Doss, 6 December, 1990.

2. Frank Cohoon, to Joe Morris Doss, 24 December, 1990.

3. Jean Smelker, M.D., to Joe Morris Doss, 26 November, 1990.

4. Samuel E. West, Ibid.

5. *Setting Free the Ministry of the People of God*, ed. Gerald Charles Davis, Eric Chogn, and Boone Porter (Cincinnati: Forward Movement Publications, 1984) 14.

6. *American Indian Mission and Ministry*, ed. David R. Cochran, Robert Rodenmayer, and H. Boone Porter, Jr. (New York: Executive Council of the Episcopal Church, 1968) 3.

7. Davis and others, eds., *Setting Free the Ministry of the People of God* 21.

8. Cohoon, Ibid.

9. William J. Gordon, Jr., to Joe Morris Doss, 4 December, 1990.

10. H. Boone Porter, Jr., "Hispanic Roots of Episcopal Worship," *OPEN* (September 1989) 1-7.

11. William J. Gordon, Jr., Ibid.

12. Ormonde Plater and Joe Morris Doss, "A Proposal for Renewal of the Diaconate in Louisiana," submitted to the Commission on Ministry of the

Diocese of Louisiana by the Committee on Non-Stipendary Ministry, 1975.

13. Ormonde Plater, to Joe Morris Doss, 23 March, 1991. Taken from his research notes for *Many Servants: An Introduction to Deacons* (Cambridge, MA: Cowley Publications, 1991).

14. Peter Moore to Joe Morris Doss, 24 November, 1990.

15. Frank Cohoon, Ibid.

16. Cohoon and others, eds., *American Indian Mission and Ministry* 20f.

17. Jay Lowery to Joe Morris Doss, 11 January, 1991.

18. Walter Guettsche to Joe Morris Doss, 27 November, 1990.

19. George Harris to Joe Morris Doss, 22 November, 1990.

20. Samuel E. West, Ibid.

21

Hunting the Hairy Elephant and Other Primeval Adventures

H. Boone Porter

[Editor's Note: The following essay is based upon one of Boone Porter's standard lectures in his introductory liturgics course. Many of his students will recognize it, and others will know it for the first time. This essay is typically Boone in that nothing less than the whole sweep of human history provides the context for his exposition of the meaning of liturgy.]

WHAT IS UNDERNEATH OUR PRESENT BOOK OF COMMON PRAYER? WHAT ideas, spiritual insights, and disclosures of God's power lie behind it? These are appropriate questions, but how vast is the answer! How many triumphs and tragedies, how many struggles of the spirit, how many graces given by God, how many mysteries are involved in the answer!

I would say that what lies back of the Prayer Book is the history of the human race. Obviously that cannot be surveyed in one lecture or essay. We can, however, evoke some glimpses of our past and some resulting implications for human spirituality.

Worship was not invented in this century or in the sixteenth or in the fourth or in the first. Worship goes back to creation. God is such a God, that beings such as people need to worship him. God has so made the universe that his wisdom and power are displayed, and it is part of our humanity to recognize this and respond to it. It is also part of our humanity to recognize that we need all the help we can get from invisible forces and powers in order to live. And when did all this start? It started, as the Bible says, "in the beginning."

Human beings are part of the animal kingdom. As the beautiful and suggestive story of Genesis puts it, we were created along with other mammals on the Sixth Day. Yet we are different. The man and the woman stand upright. Unlike most other animals, the man has broad shoulders and the woman a broad bosom. They are gloriously naked. Their eyes look ahead with stereotropic vision. Their mouths can speak, their faces can express a thousand feelings. Their hands can handle and shape things. As Genesis puts it vividly and poetically, the man and the woman look sort of like God. (This makes theologians uncomfortable. They prefer to define the image of God in man as free choice, dominance of nature, intelligence, self-consciousness, etc. I'm not against these, nor is the Bible, but Genesis makes its point in a more memorable manner.)

Being like God is the plus side. There is much on the minus side. We don't have the big teeth to chew rough food or to fight. We don't have the noses to pick up a vast variety of smells. We don't have the fierce claws which so many animals have, or the hooves on which some can run so fast. We don't have fur to keep warm. Furthermore, we are weaklings. Our muscles are third rate. Much smaller animals are much stronger than we. Try outrunning a rabbit! You will probably fall down from a heart attack before you catch it. Try catching a racoon with your bare hands. If you have any fingers left, you will not try again.

Of great importance, we lack the detailed instincts of almost all other animals. We instinctively eat, yes, but nothing inside automatically tells us what to eat, where to get it, and what not to eat. We instinctively procreate, but nothing inside automatically tells how to care for children and raise them. Animals, from ants on up, have fantastic internal apparatus directing them how to live and how to face the problems of life. We do not.

A baby bear, given food and drink and parental protection, soon grows up to be a big bear. A baby human, given nothing but food and drink and protection, would only grow up to be a big baby. To become a man or woman requires something else; that something else is what we are talking about. So we have to think and figure things out. We have to use our powers of speech to discuss, to teach, and to learn. Of course not everyone wants to, and there is a problem.

We also need qualities of character. We need training in patience, willingness to accept correction and discipline, hope in facing problems, dependability, and likable qualities which will encourage others to help us. For us, cooperation is essential. You generally can't catch a wild animal to eat alone. You need help, either in hunting or at least in fashioning the necessary weapons. You need help to clothe yourself in winter—fig leaves are notoriously chilly. You need help to build a hut or wigwam or dig a cave or make a boat. Membership in a family, tribe, or community is essential—but again, this is not automatic. We sometimes rebel, and some people always rebel.

So there is a further big difference between ourselves and our furry cousins. They do what they need to do to survive. Humans, on the other hand, sometimes do and sometimes don't. There is a great gap between what we should do and what we actually do.

These characteristics of mankind are as old as our kind of human who is perhaps forty or fifty thousand years old. Civilization as we know it goes back to about 3000 B.C. So the whole of civilized history is just the brief chapter of "these last days." Most of the human story was lived in primitive, so-called pre-historic times. Few people, but hundreds of generations, lived in those thousands of years in which the human gene pool sorted itself out, and we acquired our predispositions, proclivities, and sensitivities. I see those vast uncounted millennia as the great and mysterious well from which human spirituality flowed out. And it flowed early. Age-old human graves show people buried with weapons and tools, expressing some belief in an afterlife. The wonderful cave paintings of southern France, among the all-time great achievements of pictorial art, certainly originated for religious purposes.

Let us imagine ourselves in North America, say twenty thousand years ago, on the edge of the glacier. There would be snow on the ground much of the time. We trudge along in a hungry group of perhaps three or four dozen men, women, and children. We would keep together. Any child who fell back would be a prey to the pack of wolves that followed a quarter of a mile behind us, not yet domesticated as dogs. If we could find a wounded deer caught in a snow drift it would be a welcome snack for the group. But best of all would be a big animal, a hairy elephant or mammoth or a wooly rhinoceros, or (perhaps further south) a giant ground sloth. If we saw the tracks of a mammoth the young men would soon be buzzing with excitement. The older ones would cautiously look over the landscape. The hunters, the approved and recognized men, would finally set out.

You have to be pretty good to kill a huge animal with sticks and stones, but it can be done. Perhaps one brave fellow can run up in front of the animal and anger it by throwing snowballs or stones and then when it chases him, run out on a pond or frozen swamp with ice known to be thick enough to hold up a man but not thick enough to hold a large animal. When the animal flounders in the icy mud and water, the men can close in and ultimately kill it with their spears.

Or, in an open place, the hunters could surround the animal in a big circle. Those behind it can throw stones at it. When it turns to attack them, those on the other side who are back of it can throw their stones. When it turns to the right it can be pelted from the left; when it turns to the left it can be pelted from the right. Again, it takes considerable skill and bravery to hunt in this way. No one can break ranks from the circle because which ever way the animal turns there always have to be others back of it, or else someone will get killed. Perhaps it took hours to break a big animal down in this way. But again, it could finally be exhausted and be the victim of human spears.

This was certainly a hard way to earn a living. Men were killed from time to time. All risked their life in the process of getting food for their families. A boy would not be allowed to hunt until he had the knowledge, the skill, the patience, and the bravery to be totally trusted. His loyalty to fellow hunters and to his people had to be absolute. He had to be imbued with the traditions and beliefs of his people. He had to be tested. He had to undergo circumcision or some other painful ceremony. He had to be rid of contrary and negative features of human personality and to be invested with the virtues of a true man. Similarly, a girl could not be entrusted with the pains and responsibilities of wifehood and motherhood until she had been tested and initiated. So here we have the concept of initiation, of coming of age, the mysterious reality of spiritually belonging to the family and community within which it was possible to be an authentic man or woman.

Early Christians knew nothing about primitive anthropology. When they compiled their elaborate baptismal liturgies, they had never heard of the customs of primeval people. Yet they too found that a new member must be remade. They were not threatened by animals in the jungle, but they might be eaten by animals in the Roman arena for entertainment of their pagan fellow citizens. The new Christian also had to be willing to die if necessary. In Christian baptism, however, we join not just a local family or community (although that may be part of the picture), but the church is made up from every people, nation, tongue, and tribe—a community ultimately intended to embrace the entire human race—all indeed who have the family likeness of looking like God! When we speak of the sacrament of baptism making us brothers and sisters of all other human beings, there is profound meaning in this mystery.

There are many other things in primeval life which have shaped the human soul. We can think of the whole question of fire, how to get it; how to preserve it; and how to use it; and the spiritual significance of its light in the darkness. Or we can think of the treatment of the dead. Or we can think of events during the cycle of the year, as in the joyful greeting of spring at the vernal equinox. At that time of year, presumably when there is a full moon, we can imagine our primitive ancestors staying up all night to sing and dance around the bonfire, to rehearse the ancient stories of the tribe, to offer sacrifice, and to eat and drink. In some cases, the sacrifices may have been human. Perhaps new adults reached the final stage of their initiation at this same time. When we celebrate the Easter Vigil, we are doing something that has most profound roots in nature and in the human soul.

One of the questions that faced primitive people was their relation to the animals whom they killed for food and clothing, and for bone tools, teeth and claws as decorations, and other purposes. Hunters do not usually kill animals because they hate them, but because they like them and often admire them. Primitive people recognized, as we do, that animals, especially mammals, have many similarities to ourselves. Yet if hunting is the means of one's livelihood, one must do what one must do. Some expression of respect and gratitude was appropriate to the species of animal, or to the spirit which presided over it. Often this was focused on some one particular kind of animal with which one had a close relationship. In northern Japan the Ainu were great hunters of bears, and in modern times they still kill a bear each year and dress the body in special robes and set it up by an altar and carry out intricate and interesting acts of worship. In Alaska, Eskimo Episcopalians at Point Hope still perform special actions when they kill whales in the summer, which are so much part of their life and culture. The skull of the whale is always returned to the sea, and the jaw is set up in a special place near the village.

For the ancient Hebrews, the special animal was of course the lamb, which was not worshiped but which was involved in many ceremonies worshiping the God who provides fertility and food. We have of course inherited the lamb. A lamb is our totemic animal; it gives its name and title to our tribe. Our Lamb has been killed and sacrificed, and we eat from it food and drink. Yet in the mysterious providence of God, this same Lamb is also our shepherd who leads us by still waters, and through the valley of the shadow of death. The Spirit which governs the flock is the Holy Spirit given to us, which anoints our heads with oil and which consecrates the cup which runs over.

After this brief excursion through so many thousands of years of human history, we may return, perhaps reluctantly, to the twentieth century. Looking at our present Book of Common Prayer, we can see why baptism has been put forward, not simply as a blessing of children (valuable as that may be) but as the mystery on which is founded a fully Christian and even fully human life. We can see why the Easter Vigil has re-emerged as the most important and solemn service of the entire year. We can see why the Holy Eucharist is, on the weekly Day of Light, our response to our creator, our appropriation of the redemption by our Lamb, the opening of our hearts to the illumination of the Holy Spirit, and the affirmation and recognition of our true identity as human beings, created to be in some sense even like God.

22

H. Boone Porter
A Select Bibliography

This bibliography does not include book reviews, nor Boone Porter's writings for *The Living Church* which appeared almost weekly during his tenure as editor.

1950-1959

"Edward Bouverie Pusey." *Holy Cross Magazine* 61:9 (September 1950) 265-272.

"The Eucharist and the Anglican Chrysostom." *Holy Cross Magazine* 63:3 (March 1952) 81-83.

"The Prayer for Christ's Church." *Holy Cross Magazine* 63:5 (May 1952) 134-138.

"Cosin's Hours of Prayer: A Liturgical Review." *Theology* 56:392 (February 1953) 54-58.

"The Canonical Hours in Classical Anglicanism, Part I." *Holy Cross Magazine* 64:3 (March 1953) 75-77.

"The Canonical Hours in Classical Anglicanism, Part II." *Holy Cross Magazine* 64:4 (April 1953) 108-111.

"Font and Sepulchre." *Holy Cross Magazine* 64:9 (September 1953) 277.

"The Ash Wednesday Rites." *Holy Cross Magazine* 65:2 (February 1954) 35-37.

"Laying Hands on the Sick: Ancient Rite and Prayer Book Formulae." *Anglican Theological Review* 36:2 (April 1954) 83-88.

"Maxentius of Aquileia and the North Italian Baptismal Rites." *Ephemerides Liturgicae* 69:1 (1955) 3-8.

"The Embertide Prayers." *Holy Cross Magazine* 66:2 (February 1955) 47-48.

"The Sign of the Cross and Holy Baptism." *Holy Cross Magazine* 66:9 (September 1955) 261-265.

"The Origin of the Medieval Rite for Anointing the Sick or Dying." *Journal of Theological Studies* 7: Part 2, 1956.

"The Eucharistic Piety of Justin Martyr." *Anglican Theological Review* 39:1 (January 1957) 24-33.

"Concelebration." *Holy Cross Magazine* 68:3 (March 1957) 74-77.

"Easter and After." *Holy Cross Magazine* 68:6 (June 1957) 163-165.

"The Cross: The Wisdom and Power of God." *Holy Cross Magazine* 68:9 (September 1957) 259-261.

"What is Best on Sunday Morning?" *Holy Cross Magazine* 70:10 (October 1957) 295-298.

"The Liturgical Movement and the Sacred Ministry: I, The Diaconate; II, The Priesthood." *Sharers: Associated Parishes Publication* 4:1 (Winter 1958) 1-4.

"The Liturgical Movement and the Sacred Ministry, III: The Episcopate." *Sharers: Associated Parishes Publication* 4:2 (Spring 1958) 1-4.

"The Rites for the Dying in the Early Middle Ages, I: St. Theodulph of Orleans." *Journal of Theological Studies* 10: Part 1, 1959.

"The Rites for the Dying in the Early Middle Ages, II: The Legendary Sacramentary of Rheims." *Journal of Theological Studies* 10: Part II, 1959.

"Oil in Church." *Sharers: Associated Parishes Publication* 5:3 (Summer 1959) 5-9.

"Commemorating Our Lord's Blessed Baptism." *Sharers: Associated Parishes Publication* 5:4 (Fall 1959) 5-7.

William Augustus Muhlenberg: Pioneer of Christian Action. New York: The National Council, 1959.

1960-1969

The Day of Light: The Biblical and Liturgical Meaning of Sunday. Greenwich: The Seabury Press, 1960. Reprinted, Washington, D.C.: The Pastoral Press, 1987.

Sister Anne: Pioneer in Women's Work. New York: The National Council, 1960.

"A Sunday in South India." *Sharers: Associated Parishes Publication* 4:2 (Trinity 1960) 1-5.

"Holy Baptism: Christ's and Ours." *Holy Cross Magazine* 72:1 (January 1961) 1-4.

Truman Heminway: Priest—Farmer. New York: The National Council, 1961.

Samuel Seabury: Bishop in a New Nation. New York: The National Council, 1962.

"The Law of the Prayer Book and the Authority of Worship." *Anglican Theological Review* 44:2 (April 1962) 144-155.

"An Ecumenical Eucharist." *Studia Liturgica* 3:3 (Winter 1964) 180-182.

"Modern Experience in Practice." In *New Forms of Ministry.* David M. Paton, editor. London: Edinburgh House Press, 1965.

"Principles and Suggestions for Liturgical Renewal in Parish Life." *Studia Liturgica* 4:3 (Autumn 1965) 166-178.

"Christian Social Concern and the Liturgy." In *Experiments in Community.* Washington, D.C.: The Liturgical Conference, 1967.

Ordination Prayers of the Ancient Western Churches. London: S.P.C.K., 1967.

A Prayer Book for the Armed Forces. Editor. New York: The Seabury Press, 1967.

Growth and Life in the Local Church. New York: The Seabury Press, 1968.

"The Paschal Vigil." *Bulletin of the General Theological Seminary* 55:3 (May 1969) 19-21.

1970-1979

"The Theology of Ordination and the New Rites." *Anglican Theological Review* 54:2 (April 1972) 69-81.

Canons on New Forms of Ministry 1973. Kansas City: Roanridge, 1973.

"Holy Baptism: Its Paschal and Ecumenical Setting." *Response* 13:1 (Easter 1973) 5-11.

"Women Priests: Some Recent Literature." *Anglican Theological Review. Supplementary Series,* No. 2 (September 1973) 83-85.

"What Does the Daily Office Do?" *Anglican Theological Review* 56:2 (April 1974) 170-181.

"Liminal Mysteries: Some Writings by Victor Turner." *Anglican Theological Review* 57:2 (April 1975) 215-219.

"A Traditional Reflection on Diaconate in Relation to 'Omniverous Priesthood.'" *Living Worship* 12:9 (November 1976).

"Ministerial Priesthood and Diaconate." *Worship* 51:4 (July 1977) 326-331.

Keeping the Church Year. New York: The Seabury Press, 1977.

Jeremy Taylor: Liturgist. London: S.P.C.K, 1979.

1980-1989

"Toward an Unofficial History of Episcopal Worship." In *Worship Points the Way.* Malcom C. Burson, editor. New York: The Seabury Press, 1981.

"An American Assembly of Anaphoral Prayers." In *The Sacrifice of Praise.* Bryan D. Spinks, editor. Roma: Edizioni Liturgiche, 1981.

"Church and Ministry from Hippolytus to the Conciliarists." In *Church and Ministry.* David C. Brockopp and others, editors. Valparaiso: Institute of Liturgical Studies, 1982.

"Church Order and Missionary Expansion." *Anglican Theological Review* 66 (July 1984) 284-292.

"The Legacy of Roland Allen." In *Setting Free the Ministry of the People of God.* Gerald Charles Davis, editor. Cincinnati: Forward Movement Publications, 1984.

A Song of Creation. Cambridge, MA: Cowley Publications, 1986.

"Episcopal Anaphoral Prayers." In *New Eucharistic Prayers.* Frank C. Senn, editor. Mahwah, NJ: The Paulist Press, 1987.

"Day of the Lord: Day of Mystery." *Anglican Theological Review* 69:1 (January 1987) 3-11.

"Hispanic Roots of Episcopal Worship." *OPEN* (September 1989) 1-7.

1990-

"Hispanic Influences on Worship in the English Tongue." In *Time and Community.* J. Neil Alexander, editor. Washington, D.C.: The Pastoral Press, 1990.

"Authority: Popular Views and Opinions." *St. Luke's Journal of Theology* 34: Special Issue (May 1991) 51-54.

"Be Present, Be Present." *Studia Liturgica* 21:2 (1991) 155-164.

"Bible Reading in Church," *OPEN* (Fall 1991) 9.

Contributors

A. MacDonald Allchin is a priest of the Church of England and Director of St. Theosevia Centre for Christian Spirituality in the University of Oxford. He is an Honorary Professor in the University College of North Wales, Bangor. He is also the author of numerous articles and books, including *Participation in God* (1988), *Profitable Wonders: Aspects of Thomas Traherne* (with Anne Ridler and Julia Smith) (1989), and *Praise Above All: Discovering the Welsh Tradition* (1991).

Paul Bradshaw is Professor of Liturgy and Director of Graduate Studies in the Department of Theology at the University of Notre Dame. Editor-in-chief of the international journal, *Studia Liturgica*, he has published many articles and books in the field of liturgical studies, most recently *The Search for the Origins of Christian Worship* (1992).

Barbara Carey is a lay Episcopalian who has been active in the liturgical and musical affairs of the church for many years. She is a professional musician who teaches privately and part-time at New Mexico State University in Carlsbad, and has published widely in the areas of creativity and leadership development for the American Association of University Women, and for *The Living Church*.

Joe Morris Doss is Rector of St. Mark's Episcopal Church, Palo Alto, California. and is a past president of Associated Parishes. He studied under H. Boone Porter at the General Theological Seminary where he received the Master of Sacred Theology (1971) and an honorary Doctor of Divinity (1982). He is the author of *Law and Morality: The Death Penalty* (1988).

Reginald H. Fuller is Professor Emeritus of the New Testament at the Virginia Theological Seminary where he taught from 1972 to 1985. Dr. Fuller, who was a member of the Episcopal-Lutheran Dialogue (U.S.A.), previously served on the faculties of Seabury-Western Theological Seminary, Evanston, Illinois, and Union Theological Seminary in New York City. His most recent book is *He That Cometh* (1990).

Marion J. Hatchett is a priest of the Episcopal Church and Professor of Liturgics and Church Music in the School of Theology, the University of the South, Sewanee, Tennessee. Dr. Hatchett has written the *Commentary on the American Prayer Book* (1981), numerous historical studies, as well as a variety of supplemental liturgical and musical resources to accompany the *Book of Common Prayer, 1979*, and *The Hymnal, 1982*.

Aidan Kavanagh, O.S.B. is a monk of the Archabbey of St. Meinrad and Professor of Liturgics in the Divinity School, Yale University. A widely published and influential writer on a variety of topics, Dr. Kavanagh has made particular contributions to the study of Christian initiation and liturgical theology.

Ralph N. McMichael, Jr. is Instructor in Liturgics at Nashotah House Theological Seminary. He has served parishes in Texas and Louisiana, and has published several articles on orders, the eucharist, and liturgical language.

Leonel L. Mitchell is a priest of the Episcopal Church and Professor of Liturgics at the Seabury-Western Theological Seminary, Evanston, Illinois. Dr. Mitchell has written on a variety of subjects, including Christian initiation, ritual studies, and liturgical theology. He is the author of *Worship: Initiation and the Churches* (1991).

Anne Perkins has done public relations for New York's Union Settlement Association, the social welfare agency founded by Union Theological Seminary, and now serves on the Settlement Board. In 1989 she earned the M.Div. degree from New York Theological Seminary. She works for a small foundation with interests in public health, and part-time as a chaplain at the New York University Medical Center.

Ormonde Plater has been a deacon at St. Anna's Church in New Orleans since 1971, where he coordinates ministry to the sick. He has written *Many Servants* (1991) and *Deacons in the Liturgy* (1992), and is co-author of *Cajun Dancing* (1993). Deacon Plater is a member of the Council of Associated Parishes.

H. Boone Porter is Senior Editor of *The Living Church* and has taught at Nashotah House and The General Theological Seminary. Dr. Porter is the author of major historical studies on liturgical time, ordination rites, and English liturgiology, in addition to numerous shorter works on liturgical and pastoral subjects.

Charles P. Price is the William Meade Professor Emeritus of Systematic Theology at Virginia Theological Seminary, where he taught from 1956 to 1963, and from 1972 to 1989. Presently on the Anglican-Roman Catholic Commission (U.S.A.) and the General Board of Examining Chaplains, he is the author of *Introducing the Proposed Book of Common Prayer* (1977), *Principles of Christian Faith and Practice* (1977), and co-author with Louis Weil of *Liturgy for Living* (1979).

Frank C. Senn is pastor of Immanuel Lutheran Church in Evanston, Illinois, and received his doctorate from the University of Notre Dame. Dr. Senn was a member of the Lutheran-Episcopal Dialogue in the U.S.A., Series II, and the author or editor of several books. His most recent book is *The Witness of the Worshipping Community* (1993).

Bonnell Spencer, O.H.C. is an Episcopal priest and a monk of the Order of the Holy Cross, and has spent many years in religious education in both the United States and Ghana. The author of numerous books and articles, Fr. Spencer has served as a member of the council of Associated Parishes, and was a member of the Episcopal Church's Standing Liturgical Commission from 1964 to 1976.

Byron David Stuhlman is a graduate of Yale College and the General Theological Seminary, where he studied under H. Boone Porter. Dr. Stuhlman received his doctorate from Duke University under the direction of Geoffrey Wainwright, and is presently completing a visiting appointment in the Department of Religion at Hamilton College in Clinton, New York. His latest book is *Redeeming the Time: An Historical and Theological Study of the Church's Rule of Prayer and the Regular Services of the Church*.

Thomas J. Talley is Professor Emeritus of The General Theological Seminary where he succeeded H. Boone Porter and held the chair of Professor of Liturgics from 1971 through 1989. Dr. Talley, who did his doctorate under Boone Porter, is the author of *The Origins of the Liturgical Year* (2d ed., 1991) and *Worship: Reforming the Tradition* (1990).

Louis Weil is Professor of Liturgics at the Church Divinity School of the Pacific in Berkeley, California. He is a past president of the North American Academy of Liturgy and a former member of the Episcopal Church's Standing Liturgical Commission. He has authored several books and articles in the areas of pastoral liturgy and initiation, his most recent book being *Gathered to Pray* (1986).

John Wilkinson is priest in charge of Christ Church, Victoria Road, Kensington, England. He is a Canon of St. George's, Jerusalem, where he last worked as Director of the British School of Archeology. He has gained a great deal by his association with Dumbarton Oaks.

Nathan Wright is Senior Priest, St. Philip's Church, New York City. He has published books and articles in sociology, economics, education, and political science. As a theologian/historian, Dr. Wright received an international first prize for his work in liturgy in the early church from the Christian Research Foundation based at Harvard University. He is one of the founders of the Black Theology movement. A doctoral dissertation has been written at Rutgers University on Dr. Wright's educational thought.